DATE DUE

		PRINTED IN U.S.A.

Age of Opportunity

BOOKS BY LAURENCE STEINBERG

You and Your Adolescent: The Essential Guide for Ages 10 to 25

Rethinking Juvenile Justice (with Elizabeth S. Scott)

The Ten Basic Principles of Good Parenting

*Beyond the Classroom: Why School Reform Has Failed and
    What Parents Need to Do*

*Crossing Paths: How Your Child's Adolescence Triggers Your
    Own Crisis (with Wendy Steinberg)*

Age of Opportunity

Lessons from the
New Science of Adolescence

Laurence Steinberg, Ph.D.

AN EAMON DOLAN BOOK
Houghton Mifflin Harcourt
Boston   New York   2014

Copyright © 2014 by Laurence Steinberg

For information about permission to reproduce selections from this book, write to Permissions, Houghton Mifflin Harcourt Publishing Company, 215 Park Avenue South, New York, New York 10003.

www.hmhco.com

Library of Congress Cataloging-in-Publication Data is available.
ISBN 978-0-544-27977-3

Book design by Greta Sibley

Printed in the United States of America
DOC 10 9 8 7 6 5 4 3 2 1

For Ben, who taught me much about adolescence,
but even more about maturity.

Contents

Introduction

When a country's adolescents trail much of the world on measures of school achievement, but are among the world leaders in violence, unwanted pregnancy, STDs, abortion, binge drinking, marijuana use, obesity, and unhappiness, it is time to admit that something is wrong with the way that country is raising its young people.

That country is the United States.

It is not surprising that so many young people fare poorly in school or suffer from emotional or behavioral problems. Our current approach to raising adolescents reflects a mix of misunderstanding, uncertainty, and contradiction, where we frequently treat them as more mature than they really are, but just as frequently treat them as less so. A society that tries twelve-year-olds who commit serious crimes as adults because they are mature enough to "know better," but prohibits twenty-year-olds from buying alcohol because they are too immature to handle it, is deeply confused about how to treat people in this age range. Similarly, a society that lets sixteen-year-olds drive (statistically among the most dangerous activities there is), but doesn't allow them to see R-rated movies (an innocuous activity if there ever was one) is clueless.

The classic stereotype of adolescence is that it is a time characterized by confusion. Adolescence *is* a confusing time, but it's not the people in the midst of it who are confused. Indeed, adults are far more bewildered by adolescence than are young people themselves.

Some years ago, I received a call one evening from a friend who asked

me to watch his ten-year-old son while he dashed out to take care of a problem involving his sixteen-year-old daughter, whom I'll call Stacie. She had
just called to ask her dad to come and pick her up. She had been arrested
for shoplifting—she had attempted to steal a bathing suit from one of the
department stores that anchored the high-end mall not far from where we
lived. She and her two friends, who also had stolen a few small things from
the store, were being held at the local police station. My friend's wife was out
of town on a business trip, and he couldn't leave his son home alone.

My friend and his daughter returned about an hour later, and he stood
and stared at her as she walked through their foyer past me, avoiding any
eye contact, and climbed up the stairs to her bedroom. No one said a word.

He and I sat down in the living room to try to make sense out of what
had happened. His daughter was a good kid, a straight-A student who had
never been in trouble. The family had plenty of money, and Stacie knew
that if she needed clothes, all she had to do was ask. Why on earth would
she steal something that she could have purchased so easily? When he had
asked his daughter this on their ride home from the station, she had no answer. She just shrugged and looked out the window. My guess is that she had
no idea. Nor was she especially concerned about finding out why.

My friend, also a psychologist, wanted Stacie to see a therapist so that
she could better understand her behavior. At the time, I thought it was a
reasonable request. Now, though, I'm not sure I would have encouraged
this response. I'm all in favor of psychotherapy when a teenager has an obvious emotional or behavioral problem, like depression or chronic acting
out. But no amount of probing Stacie's unconscious was going to uncover
why she stole the bathing suit. She didn't take it because she was angry with
her parents, or because she had low self-esteem, or because she had some
psychological hole that needed to be filled with something tangible and
immediately gratifying. Holding Stacie accountable for what she did was
important. It would be appropriate to demand that she make amends to the
store and to punish her in some way—ground her, withhold her allowance,
temporarily take away some privilege.

But pushing her to understand what she did was futile. She shoplifted
because when she and her friends were wandering through the store, stopping occasionally to experiment with cosmetics or rummage through the
stacks of clothes on the display tables, it seemed like it might be fun to see
if they could get away with it. It really wasn't any more complicated than

that. Later in this book, I'll discuss how the research my colleagues and I are doing on the adolescent brain explains just why Stacie did what she did, and why it is pointless to seek the answer through introspection.

We need to start thinking about adolescence differently. Fortunately, over the past two decades, there has been tremendous growth in the scientific study of adolescence. The good news is that the accumulated knowledge, which comes from behavioral science, social science, and neuroscience, provides a sensible foundation that can help parents, teachers, employers, health care providers, and others who work with young people be better at what they do. Parent more intelligently. Teach more effectively. Supervise and work with young people in ways that are more likely to succeed. Understand why good kids like Stacie often do such obviously ill-advised things.

The bad news, though, is that a lot of this knowledge has yet to influence the ways in which we raise, educate, and treat young people.

This book synthesizes and explains what those of us who study adolescence have learned about two intersecting sets of changes. The first, in how adolescence as a stage of life has been transformed, demands that we radically reform how adolescents are raised, schooled, and viewed by society. The second, in our knowledge about adolescent development, exposes why what we've been doing hasn't been working, and reveals how we need to alter our policies and practices. My purpose is to start, stimulate, and inform a national conversation, grounded in the latest science, about how to improve the well-being of American adolescents.

A little about me: I am a developmental psychologist specializing in adolescence. Over the course of my forty years in this field, I have conducted research on tens of thousands of young people, across the United States and around the world. These studies have been funded by a wide variety of organizations, from public agencies like the National Institutes of Health to private philanthropies like the MacArthur Foundation.

Many books about teenagers are published every year that are based mainly in the author's experiences as a parent, teacher, or clinician. In contrast, I approach the topic from the perspective of a researcher, albeit one who also has been the parent of a teenager. This is not to say that personal observations or case studies are without value, only that they often tell just a small part of what is usually a very complicated story. Simply put, I place more weight on objective, scientific evidence than on anecdotes.

The studies in which I've been involved have included young people from all ethnic groups and all walks of life — from affluent suburban teens and rural adolescents to inner-city youth who come from some of the poorest and most dangerous communities in America. They have included young people who are suffering from emotional or behavioral problems as well as those who are flourishing psychologically. I've done research on teenagers who are lucky enough to attend some of the nation's finest private schools and on their same-aged peers who spend their days incarcerated in jail or prison. The research projects I've helped to direct have run the gamut from studies of small samples that use techniques like brain imaging or face-to-face interviewing to studies of thousands of adolescents, utilizing information from questionnaires. The basis for this book is a mix of my own research and that conducted by other scientists, often working from other disciplines. In the pages that follow I draw extensively on psychological research, but I also look at what we are learning about adolescence from sociology, history, education, medicine, law, criminology, and public health, and especially from neuroscience.

My use of brain science in this book deserves special mention. In the last few years, after enjoying a period of uncritical acceptance, the use of neuroscience to explain everyday behavior has come under attack. Its critics have pointed out — often correctly — that many of the claims put forth in popular-science books about the brain are exaggerated, that neuroscience frequently doesn't add to the explanation of human behavior beyond what we already know from psychology and other social sciences, and that our fascination with brain science is leading to a misunderstanding of important aspects of human nature. And they have rightly cautioned about the rush to embrace the promise of neuroscience to transform the ways in which various social institutions, like our courts, operate. I share many of these concerns.

My intention in grounding this book in the science of adolescent brain development is not to reduce adolescence to little more than a network of neurons, to suggest that everything that adolescents do is dictated by biology alone, or to imply that adolescents' behavior is fixed and not shaped by external forces. In fact, I argue just the opposite — that the main lesson we are learning from the study of adolescent brain development is that it is possible to influence young people's lives for the better. It was once said that advances in the study of genetics taught us just how important the environment is. What we're learning about the adolescent brain offers a similar message.

The study of adolescent brain development has been attacked in some circles as little more than an effort to use biology to oppress a less powerful group of people. Many youth advocates contend that adolescent brain science is a sham, or even some sort of conspiracy, and that alleged differences between adolescents and adults in how their brains function are figments of scientists' imagination, concocted to give high-tech credibility to a tired old story grounded in untrue stereotypes about teenagers. At the turn of the twentieth century, the inexorable source of adolescent immaturity was said to be raging hormones. Today it is said to be an immature cerebral cortex. Either way, in the view of some critics, it is little more than a prejudice against young people cloaked in pseudoscience.

I, too, believe that we shouldn't falsely stereotype teenagers, but the idea that adolescent brain science is bogus ignores fifteen years of important progress in the study of brain development. It is now well established that there are substantial and systematic changes in the brain's anatomy and functioning during the years between puberty and the early twenties. I know of no credible neuroscientist who contests this. This does not mean that adolescents' brains are defective, but it does mean that they're still developing. Pointing this out is no more biased against teenagers than it is prejudiced against babies to note that infants can't walk as well as preschoolers. Adolescence is not a deficiency, a disease, or a disability, but it is a stage of life when people are less mature than they will be when they are adults.

A word or two about terminology. Much has been written in recent years about what we should call people in their early twenties—"emerging adults," "twixters," and "adultescents" have all been suggested—and, as well, whether we should view the early twenties as a unique stage of development, the first part of adulthood, or an extension of adolescence. In this book, I use the term "adolescence" to refer to the period from ten until twenty-five. This may come as a surprise to readers who think of adolescents as teenagers and may bother those who balk at the notion of referring to people in their early twenties by the same label we use to describe people in their early teens.

I lean toward seeing the early twenties as an extension of adolescence not to disparage people this age or to insinuate that they're emotionally immature, but because I think society has changed in ways that now make the term apt when referring to the period from ten to twenty-five. Conventionally, "adolescence" has meant the stage of development that begins with puberty and ends with the economic and social independence of the young person from his or her parents. As I will explain, by that definition, ten to twenty-five isn't far off the mark today. There is also evidence from brain science that the brain doesn't completely mature until sometime during the early twenties, so applying the term "adolescence" to people this age is also consistent with what we are learning from neuroscience. Regardless of what we call it, the period of time during which people are no longer children but not quite fully independent adults has grown longer and longer, and it continues to do so. This elongation of adolescence has created tremendous inconsistency and misdirection in the ways in which we treat young people at home, in school, and in the broader society.

A brief road map of the chapters that follow may be helpful. In the first chapter, I discuss why now is the time to rethink the way we are raising young people — not only because we have made so little progress in the past three decades, but because new discoveries about the adolescent brain can guide us toward a more intelligent way of raising them. Chapter 2 explains the recent discoveries about the adolescent brain and why these revelations are so important. In chapter 3, I examine the ways in which adolescence itself has changed, more than doubling in length over the last century — from about seven years to about fifteen. Chapter 4 applies the science of adolescent brain development to the question of why young people act the way they do. Building on this look at the adolescent brain, chapter 5 explains why risky behavior is so common in adolescence and why teenagers' inclinations to behave recklessly are especially aroused when they're with each other. Chapter 6 explains why the most important contributor to success and well-being in adolescence is strong self-control. With this foundation in place, I then explore how lessons from the science of adolescent brain development can help us do a better job as parents (chapter 7) and educators (chapter 8) to promote adolescents' well-being and place them on pathways to success. I then consider some of the broader social implications of our new understanding of adolescence, explaining in chapter 9 how its transformation is widening the divide between the haves and the have-nots, and discussing in chapter 10 how our social and legal policies can be more intelligently aligned with the latest science. In a concluding chapter, I offer a series of recommendations — for parents, educators, policymakers, and other adults concerned with the well-being of adolescents — that I believe will benefit young people as well as the adults who care about them.

I began this introduction with a call to action. But I recognize that not all readers will agree with the urgent tone I used. Some experts will claim that our young people are faring better than they used to. And in some respects, those claims are accurate. Fewer of today's teens drink alcohol or smoke cigarettes than their parents did. Youth crime is lower today than it was twenty years ago. Teen pregnancy has decreased. This is all good news.

But given how much we have spent over the past thirty years in trying to improve young people's behavior and well-being, celebrating where we are today is a bit like throwing a parade for a team that's marginally better than it used to be but still stuck at the bottom of the standings. Some problems are less prevalent today than in the recent past, but their levels still remain unacceptably high, and the United States lags far behind the rest of the developed world on most indicators of adolescent achievement and health. That is neither good enough nor reflective of what we could accomplish with a more informed understanding of adolescence and a radically different approach to raising young people. What I propose in the pages that follow is nothing short of an entirely new way of thinking about what adolescence is, one that is based on cutting-edge, transformative science. I'm confident that if we adopt this viewpoint, we will see vast improvements in our young people's well-being.

1   *Seizing the Moment*

Now is the right moment to reassess how we're raising our young people, for several reasons. During the last fifteen years, we've learned a great deal about adolescence as a stage of development, in part because of tremendous advances in our understanding of how the brain changes during this period. Whereas it was once thought that brain development was more or less complete by the end of childhood, new research shows that the brain continues to mature well into one's twenties. Insights into how brain development unfolds, and the implications of these neurobiological changes for adolescents' behavior, expose many errors in the ways we raise young people. Some of the most important goals of this book are to share the results of this brain science, explain why so much of what we've been doing is unwise, and suggest how we can learn from, take advantage of, and build on our new understanding of what young people need in order to develop into happy, well-adjusted, and successful adults.

Another reason to rethink adolescence now is that adolescence itself is changing, and in ways that make our prevailing views of it outdated, wrong, and even dangerous. As I've noted, this stage of life, which once lasted just a few years, is now a much longer period, lengthened at the front end by the earlier onset of puberty and at the back end by the increasingly protracted transition of young people into careers, marriages, and financial independence. Simply put, children are entering into adolescence earlier than ever, but adolescents are taking longer to become adults.

The ramifications of this change are important, but they're complicated.

In general, the earlier age at which children now mature physically is much more worrisome than most people recognize, because it doesn't bode well for physical or mental health — earlier puberty places people at significantly greater risk for a host of physical, mental, and behavioral problems, including depression, delinquency, and even cancer. On the other hand, the delayed transition into adulthood, which has prompted a lot of handwringing about the values and attitudes of today's young adults, isn't nearly as problematic as the popular media have suggested, and as we'll see, it may even be beneficial. The underlying causes and likely consequences of today's prolonged passage into adulthood are greatly misunderstood, and people in their midtwenties are being unfairly criticized as a result.

Regardless of what we think about the lengthening of adolescence, though, the fact that the transition from childhood into adulthood now takes fifteen years demands that we rethink what it means to be an adolescent and how we ought to behave as parents, educators, and adults who work with and care about young people.

The third and most important reason to reevaluate how we are raising the next generation grows out of an incredibly exciting discovery about brain development, a discovery that hasn't drawn the kind of attention it deserves: adolescence is a period of tremendous "neuroplasticity," the term scientists use to describe the brain's potential to change through experience.

You're likely familiar with the idea that the early years — "zero to three" is the popular shorthand — are a time during which children's experiences make a major, lasting difference in how their brains develop and their lives unfold. And this is true. But most people don't realize that adolescence is a second period of heightened malleability. Scientists' discovery that the brain is highly plastic during the early years has rightly prompted renewed interest in what we as a society can do to take advantage of this opportunity to offer young children the kind of experiences that will benefit them most. We must now make a similar commitment to adolescents.

The fact that the adolescent brain is malleable is both good and bad news, though. As neuroscientists are fond of saying, plasticity cuts both ways. By this they mean that the brain's malleability makes adolescence a period of tremendous opportunity — and great risk. If we expose our young people to positive, supportive environments, they will flourish. But if the environments are toxic, they will suffer in powerful and enduring ways.

Adolescence Is the New Zero to Three

The idea that the brain is plastic—that it is altered by experience—may strike some readers as startling, or even profound, but it actually is a mundane observation to anyone who studies the brain. Any instance of learning must necessarily alter the brain's anatomy. Whenever anything is retained in memory, it must cause some underlying and enduring neural change; otherwise it couldn't be remembered.

Until recently, it was believed that no period of development came close to the early years in terms of the potential impact of experience on the brain. Because the brain approaches its ultimate adult size by the age of ten or so, many had assumed that brain development was more or less complete before adolescence began. We now know, however, that internal transformations in brain anatomy and activity are not always reflected in the organ's outward appearance. In fact, it is only within the past twenty-five years that scientists discovered that systematic and predictable patterns of brain maturation even take place during adolescence, much less that patterns of brain development during this stage might be influenced by experience.

All this is changing, though. And adolescence is emerging as a period of brain growth that is far more sensitive to experience than anyone previously imagined.

Not only is the brain more plastic during adolescence than in the years that immediately precede it, but it is also more plastic during adolescence than in the years that follow it. The drop in plasticity as we mature into adulthood is just as significant as the increase in plasticity as we enter adolescence. In fact, adolescence is the brain's *last* period of especially heightened malleability. One reason psychological problems are easier to treat in adolescence than they are in adulthood is that the problems become more entrenched as we get older.

The brain's malleability doesn't only permit change for the better, it also allows change for the worse. Infants who receive cognitive stimulation, like having their parents read to them, thrive because this exposure is taking place at a time when the brain is still being shaped by experience. But babies who are neglected or abused early in life can suffer especially long-lasting damage, because the maltreatment has occurred at an age when it is easier for the brain to be harmed by deprivation and other kinds of negative experiences. In other words, the discovery that the brain is highly plastic during adolescence is good news in principle, but it is only good news if we take advantage of it, by providing the sorts of experiences to young people that will facilitate positive development and protecting them from experiences that will hurt them.

Causes for Concern

American adolescents are not doing well. Many of the encouraging trends in indicators of adolescent well-being that we saw over the past twenty years have leveled off or have even reversed. Declines in rates of teen pregnancy and smoking have more or less stalled. Adolescents' drug use is on the rise, as is attempted suicide, bullying, and the need for remedial education among college freshmen. Much of the progress we made in the late 1990s has ended, and some of it is actually unraveling.

Right now we are neither adequately protecting young people from harm nor taking advantage of the opportunity to promote enduring positive development. The problem doesn't appear to be one of insufficient spending. Indeed, we waste an incredible amount of money in our current approaches to raising young people. The United States spends more per student on secondary and postsecondary education than almost any other country in the world, so it's unlikely that our mediocre school achievement or worrisome college attrition is due to a lack of financial resources. We spend millions of dollars each year on a collection of unproven, ineffective, and only marginally successful programs designed to dissuade adolescents from drinking, drug use, unprotected sex, and reckless driving. And as the world's leader in prison population, we spend nearly $6 billion each year incarcerating adolescents, many of whom have committed nonviolent crimes and who could be managed in the community at a fraction of the cost. If we have a youth-violence problem, it isn't because we don't spend enough on punishing lawbreakers.

Here are some specific examples of why I think we should be concerned.

- There have been no gains in scores on standardized tests of high-school achievement since the 1970s. American adolescents continue to underperform teens from many industrialized countries that spend a lot less on schooling. Although our elementary-school students fare well in international comparisons, and our middle-school students place somewhere in the center of the rankings, the performance of our high-school students is undeniably lackluster, and in math and science, well below that of our chief economic competitors. This underachievement is costly: one-fifth of four-year college entrants and one-half of those entering community college need remedial education, at a cost of $3 billion each year. That's money that could be spent on making college cheaper and more accessible to more people.

- The United States once boasted one of the world's highest college-graduation rates. It now doesn't even make the top ten, and a large proportion of American college graduates obtain their degrees from for-profit universities of questionable quality. One-third of students who enroll in college *never* graduate; the United States has one of the lowest college-graduation rates in the industrialized world, despite the fact that the economic returns on college completion in America are among the world's highest.

- Low achievement is not the only problem, by any means. American adolescents' mental and physical health is poor as well. One in five American high-school seniors abuses alcohol (abuses, not just uses) at least twice a month. The proportion of students who smoke marijuana every day is the highest it's been in twenty years. American adolescents are among the most frequent binge drinkers and users of illegal drugs in the world. And the use of illicit drugs by teenagers and young adults is on the rise.

- Nearly a third of young women in the United States will get pregnant at least once by age twenty. The United States continues to lead the industrialized world in teen pregnancies and STDs, and ranks near the top in adolescent abortions, despite the fact that rates of sexual activity among teenagers in many other countries are higher. The rate of regular condom use among sexually active high-school students, which had been rising, has remained flat for some time now. One-third of sexually active teenagers do not protect themselves against STDs.

- The birth rate among unmarried women increased by 80 percent between 1980 and 2007. In 2011, nearly one-third of the women who gave birth had never been married. Having a child outside of marriage increases the risk of young women and men curtailing their education, depresses parents' lifetime earnings, and increases the odds of living in poverty. Having children outside of marriage undermines the quality of mothers' and fathers' parenting, stunting children's intellectual growth and elevating their risks for emotional and behavioral problems. Children born to unmarried parents themselves are more likely to have babies outside of marriage, perpetuating the same problems in the next generation.

- Aggression continues to be a widespread problem. According to the Centers for Disease Control and Prevention, 40 percent of high-school boys in the United States have been in a physical fight in the past year, and of these, more than one in ten were injured severely enough to warrant medical attention. The United States has one of the highest rates of youth violence in the developed world, as well as the highest rate of violent deaths among adolescents. According to the CDC survey, nearly 10 percent of high-school males regularly carry a gun.

- Each year, nearly three hundred thousand teachers, or about 8 percent of the profession, are physically threatened by students. In more than 150,000 of these incidents, teachers actually have been physically attacked. Nearly two-thirds of our high schools have security guards who carry firearms.

- Twenty percent of all high-school-aged boys in America take prescription medication for ADHD, a figure that is nearly double the prevalence of ADHD among boys this age. Many experts believe that adolescents are being medicated so that they are easier to manage at home and in school. Rates of ADHD are similar around the world, but the United States consumes more than 75 percent of the world's ADHD medication. A country that has to resort to arming its school personnel or drugging its students to establish order in its classrooms is not winning the war on poor achievement or youth violence.

- Adolescent obesity is three times more common now than it was in the 1970s. The United States, where approximately one-sixth of the adolescent population is classified as obese and another sixth as overweight, leads the world in adolescent obesity and diabetes.

American adolescents may be near the bottom of the international rankings in school achievement, but they are near the top in soft drink and french fry consumption.

- The percentage of American high-school students who try to kill themselves each year — about 8 percent of the high-school population — is no different today than it was twenty years ago. The rate of adolescent suicide in the United States is consistently higher than the international average, and suicide attempts and suicidal ideation among American high-school students are both on the rise. International surveys that measure less severe signs of psychological distress, such as headaches, stomachaches, insomnia, or unhappiness, find that American teenagers are among the world's most miserable.

- Problems in mental health are by no means limited to younger teenagers or high-school students. According to one recent national study of more than forty thousand people, in any given year nearly one-half of all American young people between the ages of nineteen and twenty-five suffer from a diagnosable psychiatric disorder, most commonly substance dependence but also depression, anxiety, and certain types of personality disorders. Nor are these problems limited to people from poorer families: in this study, rates of mental illness among young people in college were only marginally lower than those among young adults who weren't in school.

- Adolescents' psychological problems have gotten worse over time. A study that compared contemporary young peoples' mental health with that of their peers seventy-five years ago, using an identical measure of psychological functioning, found that five times as many teenagers and young adults today score above the test's cutoff for a serious psychological problem than their counterparts did in the past, even after taking into account the fact that people today are more likely to admit to such problems than their parents, grandparents, or great-grandparents were.

Despite extensive and expensive efforts to reform our high schools, our students' test scores are no better today than they were in the 1970s. Despite massive investments in health education, sex education, and violence prevention, rates of adolescent drug abuse, obesity, depression, unintended pregnancy, and youth crime and aggression remain unacceptably high. Clearly we are doing something terribly wrong.

A New Approach

Adolescence isn't what it used to be. Today adolescence begins much earlier, it ends much later, and it is far more important in determining health, success, and happiness in adulthood than it has ever been. Moreover, because the factors that have made adolescence begin earlier and last longer are likely to persist, and even intensify, our current concept of adolescence as the "teen years" will become more outdated and harmful.

Brain science explains not only why adolescence is a vulnerable period, but why it has become far more so, a period in which young people are more susceptible than in the past to risky behavior, mental health problems, and difficulties in making a successful transition to adulthood. As I'll explain more fully in chapter 4, changes in the brain that take place when adolescence begins make us more easily excited, emotionally aroused, and prone to getting angry or upset. But these brain changes take place considerably earlier in adolescence than equally critical brain changes that strengthen our abilities to control our thoughts, emotions, and actions — a cluster of skills that psychologists call "self-regulation." There is a time lag between the activation of brain systems that excite our emotions and impulses and the maturation of brain systems that allow us to check these feelings and urgings — it's like driving a car with a sensitive gas pedal and bad brakes. When our capacity for self-regulation isn't strong enough to rein in our arousal, problems are more likely to result — problems such as depression, substance abuse, obesity, aggression, and other risky and reckless behavior.

The longer you drive a car with an overly responsive accelerator and poor brakes, the greater your chances of getting into an accident. Similarly, a longer period between the start of adolescence (when the brain becomes more easily aroused) and when it ends (when brain systems that govern self-regulation have finally matured) means a longer period of imbalance, and greater exposure to all sorts of problems.

Although adolescence generally is a time of heightened vulnerability, some young people are undoubtedly more vulnerable than others. Thankfully, most adolescents don't become depressed, flunk out of school, develop substance-abuse problems, or end up in jail. What separates those who can weather the storms of the period from those who can't? And what is it about those who don't merely survive, but actually thrive during this time?

The capacity for self-regulation is probably the single most important contributor to achievement, mental health, and social success. The ability to exercise control over what we think, what we feel, and what we do protects against a wide range of psychological disorders, contributes to more satisfying and fulfilling relationships, and facilitates accomplishment in the worlds of school and work. In study after study of adolescents, in samples of young people ranging from privileged suburban youth to destitute inner-city teenagers, those who score high on measures of self-regulation invariably fare best—they get better grades in school, are more popular with their classmates, are less likely to get into trouble, and are less likely to develop emotional problems. This makes developing self-regulation the central task of adolescence, and the goal that we should be pursuing as parents, educators, and health care professionals.

The good news is that the brain systems that govern self-regulation are especially malleable in adolescence. This knowledge should force us to more closely consider the quality of the experiences we provide young people, at home, in school, and, for older adolescents, in the workplace. At the same time, we should avoid exposing adolescents to potentially dangerous situations before they've developed self-control, and even worse, to experiences that actually compromise the normal development of these regulatory systems. In chapters 5 through 8, I discuss the importance of self-regulation, how parents and schools can encourage it, and what we can do to protect adolescents while it's still maturing.

The ever-widening gap between the beginning and end of adolescence has made it a more perilous time than ever for all young people. But it's especially hazardous for those who have the fewest resources for coping with the new realities of this stage of life.

The lengthening of adolescence fuels the growing divide between the haves and have-nots in ways that haven't been recognized, much less addressed, by educators and policymakers. This group of our most at-risk youth includes, not surprisingly, those millions who grow up in poverty, but it also includes a growing number of kids from working- and even middle-class families.

Ever since it became clear that adolescence rivals zero to three in terms of brain plasticity, experts have debated which period deserves more of our resources. To me, this is a little bit like asking whether it is more important to breathe or eat. Suffocation will certainly kill you faster than starvation, but if you don't eat, no amount of breathing is going to keep you alive for very long. By the same token, investing in the early years is vitally important, but if that's all we do, by the time these young children become adolescents, we will have squandered much of this early investment. Making sure that infants get off to a healthy start is critical, but we need to remember that early intervention is an investment, not an inoculation.

As I'll show in the pages that follow, many of our assumptions about adolescence are wrong. These assumptions lead parents to make mistakes they could have avoided, schools to ignore the cultivation of essential skills, legislators to pass misguided laws, and those who hope to influence adolescents with their messages to use strategies that are doomed to fail.

As a second and final stage of heightened brain plasticity, adolescence is probably the last real opportunity we have to put individuals on a healthy pathway and to expect our interventions to have substantial and enduring effects. In order to grasp how essential plasticity is to adolescence and how influential it is on our entire lives, we must explore the remarkable and sometimes surprising mechanisms of brain plasticity — as we will do in the next chapter. As I'll explain, it isn't impossible to help people change once they have reached adulthood. But adolescence is probably our last significant window of opportunity.

2 The Plastic Brain

I have exceptionally vivid memories of my adolescence — far richer and more specific than my recollections of either childhood or adulthood. Although I am now in my early sixties, I can recall, with astonishing clarity, not only important people, places, and events from my teen years, but even the smallest details about them: the particular sounds of different friends' voices; the way a certain girl's legs looked in the tartan skirts and forest-green tights she wore to school; the warmth and smell of the cardboard box I would hold on my lap, sitting next to my father on the short drive home from the local pizzeria.

I can remember things that happened to me as a child and as an adult, of course, but these memories are almost entirely of major events, life transitions that virtually everyone who has experienced them recalls: moving into a new home, getting a new pet, receiving a first job offer, proposing marriage, watching the birth of a child. My recollection of day-to-day life when I was a child or an adult is nebulous and not very detailed, like Woody Allen's description of *War and Peace,* which he'd just speed-read: "It was about Russia." That's about the level of detail with which I recall entire years from childhood and adulthood. But for some reason, my brain has stored memories of the most mundane things from adolescence in 3-D, high-definition format.

What's surprising about this is that my adolescence was itself very ordinary. No tragedies befell my family, nor did we win any lotteries. I was extremely fortunate in that my life as a teenager was untouched by family disruption, serious illness, death, or dramatic changes in our standard of living. Life progressed from one day to the next as steadily and predictably as a ride on an airport people mover.

To be honest, I can't think of a single reason my adolescence stands out any more than my childhood or adulthood. In fact, if I were to catalog the most important events in my life, the list would show that far fewer significant and life-changing things happened to me when I was a teenager than when I was in my thirties, a decade during which I married, became a father, changed jobs twice, lived in three different cities, and was granted tenure. Yet I recall my adolescence far more extensively and intensively.

Over the years, I've asked many colleagues and friends if this experience rings true for them, and at least 90 percent of them agree. Nearly everyone recalls adolescence more powerfully than any other stage of life.

The Reminiscence Bump

The special clarity of adolescent memories is so common that psychologists have given it a name: the "reminiscence bump." Controlled experiments, in which researchers take into account the age of the people doing the recollecting (this is necessary because on average people recall recent events more easily than distant ones), corroborate people's subjective experiences — events between the ages of ten and twenty-five are recalled more frequently than events from other periods.

This isn't because our *ability* to remember things in general is better when we're teenagers. Memory skills improve between childhood and adolescence, but our ability to remember things remains excellent until the midforties, when the mental decline that predictably takes place in later adulthood begins. Age differences in basic memory ability might account for why we're better at remembering adolescence than childhood, but they can't explain why we remember our teens and early twenties better than our thirties or early forties.

If the adolescent reminiscence bump isn't due to better memory during those years, perhaps it has something to do with the nature of the events themselves. This possibility has been the focus of a fair amount of research, since it seems very plausible. Three different versions of this basic hypothesis have been proposed.

One is that we recall adolescence more than other periods because relatively more things happen for the first time during these years (first kiss, first job, first car, first beer), and research shows that we remember novel things more than familiar ones.

Another is that events that typically take place in adolescence are generally more momentous and emotion-laden. Because many important events take place in adolescence — graduation, leaving home, losing one's virginity — it isn't surprising that we have more memories from this time of life. We recall emotionally intense events with special clarity (but not any more accuracy, it turns out). Because adolescence entails a lot of "drama," we would expect people to have more memories from this time.

Finally, some scientists have hypothesized that because adolescence is the stage during which we first develop a coherent sense of identity, we are more likely to use events that take place at this age to define ourselves, which may make them easier to remember as we grow up and incorporate these occurrences into our developing autobiographies.

All of these possibilities seem very reasonable, and all are incorrect. Although adolescence is indeed a time when many novel, emotional, momentous, and self-defining things happen, this is not the reason that it is more likely to be remembered.

Researchers have studied this by presenting subjects with lists of common words, like "book" or "storm," and asking them to write down one memory that each cue triggers. When all of the cues have been exhausted, the subjects are asked to go through the events and indicate approximately how old they were at the time each one occurred. After the events have been dated, the subjects are asked to rate each one along one or more dimensions, such as how novel, important, or emotional the event was.

You won't be surprised to hear that subjects typically recall *more* events from adolescence than from any other age period. But the events they recall are no more novel, important, emotional, or personally meaningful than events from other ages. In fact, the larger number of events we recall from adolescence is due entirely to the greater number of *mundane* events that we remember from this time. Unusual, emotion-laden, momentous, and self-defining events are recalled regardless of when they occur. But we are more likely to remember the ordinary things that happen to us during adolescence than the ordinary things that occur at other ages. There is something about this time of life that burns even trivial events deep into memory.

We are also more likely to remember music, books, and films from this age as well. Just like experiences, people, and places, the songs, the novels, and the movies we remember best are those we first encountered between the ages of ten and twenty-five. So are items from the news, which is especially surprising, since teenagers aren't exactly famous for their interest in current affairs.

The adolescent reminiscence bump is revealing for a couple of reasons. Because the bump has nothing to do with the nature of the events that happen during adolescence, there must be something special about the way our memory works during adolescence that makes this period a treasure trove of recollection.

Something is different about how everyday experiences are encoded during adolescence, as if the brain's "recording device" is calibrated to be hypersensitive at this age. When certain neurotransmitters, like dopamine, are released at the same time an event is experienced, the event is more easily remembered than when levels of these chemicals are not as high. These chemicals are released when we experience something that elicits strong negative or positive feelings. As we'll see, brain regions responsible for strong emotions are especially sensitive during adolescence. As a result, the adolescent brain is chemically primed to encode memories more deeply. The reminiscence bump doesn't exist because more emotional events take place in adolescence, but because ordinary events trigger stronger emotions.

The Adolescent Brain Is Plastic

The reminiscence bump is but one piece of accumulating evidence that the adolescent brain is particularly sensitive to its environment — one factor that makes it a period of heightened neuroplasticity. One reason we are so much more likely to recall events from adolescence is that the brain's amplified sensitivity to the environment leads us to encode experiences more deeply, in more detail, and more unshakably. It's no coincidence that so many autobiographies and works of fiction are set during adolescence, or that it has been so often described as a period of rebirth. Novelists, playwrights, philosophers, and authors of coming-of-age memoirs may not have been aware of the period's underlying neurobiology, but they were absolutely on target in drawing attention to just how formative a stage adolescence is.

Until recently, neuroscientists believed that developmental plasticity is mainly a characteristic of early life. The reasons for this belief are easily understandable, since we know that the brain is developing rapidly during this phase, and because many basic abilities are improving (like vision), emerging (like language), and consolidating (like gross motor skills) during this time. More of our brains are being "built" during the early years than at any other point in our lifetimes.

Once these early-developing brain systems have matured, it is very hard to alter them. This helps explain why the effects of extreme deprivation early in life are so difficult to reverse. Infants who have been kept in orphanages without adequate environmental stimulation will not develop normally if they aren't removed from these harmful environments before they're two years old. In one of the most extensive studies of institutionally reared infants ever conducted, the researchers compared Romanian children who were randomly placed into foster care with a matched group that remained in the orphanage past age two. They found significantly less intellectual impairment among the children in the foster-care group — they had substantially higher IQs, for example — than among those who remained institutionalized. The children who had been placed in foster care were also far less likely to suffer from emotional and behavioral problems.

We now know that adolescence is a similarly remarkable period of brain reorganization and plasticity. This discovery is enormously important, with far-reaching implications for how we parent, educate, and treat young people. If the brain is especially sensitive to experience during adolescence, we must be exceptionally thoughtful and careful about the experiences we give people as they develop from childhood into adulthood.

We must also revisit our steadfast belief in the unique importance of the first years of life. The brain *is* especially malleable during the first few years, and yes, it does lose some of this malleability after infancy. But new evidence shows that brain plasticity increases during adolescence and remains at this relatively higher level until adulthood. Whether the brain is as plastic in adolescence as it is early in life isn't really the right question, because, as I'll explain, the brain is plastic in different places during these time periods.

This revision in how we think about brain plasticity is not the first time our ideas about the malleability of the brain have changed in the last two decades. Until fairly recently, it was thought that the brain loses almost all of its plasticity once we become adults, and that there was little that could be done to keep the brain malleable. This, it turns out, is just plain wrong. The adult brain is not as plastic as it is at younger ages, but *less* plasticity is not the same as *no* plasticity. (Whether we know precisely what needs to be done to take advantage of this is a different matter, and unproven claims about how to "change the adult brain" abound.) It was also once thought that we are born with a finite number of brain cells and we produce no new neurons as we age. This isn't true, either.

Plasticity Has a Purpose

Using the word "plastic" to describe the brain can be confusing, because that word has two very different connotations. The things we use each day that are made of plastic, like the keyboard on which I am typing these words, tend to be hard and stiff, not malleable at all. We don't generally think of plastic objects as ones whose form we can easily change in any permanent way. I can squeeze the plastic water bottle that is sitting on my desk, but the bottle returns to its original shape as soon as I loosen my grip.

When we say the brain is plastic, we mean something that is truer to the actual derivation of the word. "Plastic" comes from the Greek word *plastikos,* derived from the verb *plassein,* which means "to mold." A plastic brain is a brain that can be molded — like industrial plastic before it has been hardened into its final shape. In this sense, the word "plastic" is in fact an excellent way to describe the brain at certain points in development, because just as plastic can be transformed from a soft, malleable state into one that is hard and rigid, so too does the brain change from being relatively more moldable to being relatively more fixed. The adolescent brain is more like plastic in its soft, pliable form than in the form it takes after it has been allowed to harden.

Most of us accept that our development is affected by what happens to us as we grow up — that who we become is the product not only of the genes we inherit from our parents but the experiences we have throughout life. It is easy enough to envision, if only in the most rudimentary sense, where the genetic influences on who we become reside — they are encoded in the DNA that is contained in all of our body's cells. And we know how these genetic influences ended up inside of us. They have been a part of us since conception, transferred through the selective merging of the genetic material carried by each of our parents.

It is harder to imagine how the *experiences* that shape who we are get inside of us, or where these experiences live once they do. You probably wouldn't be surprised to learn that researchers have found that children whose parents beat them become more aggressive, or that adolescents find it easier to form close romantic relationships if they've been raised by happily married parents, or that preschoolers whose parents regularly read to them find it easier to learn once they start kindergarten. You also most likely have an intuitive sense of why spanking produces aggression, exposure to a happy marriage helps children develop more satisfying relationships later in life, and intellectual stimulation at home enables children to learn in school.

But accepting that certain experiences produce certain outcomes, or even having a reasonable psychological theory about why they do, isn't the same as understanding the underlying biological processes that connect experience with development. *How* does being spanked influence a child's inclination to hit others? *How* does growing up with parents who express affection toward each other shape a child's own capacity for intimacy? *How* does being read to facilitate intellectual development?

Plasticity is the process through which the outside world gets inside us and changes us. If experiences did not actually change the brain, we would never be able to remember anything.

Because plasticity is what allows us to learn from experience, it enables us to adapt to the environment. The fact that your brain was changed the first time you were burned by a flame is what makes you avoid sticking your hand into a fire whenever you see one, no matter how enticing the colors may be.

Brain plasticity is a fundamental component of our evolutionary heritage. Without it, our ancestors couldn't have remembered which contexts were safe and desirable, because they supplied food or water, for example, and which were to be avoided, because they were dangerous. The malleability of our brains greatly benefits us because it allows us to acquire new information and abilities. Periods of heightened plasticity, like infancy or adolescence, are therefore good times to intervene in order to promote positive development.

But this malleability is a risk as well, because during these times of heightened sensitivity, the brain is also more vulnerable to damage from physical harms, like drugs or environmental toxins, or psychological ones, like trauma and stress. Plasticity opens the brain's windows to the outside world, but open windows can let in pollen, noise, and mosquitoes just as easily as ocean breezes, birdsong, and the fragrances of flowers. When these windows are open especially wide, as they are in infancy and adolescence, we must be especially attentive to what comes in through them.

Building a Better Brain

There are two types of brain plasticity. "Developmental plasticity" refers to the malleability of the brain during periods in which the brain is being built, when its anatomy is still changing in profound ways. Some of these changes involve the development or loss of brain cells, but the most important changes involve the brain's "wiring" — that is, how its one hundred billion neurons are interconnected.

Just as some homes are wired and plumbed more efficiently and effectively than others, some children's brains become better organized during plastic periods than do others'. And just as expert electricians and plumbers know how to build a residential infrastructure that works especially well, developmental neuroscientists — experts in brain development — are coming to understand what it takes to build a better brain.

Imagine if every single outlet in your home were connected with every other one, regardless of their locations. Picture each outlet in your kitchen connected to each one in your bedroom, each one in every hallway, and so on. If you had just four rooms with only four outlets in each, every outlet would have fifteen different wires coming out of it. Visualize the rat's nest of wires that would be hidden behind your walls and contemplate how inefficient this configuration would be. Electricity would flow along wires to outlets that didn't need it, wasting energy and time. Greater efficiency is why we arrange the outlets in our homes along clusters that connect via separate circuits.

The brain also works well because its neurons are not all interconnected — they are selectively linked. At birth, we have most of the neurons we will ever have. During the early years of life, our brains don't produce many new neurons, but they make billions of connections between neurons. This process is so extensive that neuroscientists often call it "exuberant." In the first six months after birth, one hundred thousand new connections between neurons are formed *every second*. Now, that's exuberance.

Because it is inefficient for each neuron to be connected to every other neuron (nor is it physically possible — if every neuron were connected with every other one, the amount of wiring in your head would require an area about the size of Manhattan), it is important that the brain's network be well organized. The exuberant production of neuronal connections in infancy is overkill.

Much of developmental plasticity therefore involves eliminating unnecessary connections, a process called "pruning." At one year of age, there are about twice as many connections between neurons as there are in the adult brain. Pruning makes the brain function more effectively, the way that thinning a tree allows the remaining branches to grow stronger. It's part of a more extensive process through which the circuitry of the brain is remodeled — through which connections between neurons are created, strengthened, weakened, or eliminated.

Brain regions that regulate basic sensory abilities, like vision and hearing, are pruned very early in life and don't change much after that unless the brain is damaged by injury or disease. Regions that control higher-level cognitive functions, like making complicated decisions, take much longer to be pruned, and many of these brain systems are not fully mature until the early or mid twenties. These regions are the focus of pruning during adolescence, which is why our ability to perform these functions can be forever shaped by our adolescent experiences.

Adult Plasticity

Developmental plasticity is the process through which experience sculpts the developing brain, which continues until about the midtwenties. The other type of plasticity is "adult plasticity." Because every time we learn something there must be some enduring biological change in the brain, the brain must possess a certain degree of plasticity at all ages. If this weren't true, it would be impossible to acquire new knowledge or abilities in adulthood. Because we can always learn new things, however, there is always some amount of plasticity in the brain, no matter how old we are. But the two kinds of plasticity differ significantly.

First, adult plasticity doesn't fundamentally alter the neural structure of the brain, whereas developmental plasticity does. Developmental plasticity involves the growth of new brain cells and the formation of new brain circuits. Adult plasticity mainly involves fairly minor modifications to existing circuits. It's like the difference between learning how to read (which is a life-altering change) and reading a new book (which usually is not).

Second, brain systems are far less malleable during periods of adult plasticity than they are during periods of developmental plasticity. In fact, the developing brain is chemically predisposed to be modified by experiences, like clay when it is still soft, whereas the adult brain is predisposed to resist modification — like that same clay once it has hardened. This is the reason we don't become better at seeing or hearing after we have matured beyond infancy, or why we have so much more trouble learning to ski or surf as adults than as children. By the time we are adults, the brain systems that regulate vision, hearing, and coordination have hardened. This is also why it is far easier to learn a foreign language before adolescence than after — brain systems responsible for language acquisition have matured by then.

Finally, because the developing brain is so much more malleable, it can be influenced by a far wider range of experiences than can the mature brain. When the brain is developing, it is shaped by experiences that we aren't even aware of. Once the brain has matured, we need to pay attention to and give meaning to our experiences in order to be affected by them in an enduring way.

The developing brain is sculpted both by passive exposure and by active experience. That means that before our brain has fully matured, we can be affected, in potentially permanent ways, by *every* experience, whether it's positive or negative, whether we understand it or not — in fact, whether or not we're even aware of it. It's not surprising, then, that we recall things from adolescence more easily than we do from adulthood. Even if I wasn't trying to remember that girl's green tights or driving home with the pizza box on my lap, the images and sensations they produced in me at that time were being recorded. The incidental plasticity of adolescence doesn't explain why each of us remembers the particular things we do from this time, but it may explain why we remember more of them.*

All Plasticity Is Local

The brain isn't built all at once. Different brain systems mature along different timetables and have different periods of developmental plasticity, sometimes referred to as "sensitive periods." Brain systems that regulate the most fundamental human abilities, like vision, hearing, and the ability to learn, have very early and brief sensitive periods, typically during the first months of life. Systems that regulate somewhat more complex abilities, like language or bonding with a parent, have a later and longer period of plasticity — spanning the first two years of life.

Brain systems that control our most advanced abilities, like logical reasoning, planning, and many aspects of self-regulation, have a much more protracted period of plasticity. Many aspects of these systems don't fully mature until the early or even mid twenties.

Although brain systems that develop early, and that govern our most basic and essential abilities, are also affected by experience, they are less easily influenced by small variations in the environment than are systems that regulate more complex functions. The early maturation of these basic brain systems is mainly driven by a biological program that is encoded in our genes, a program that unfolds both in the womb and in the very early months of life. This makes good sense. The more limited plasticity of these basic systems increases our likelihood of acquiring a solid neural foundation on which more advanced abilities are built, regardless of the environment into which we are born.

Take vision, for example. Although some visual stimulation is needed

---

* You may be wondering why, if the brain is also highly plastic very early in life, we have difficulty recalling events from this time. Few of us can remember events that happened before we were three or so. It is thought that the production of new neurons during infancy in the hippocampus, a part of the brain that is important for memory, disrupts previously encoded events (the development of new neurons slows considerably after the very early years). In other words, during infancy one type of plasticity (the development of new neurons) disrupts the effects of another (the development of new neuronal connections).

early in life to develop the ability to see, the level and type of experience necessary to make this happen is the sort that virtually all infants encounter. The development of normal vision does not require fancy mobiles, expensive objects for the baby to focus on, or a special environment. Similarly, almost all infants develop the basic ability to produce and understand speech, because the main experience that is necessary to drive language development is simply hearing other people speak, something nearly all babies are exposed to.

The development of abilities like vision and speech is said to be "experience expectant," because we can expect to find the experiences needed to stimulate these processes in the typical environments that humans encounter. All babies, no matter where they are born, have things to look at, and nearly all of them hear the sounds of human voices. If you were to raise an infant in total darkness or without hearing any human speech, vision and language wouldn't develop as they should, but it takes this sort of extreme environmental deprivation to produce such an aberrant outcome.

In contrast, because brain systems that govern more complex abilities are relatively more malleable, variations in experience more strongly shape their development and final form. These sorts of abilities are referred to as "experience dependent," because their ultimate shape depends so much on the particular environment in which their underlying brain systems mature.

Seeing, hearing, learning, and moving are essential regardless of the world into which we are born. One reason it's so tiresome to hear about the "extraordinary" accomplishments of other people's newborns is that they rarely are any different from the achievements of any other infants. Normally developing babies who grow up in good-enough environments pretty much all develop in the same ways and along the same timetable.

The abilities that develop in adolescence, however, are not as necessary for survival as are those that develop early in life. You can live without being able to reason logically, plan ahead, or control your emotions (the plenitude of illogical, impetuous, and short-tempered adults attests to this). These skills are adaptive in many contexts, but they are not as essential as being able to see, listen, learn, or move. More to the point, their value depends on the environment in which the individual develops.

Unlike elementary skills, whose development is tightly regulated by preprogrammed biology, evolution left more room for variation in the development of complex abilities. That's why there's so much variation in how well different people reason, plan for the future, and control their emotions, but far less variation in how well people see, hear, and walk.

In the past, not all environments demanded especially advanced cognitive abilities. People growing up in societies where basic survival was a day-to-day challenge may have had to run fast to escape predators, but they probably didn't need to elaborately plan things out months in advance. Indeed, people who spent too much time thinking before they sprinted were probably more likely to end up as some other animal's dinner.

In today's world, though, where formal education is increasingly important for success, people who are bad at reasoning, planning, and self-regulation are at a serious disadvantage, and the fact that the development of these abilities is highly sensitive to environmental influence is a mixed blessing. The brain systems responsible for these advanced capabilities remain plastic for a very long time, which permits these capacities to be shaped and fine-tuned by experience. For people who grow up under favorable circumstances, the plasticity of these brain systems is wonderful. For those who don't, this same plasticity can be disastrous.

And it isn't just early experience that matters. It is true that these advanced capacities can't be acquired if their basic foundation is not put in place during the first years of life — it is impossible to develop the ability to plan ahead without the ability to learn from experience. But successful brain development during the early years does not guarantee that these advanced skills will develop to their fullest extent. In order for that to happen, the brain needs certain kinds of experiences beyond those it encounters in early childhood.

This is why debates about when the brain is most plastic are pointless. Asking when the brain is most plastic, or asking when plasticity is most important, is best answered with another question: "Most plastic or most important *in what regions, and for what purposes?*" The very same experience can affect different parts of the brain at different points in development, depending on which parts are most malleable when the experience happens. A study of the impact of child sexual abuse on the brain found, for example, that the region adversely affected by the abuse differed depending on the age at which it occurred. Abuse during early childhood affected the hippocampus, a part of the brain important for memory. Abuse during adolescence, however, affected the prefrontal cortex — a part of the brain that is especially plastic at that age, and which governs self-control.

If all we cared about was raising people who can learn, converse, and form attachments, we could content ourselves with providing adequate stimulation during the early years. But if we also care about raising children who can navigate the complex landscape of other people's needs, motivations, and intentions; who can make plans and follow them; who can think about the longer-term consequences of their actions; and who can regulate their behavior, emotions, and thinking, we can't just provide stimulation during the early years, cross our fingers, and then hope for the best. In order to achieve these goals, we need to provide appropriate stimulation when the brain systems that regulate these higher capacities are plastic, and to focus especially on the periods of greatest malleability.

Your Most Important Network Is Not on Facebook

In order to understand how and why the brain is so plastic in adolescence, you need to know a little bit about how the brain works.

The brain functions by transmitting electrical signals across circuits that are composed of interconnected cells, called neurons. Each neuron has three parts—a cell body; a longish projection called an axon, which terminates in many small tips; and thousands of tiny, antennae-like branches, called dendrites, which themselves split off into smaller and smaller spines, like a plant's root system. In the adult brain, each neuron has about ten thousand connections. Collectively, neurons and the projections that connect them are called "gray matter."

When electrical impulses travel along a neural circuit, they leave one neuron through its axon and enter the next one through one of the receiving neuron's dendrites. The transmission of current from one neuron to another can be thought of as the passage of information along that particular pathway, like runners on a track team passing a baton during a relay race. Everything we think, perceive, feel, or do depends on the flow of electrical impulses across the brain's circuits.

The axon of one neuron is not actually connected to the dendrites of another, though, the way an electrical wire in your home is connected to a light switch, or the way the prongs of an appliance plug touch the active contacts inside an outlet. There is a tiny gap, called a synapse, between the tip of one neuron's axon and another neuron's dendrite. In order for an impulse to be relayed to a neighboring neuron, the electrical charge has to "jump" across this gap. How does this happen?

The transfer of current across the synapse when a neuron fires is enabled by the release of chemicals called neurotransmitters. You've probably heard of some of the most important neurotransmitters, like dopamine or serotonin. (Dopamine plays a very important role in the adolescent brain, for reasons I'll explain in chapter 4.) Many of the most widely prescribed antidepressants work, for instance, by altering the amount of serotonin in brain circuits that control mood.

When neurotransmitters are released from the "sending" neuron and come into contact with the receptors on the dendrites of the "receiving" neuron, a chemical reaction occurs on the other side of the synapse that triggers a new electrical impulse, which travels on its way to the next neuron in the circuit, jumping across the next synapse with the help of neurotransmitters. This process is repeated whenever information travels through the brain's elaborate circuitry.

Each neurotransmitter has a specific molecular structure that fits into a receptor which is precisely designed for it, the way a key fits into a lock. An impulse that stimulates a neuron to release dopamine will trigger a response in a neuron that has dopamine receptors, but not in one that only has receptors for a different neurotransmitter. This enables the brain to stay organized — if any time a neuron fired it activated every other neuron in the neighborhood, all helter-skelter, it would be impossible to maintain well-defined brain circuits — an enormous challenge in an organ that packs one hundred billion neurons, each with ten thousand connections, into the space inside your skull. This way, when a neuron that is part of a circuit that regulates mood fires, it affects how you feel, not whether you move your big toe.

Cells other than neurons also play a role in transmitting electrical impulses along brain circuits. These cells, known as "white matter," provide support and protection for neurons and compose a fatty substance, called myelin, that surrounds the axons of certain neurons, like the plastic sheath around electrical wires. Myelin insulates brain circuits, keeping the impulses flowing along their intended pathways rather than leaking out. Circuits that are coated in myelin carry impulses about a hundred times faster than circuits that are not myelinated, making them much more efficient, especially if the circuits cover a large territory. Multiple sclerosis is a disease in which the body's myelin becomes damaged, which interferes with the transmission of electrical impulses in the brain and the rest of the nervous system, making it hard to control muscles.

The amount of myelin in the brain increases well into our late forties, insulating more and more brain circuits as we mature. Along with remodeling the connections between neurons, the myelination of brain circuits is the other main contributor to brain plasticity. But whereas the remodeling of neuronal connections leaves the brain open to more change — circuits that are strengthened today can be weakened at some later point, and vice versa — myelination stabilizes the circuits that have already been formed, rather than creating new ones. One of the reasons that the brain becomes less plastic once we reach adulthood is that there is an increase during adolescence in certain brain proteins that impede the formation of new synapses and in other proteins that promote myelination, both of which make it more difficult for the brain to alter its connections between neurons.

Experience in the Zone Changes the Brain

Comparisons between the electrical circuits in our homes and those in our brains are helpful up to a point, but the analogy doesn't work in one very important way. In your home, the more often you use an electrical circuit, like the one inside a light bulb that makes the bulb glow when you turn it on, the more likely it is to wear out and need replacing. Just the opposite is true in your brain, though. The more often you activate a particular brain circuit, the stronger it becomes — the connections between the neurons actually multiply as a result of the experience. Perhaps the most well-known example of this comes from a study of London taxi drivers, who must pass an extensive test of their knowledge of London's streets before being licensed. Repeated scans of their brains revealed an increase in gray matter over the course of their training — that is, an increase in the connections between neurons — specifically in brain regions that govern memory for geographic information.

In other words, the very connections between neurons that allow us to do something — think a particular thought, feel a particular feeling, perform a particular act, remember a map of city streets — are strengthened each time we do it. This is why things become simpler with practice, why objects become easier to recognize the more often we see them, or why studying something helps us retain the information and recall it when we need it — the brain circuits that regulate these acts become stronger each time we use them.

Brain plasticity doesn't just strengthen the brain circuits we use; it also eliminates the ones we don't. When a brain circuit is not used, its connections become weaker and weaker. Axons retract, spines die off, and as a result, synapses start to disappear, often to the point that the circuit finally ceases to exist. This process is called "synaptic pruning."

Imagine a hilly meadow between two villages. Hundreds of lightly trodden paths connect one village to the other. Over time, people discover that one path is more direct than others. As people begin using this path more often, it becomes wider and deeper — like a brain circuit that has been strengthened by experience. Because the other paths aren't used anymore, the grass grows back and those paths disappear — just like a brain circuit whose synapses have been pruned. The difference between a brain region that has been pruned and one that hasn't is the difference between a highway system composed of a large number of narrow dirt paths and one that is made up of an efficiently organized network of a smaller number of superhighways.

Experience also affects myelination, which makes a circuit not only more efficient, but more durable. When we practice something, learn a new skill, or receive training designed to strengthen some sort of cognitive ability, the activity stimulates the growth of white matter in the expected brain regions (for instance, in regions responsible for finger movement in professional piano players, or eye-hand coordination in jugglers). Although some of the most famous examples of this process come from studies of physical activities such as juggling and piano playing, which have shown how practice leads to the growth of myelin, more recent studies of cognitive abilities, like memorization and meditation, have also confirmed that repetition stimulates myelination.

The brain's remarkable malleability in response to experience enables us to learn and strengthen abilities, from very basic ones (like memory) to very advanced ones (like self-regulation). This is at the heart of brain plasticity. It's not only "use it or lose it." It's also "use it and improve it." This is true at all ages, but it is much more easily and reliably accomplished before adulthood.

There is an important qualification to the mantra "use it and improve it," though. Pure repetition in and of itself is not very effective in stimulating brain change. In order to take full advantage of the brain's capacity for plasticity, the demands we place on our brain must exceed the brain's capacity to meet them. The slight mismatch between what we can do and what we push ourselves to do is what stimulates brain development. If the mismatch isn't there, or if it's so great as to be overwhelming, development won't occur. Good parents and good teachers know how to work in what is called the "zone of proximal development," the place where a child or adolescent's brain growth is most likely to occur. They engage in a process called "scaffolding," which gradually strengthens the young person's skills. I'll explain scaffolding in a later chapter.

Strengthening the brain is like going to the gym for weight training. You can maintain a certain level of strength by working out with the same weights day after day, but if you want to get stronger, you need to either increase the amount of weight you lift or the number of repetitions you perform. Something similar applies to neural circuits.

We've often heard that it takes ten thousand hours to develop expertise in something. But it's rarely noted that the ten thousand hours need to be devoted to deliberate practice that is set up to progressively challenge the brain system being trained. Merely repeating the same activity over and over again, without making it more demanding, doesn't do much.

But remember, different regions of the brain are plastic at different ages. Experience, even in the zone, is not an "equal-opportunity brain changer." As a consequence, the abilities that are most likely to be developed, strengthened, or weakened during adolescence are not the same as those that are developed, strengthened, or weakened at other ages. Adolescence is important not only *because* the brain is plastic, but because of *where* the plasticity occurs.

Priming the Brain for Future Change

The brain's ability to change in response to experience is extraordinary enough, but the story is even more remarkable. In recent years, scientists have learned that certain experiences not only stimulate neurobiological change at a given moment, but enhance the potential for further change—something referred to as "metaplasticity." In other words, plasticity actually begets more plasticity—and not merely in the circuits that were directly altered by the experience. The modification of a given brain circuit actually causes chemical reactions that induce future plasticity in *neighboring* brain circuits, too. It's as if memorizing the capitals of European countries not only made it easier to subsequently learn the capitals of countries in other continents, but also made it easier to learn how to remember things that have nothing to do with geography—like memorizing the sequence of American presidents or the multiplication tables.

One especially exciting discovery is that, during periods of heightened plasticity, learning something new can make subsequent learning easier—as if the initial dose of learning primes the brain in a way that makes it easier to learn the next time. What this means is that people who are able to maintain their exposure to novel and challenging experiences during periods of heightened brain plasticity—like adolescence—actually may be able to keep the window of plasticity open for a longer period of time. In other words, it is important to be exposed to novelty and challenge when the brain is plastic not only because this is how we acquire and strengthen skills, but because this is how the brain maintains its ability to profit from *future* enriching experiences. This is why intelligent people enjoy longer sensitive periods—periods when the brain is especially malleable—than their less bright counterparts.

The Three R's of Adolescent Brain Development

Neuroscientists study age differences in brain activity mainly through the use of functional magnetic resonance imaging, or fMRI, which allows them to identify which regions of the brain are active during different tasks. Functional imaging added a whole new dimension to our understanding of the adolescent brain. The beauty of fMRI is that it can show differences between how adolescents' and adults' brains work that aren't revealed through studies of their brains' anatomical appearance. Indeed, we now know that adolescents' and adults' brains are even more different in how they function than in what they look like.

Hundreds of studies of age differences in brain activity have been conducted over the past fifteen years, and they have revealed particularly dramatic differences among children, adolescents, and adults in brain regions that govern advanced thinking abilities, like planning ahead and making complicated decisions; in areas that are important for how we experience reward and punishment; and in regions that regulate how we process information about interpersonal relationships. The adolescent brain undergoes particularly extensive maturation in regions that regulate the experience of pleasure, the ways in which we view and think about other people, and our ability to exercise self-control. These three brain systems — the reward system, the relationship system, and the regulatory system — are the chief places where the brain changes during adolescence. Think of them as the "three R's" of adolescent brain development. These are the brain systems that are most responsive to stimulation during adolescence, but they are also the ones that are most easily harmed.

A Precarious Time

The fact that we can recall adolescence better than other periods and that this is a time of change in many brain regions are two pieces of evidence that the brain is likely to be especially plastic at this time. Another indication comes from statistics on the average age of onset of serious psychological disorders. The adolescent brain is extraordinarily sensitive to stress.

The average age of onset for serious mental health problems is fourteen. Different disorders have somewhat different age ranges when they are most likely to appear. Some have a very narrow age band, such as social phobia, which usually appears sometime between ages eight and fifteen. Others have a wide band, like panic disorder, which typically makes its first appearance sometime between sixteen and forty.

But with the exception of ADHD, separation anxiety disorder, learning disorders, and autism spectrum disorders, the age range for the typical onset of *every other major disorder* falls somewhere in the period between ages ten and twenty-five. The list of disorders that often first appear in adolescence is staggering:

- Mood disorders, such as depression and bipolar disorder
- Substance-abuse disorders, such as alcohol or drug dependence

- Most anxiety disorders, such as obsessive-compulsive disorder, panic disorder, and generalized anxiety disorder
- Most impulse-control disorders, such as conduct disorder and oppositional-defiant disorder
- Eating disorders, such as anorexia and bulimia
- Schizophrenia

Very few serious psychological problems appear for the first time before age ten. On the other hand, if someone has not developed any psychological disorders by age twenty-five, the chances that he or she will develop one later are small.

Studies of substance abuse and dependence are especially telling in this regard. The neural underpinnings of these disorders are well understood, because drug addiction can be easily studied in animals. (Many other species enjoy the same recreational drugs that humans do.)

Because all mammals go through puberty—the hormonal changes that mark the beginning of adolescence—other species can be used to see whether certain experiences have a more lasting impact when they occur before, during, or after adolescence. Experiments in which scientists have compared the brains of animals exposed to drugs either near puberty or after reaching full maturity have shown that drugs like nicotine and alcohol in early adolescence can *permanently* affect the way the brain's reward system functions, because this brain system is especially plastic at puberty. Repeated use of these and other drugs during this period can make it not only especially enjoyable to use them, but *necessary* in order to experience normal amounts of pleasure. This is the basis of addiction.

We can't conduct these sorts of experiments with human adolescents, for obvious ethical reasons. But large-scale surveys show that exposure to drugs during adolescence is more closely associated with addiction than is exposure during adulthood. Compared with people who don't drink until they're twenty-one, those who begin drinking before age fourteen are *seven times* more likely to binge drink as teenagers and *five times* more likely to develop a substance-abuse or -dependence disorder sometime in their life. Similar evidence indicates that people who begin smoking regularly before age fifteen are at greater risk for nicotine dependence as adults than are those who start in late adolescence. Parents should keep their teenagers away from alcohol, tobacco, and other drugs at all ages, but it is especially crucial to do so when they are younger than fifteen.

These correlational studies cannot rule out the possibility that people who start smoking, drinking, or using illicit drugs early in adolescence simply have personality traits that lead them both to begin experimenting early and to become addicted (such as poor self-control, which would likely contribute to both). But the animal studies tell us that something else is also going on, because the adolescent animals exposed to drugs in these studies didn't have a choice — they were randomly assigned to be exposed at this age and compared with animals chosen to be exposed for the first time as adults.

Adolescents' vulnerability to mental illness and addiction is just one reason why plasticity during this period can be so risky. Other research suggests that the adolescent brain is more susceptible to the adverse consequences of concussions than the adult brain. High-school football players who suffer concussions take longer to recover than do college players, and adolescents are more adversely affected by a second impact while the brain is still recovering from an initial hit. There is good reason to worry about the long-term consequences of playing football during a period of such heightened susceptibility to brain injury.

Taking Advantage of Plasticity

As I've already mentioned, brain plasticity can be a force for good as well as harm.

Although the science is not yet conclusive, it appears that old brains are changed when they learn new tricks, but not as much as young brains are. This is consistent with the idea that there is such a thing as "adult plasticity," but that the plasticity characteristic of the adult brain is nowhere near that of the adolescent brain. Cognitive neuroscientists are now actively studying whether people in their teens are more responsive to "brain training" than adults, and if so, which parts of the brain are more easily enhanced.

This is a challenge, though, because the brain matures in different ways at different times. If you wanted to examine the effects of seeing a scary movie on someone's emotional state, measuring how often people cried would be sensible if you were studying toddlers, but probably wouldn't be if you were studying adults. Along the same lines, the same brain training could lead to pruning in a child, myelination in an adult, and both in an adolescent. This illustrates the challenge of coming up with a common measure of "brain enhancement" that applies equally well across different ages.

One new use of brain imaging that may prove helpful for this purpose is the combined use of fMRI and a technique called "transcranial magnetic stimulation" (TMS). TMS involves the stimulation of the brain with a mild magnet that is applied to the scalp and pulsed on and off. Depending on the frequency and pattern of the magnetic pulses, activity in the region of the brain close to the magnet can be increased or suppressed. Studies have shown, for example, that people can be made more impulsive by using TMS to interfere with brain circuits that govern self-regulation. TMS is safe, and its effect on the brain can be studied even after the stimulation stops, because its impact continues for about an hour.

Because the stimulation or suppression of activity in a brain circuit looks the same regardless of the age of the individual, it is possible to apply an equal amount of magnetic stimulation to the same brain region of people of different ages and compare their degrees of activation. If adolescents showed a larger change in activity than adults in response to an identical magnetic pulse applied to an identical region of the brain, it would suggest greater plasticity in the younger age group.

TMS has been approved for use as a clinical treatment for major depression in adolescents who have not responded to other forms of therapy, but it is not yet being used in research on young people who haven't been diagnosed with a mental illness. There is some evidence from clinical trials, however, that the adolescent brain is more responsive to TMS than the adult brain.

This is consistent with the view that, generally speaking, it is easier to treat psychological problems when they first emerge than later, after they have become more intractable. To the extent that the adolescent brain is more plastic, it is crucial not only that we prevent young people from being exposed to the sorts of stressors and substances that cause psychological disturbance, but that we treat psychological problems that have emerged in adolescence as early as possible. Some moodiness during adolescence is normal, but if a teenager has shown signs of emotional or behavioral problems that persist for longer than two weeks, it's a good idea to have the situation checked out. Parents who believe their adolescent may be suffering from a problem like depression, anxiety, or substance abuse should not wait before seeking professional help. Once the window of plasticity has started to close, these problems become harder to treat.

Plasticity Increases as We Enter Adolescence

Although there isn't much direct evidence to date proving that the brain is more plastic in adolescence than middle childhood, there are several reasons to think that it probably is. Although it has not yet been proven conclusively, support for this view is slowly accumulating, and several neuroscientists have come to a similar, albeit speculative, conclusion.* There are several reasons for this.

First, psychological change during adolescence is far more dramatic than it is in middle childhood, which would suggest that the brain is undergoing more rapid or extensive modification in adolescence as well, since any change in our behavior must be linked to a change in the brain. This view of development is also consistent with anecdotal accounts, which portray middle childhood as a far less volatile time — after all, Freud went so far as to call this stage the "latency period," a time characterized by great stability and the consolidation of existing skills, rather than a major psychological overhaul. That doesn't take place until adolescence. As Rousseau wrote, we are born twice — once into existence, and once into life. The second birth he was referring to is adolescence.

Second, findings from studies of the reminiscence bump and psychological disorder suggest that adolescence is a more sensitive period than middle childhood — at least for memories and mental health problems. Remember, adolescence is not just a time of heightened recollections and emotional difficulty in comparison to the years that follow it; it entails more vivid mem-

---

* Because most research on plasticity is conducted on rodents, which have a very short period of development between birth and puberty (only about thirty days in mice), it is much harder to draw boundaries between childhood and adolescence in laboratory animals than in humans; scientists who study mice usually talk about development before puberty (which includes "infancy"), around puberty ("adolescence"), and after puberty ("adulthood"). If the course of brain plasticity is one that starts high, falls, increases, and then falls again, this would be hard to document in an animal with such a short lifespan.

ories and more psychological distress than the years that precede it, too. Again, this is not direct evidence that the brain is more plastic in adolescence than childhood, but it is certainly consistent with the idea.

Third, studies also show that the adolescent brain is more responsive to stress and arousal than the preadolescent brain. The correlation between the number of stressful life events that people have experienced (illness in the family, the loss of an important friendship, the death of a pet, a parent's job loss, and so on) and symptoms of depression, anxiety, or other psychological problems is stronger during adolescence than childhood. This heightened stress-reactivity of adolescence is another indicator that the period is one of special sensitivity to the impact of the environment.

Fourth, many patterns of change in brain activity do not follow a straight line between childhood and adulthood, but instead follow a trajectory that looks more like a right-side-up or inverted U. For instance, the brain's response to rewarding images, like pictures of smiling faces, increases in intensity between childhood and adolescence, and then declines between adolescence and adulthood. This suggests that something about the adolescent brain is different from both the child and adult brain. If plasticity was high at birth, and then gradually and steadily declined with age, we wouldn't expect to see a pattern like this.

Finally, something happens to the brain between childhood and adolescence that provides a plausible explanation for why there might be changes in plasticity at this time. That something is puberty.

Puberty and Plasticity

We tend to think of puberty as an event that transforms us into physical and sexual adults. The hormonal changes of puberty make us grow taller and heavier and develop the outward signs of sexual maturation (like breasts in females and facial hair in males). They facilitate the development of our reproductive systems. And they activate our sex drive.

But the impact of puberty on how we function is more far-reaching than its impact on our physical appearance, reproductive capability, and libido. The brain is radically transformed by sex hormones like testosterone and estrogen. These substances, whose levels increase dramatically at puberty, affect the anatomy of the brain, chemically altering the actual structure of its circuits. Sex hormones promote myelination, stimulate the development of new neurons, and facilitate synaptic pruning. Puberty makes the brain more sensitive to all sorts of environmental influences, both good and bad. And it stimulates a dramatic increase in brain plasticity, making us not only more attentive to the world, but more easily influenced by it in potentially enduring ways. For example, the fears we acquire during adolescence are especially difficult to rid ourselves of later in life.

As we leave adolescence, another series of neurochemical changes makes the brain increasingly less plastic. Closing the window of brain plasticity (although not nailing it shut) as we mature from adolescence into adulthood is a gradual process that takes place throughout the twenties, as the brain's chemistry shifts from encouraging changes in our neural architecture to favoring stability. New synapses and new neurons proliferate during adolescence, and many existing neural circuits are pruned, but these processes taper off considerably as the brain matures into adulthood.

We don't know what signals the brain to start this shift from more to less plasticity as adolescence comes to a close, but recent animal studies show that if one of the genes that controls this shift is blocked, the brain of an adult mouse retains some of the plasticity it had during its juvenile period. Even after this genetic switch has been flipped, its effects can be reversed by switching it back to its adolescent position. This research has not yet been done on humans, but if the same pattern were seen, it would have tremendous implications for restoring brain plasticity to adults who have suffered brain injury. Repairing the damage to an injured adult's brain that has once again been made plastic should be a lot easier.

The natural decline in plasticity that takes place toward the end of adolescence is not merely a reversal of the increase sparked by puberty. In fact, there is no evidence that changes in sex hormones reduce plasticity. This makes perfect sense, given that levels of sex hormones don't start to drop until much later, well into the thirties. If the brain is losing some of its plasticity in early adulthood, it has nothing to do with decreases in testosterone or estrogen.

Instead, the reduction in plasticity as one enters adulthood is probably due at least in part to experience. Many studies show that the motivation to seek out novel and exciting experiences increases shortly after puberty and then declines as we move from late adolescence into adulthood—a pattern seen in other animals as well. This built-in need to explore the world during adolescence is so strong that many of the fears we may have developed during childhood are temporarily squelched, only to reappear in adulthood, perhaps as a way of ensuring that they don't interfere with the natural wanderlust that enables us to separate from parents and reproduce outside the family. The increase in novelty seeking is a way of making sure that individuals venture out into the world at a time when the brain is primed to learn from new experiences. Because the adolescent brain isn't just more plastic — it's more "metaplastic," too — it is very likely that the learning that takes place during this quest for novelty is what helps keep the brain malleable during adolescence.

We know that brain plasticity in adulthood is facilitated by a mismatch between what the environment demands of the brain and what the brain can do. The less often we put ourselves in novel situations, the less frequently we encounter these mismatches. When this happens, and when the need to learn new things becomes less and less pressing, the brain begins to lose some of its malleability. When we leave adolescence and stop seeking out new experiences, our brains shut down the final period of extensive plasticity.

Trading Plasticity for Efficiency

As more of the brain's circuits become hardened, they become less easily modified. This makes the brain more efficient — it makes the electrical impulses travel faster — but it also makes the brain less able to change as a consequence of experience. This makes good evolutionary sense.

Adolescence is when we acquire the last set of skills and capabilities we need to be able to function independently, and most important, to survive long enough to reproduce and bring offspring into the world. During this final period of preparation for adult life, our last chance to learn what we need to know before venturing out on our own, we are sponges for information — which is why the adolescent brain is built to be so exquisitely aware of what is going on all around us, even things that we are not cognizant of. As adolescence draws to a close and the necessary knowledge and abilities have been acquired — some gained by actively seeking this information, but a large amount absorbed incidentally — the brain begins to change its "portfolio," emphasizing the effective use and preservation of existing resources over the addition of new ones. Plasticity is crucial while we're developing, but remember that all environments contain risks as well as opportunities. Once we have what we need to survive on our own, it doesn't make any sense to remain malleable enough to be potentially harmed by unfavorable experiences. It's simply not worth the risk. It's like converting one's retirement investments from high-risk equities to more conservative bonds once we reach a certain age.

When we enter adolescence, the brain is still plastic, but the biologically programmed changes of puberty open the window of plasticity wider. When we leave adolescence, we begin to close that window by progressively relinquishing — either through choice or necessity — the sorts of experiences that would otherwise keep it open.

With this in mind, the lengthy passage into adulthood that characterizes the early twenties for so many people today starts to look more beneficial than parents and pundits may think. Indeed, those who are lucky enough to be able to prolong adolescence may actually have an advantage, as long as the environment in which their adolescence is prolonged affords opportunities for continued stimulation and increasing challenge, and avoids the harms that can assault a malleable brain. Recent studies show that higher education contributes to the development of advanced cognitive abilities by improving the structure of the brain's white matter — and that college contributes to brain development above and beyond the effects of just getting older. Perhaps we should stop wringing our hands over the delayed transition into adulthood experienced by more and more young people and look at it in the more positive light it deserves.

I've noted several times that brain plasticity carries with it both opportunity and risk. As we'll see in the next chapter, this period of promise and peril has never been longer. And as a result, adolescence now matters more than ever.

3   The Longest Decade

Adolescence is longer today than it has ever been in human history.

Deciding how we define a stage of life—when it begins and when it ends—is inherently subjective. Experts use puberty to mark the beginning of adolescence because it's easy to measure, has obvious consequences (like sexual maturation), and is universal. In societies that have formal rites of passage, puberty has long been used to indicate when people are no longer children.

We may lack formal initiation ceremonies in modern society, but we still use puberty to mark the passage into adolescence. Getting consensus on when the period ends is harder. Although there are a few objective biological boundaries between adolescence and adulthood—for instance, the point at which people stop growing taller or when they can bear children—these somehow just don't feel right. Some people finish their growth spurts when they're as young as twelve or thirteen, and some can even become a parent at this age, but few of us, at least in today's world, feel comfortable labeling a thirteen-year-old as an "adult." That's why we tend to use some sort of social indicator to draw the line between adolescence and adulthood, like attaining the age of legal majority, starting a full-time job, or moving out of one's parents' home. Reasonable people may disagree about *which* social indicator makes the most sense, but they would probably agree that a cultural marker of adulthood makes more sense than a biological one.

This is why experts define adolescence as beginning in biology and ending in culture.

Of all the possible markers of the beginning and end of adolescence, menstruation and marriage are probably the best ones to use in order to see if adolescence actually has gotten longer. Both are widely experienced, and we can date both of them accurately. For most women, menarche is a memorable event, and one whose date is regularly recorded in doctors' files. Scientists in the Western world have been keeping track of the average age of girls' first menstruation since about 1840, and we have a very good idea of how the advent of puberty has changed since then. There is no comparable pubertal event for boys that screams, "I am a man," but the ages at which males and females within the same society go through puberty are highly correlated. Even though girls typically go through puberty a year or two before boys, in societies in which puberty is early for girls, it comes early for boys, too.

The age at which people marry is even more reliably documented than the age of menarche. Government officials have long noted how old people are when they take their wedding vows, and as a consequence we have accurate statistics about marriage that go back for centuries. This is certainly not to say that one must be married in order to be an adult, only that changes in the average age of marriage are useful for tracking historical trends. Trends in the age at which people complete their schooling, begin their careers, or set up independent households would also be fine ways to track historical changes in the transition into adulthood, but we haven't kept very good official records of these for nearly as long as we've been recording marriages. And although getting married, leaving school, starting a career, or setting up a home do not all take place at the same age, they tend to move in lockstep from one generation to the next. When the average age for getting married rises over time, so do the others.*

---

* In an analysis my colleagues and I conducted using Monitoring the Future, an annual survey of a nationally representative sample of Americans who graduated high school between 1977 and 2010, we looked at the correlations among the ages at which people made various transitions into adult roles. Each graduating class's average age at the time of their first marriage was the strongest correlate of how old the graduates were when they completed their last year of education, began their first full-time job, set up their own households, or had children.

Adolescence Has Gotten Longer

In the middle of the nineteenth century, adolescence lasted around five years — that's how long it took girls to go from menarche to marriage in the mid-1800s. At the turn of the twentieth century, the average American woman got her first period between fourteen and fifteen and married when she was just under twenty-two. In 1900, adolescence lasted a little less than seven years.

During the first half of the twentieth century, people began getting married at a younger age, but the age of puberty continued to decline. This froze the length of adolescence at about seven years. In 1950, for example, the average American female went through menarche at around thirteen and a half and married at twenty.

From 1950 on, though, things changed. The drop in the age of puberty continued, but people started marrying later and later. Each decade, the average age of menarche dropped by about three or four months, whereas the average age at marriage rose by about a year. By 2010, it took fifteen years for the average girl to go from menarche to marriage.

If these trends continue — and, for reasons I will explain, they probably will — by 2020, adolescence will take almost twenty years from start to finish.

What About the Boys?

The availability of information on menarche makes it easier to document the declining age of puberty among girls than boys. In order to study historical trends in the age of male puberty, researchers have had to use more ingenious methods. Several very cleverly done studies, using more indirect methods, show that boys also mature at a much earlier age today than they did in the past.

One reliable indicator of male puberty is that the boy's voice deepens, or "breaks." If you're in the business of assembling children's choirs, you pay close attention to this change, and choirmasters have long kept records that indicate when the break has occurred among their singers. According to these records, the average age at which boys' voices broke has fallen from about eighteen in the mid-1700s, to around thirteen in 1960, to about ten and a half today. The drop in voice that happens to boys when they mature usually occurs more toward the beginning of puberty, a little less than three years before maturation is complete. So we can extrapolate: if boys' voices break, on average, at ten and a half today, they're completing physical maturation when they're about thirteen. This means that the drop in the age at which boys finish puberty over the past few centuries has been similar in magnitude to that observed in girls — about three or four months per decade.

We've also been able to glean information on changes in male puberty from mortality statistics. In all cultures and times, the mortality rate among boys spikes a few years after they become adolescents. It's called the "accident hump," and it occurs because the rise in testosterone that takes place at puberty makes males more aggressive and reckless. That makes them more likely to do things that get them killed, like picking fights or doing risky things on a dare. Because many societies keep track of who dies and when, we can see whether the timing of the accident hump has shifted downward, as we'd expect to find if puberty was happening earlier. And indeed, the accident hump has also dropped by about three months per decade over the past several centuries.*

Scientists have to rely on these sorts of indirect measures to calculate whether the age at which boys go through puberty is earlier today than in the distant past. We have far better data on more recent trends because modern doctors keep better records. And these newer statistics tell a similar story. A 2012 report based on information provided by pediatricians throughout the United States documented that by 2010, boys were going through puberty as much as two years earlier than they were in the 1970s. The age at which males enter adolescence has continued to decline, just as it has among females.

Puberty may be more difficult to measure in males than females, but marriage isn't, so we can track the age of transition into adult roles just as easily among men as women. The average age at which men marry for the first time has increased. In 1950 the typical American man married at

---

* It was trending downward long before the twentieth century, so we know that the decline was not due to industrialization or the introduction of the automobile.

twenty-three; by 2011, the average age had risen to twenty-nine, an increase of about one year per decade — about the same as it rose among women.

In 1960, when boys were completing puberty at around sixteen and marrying at twenty-three, adolescence lasted about seven years. Today, with puberty ending around fourteen and first marriage taking place at around twenty-nine, male adolescence, just like female adolescence, lasts about fifteen years.

"Wait until you are married" is a piece of conventional wisdom that is getting harder and harder to follow.

How Low Can It Go?

The age of puberty declined steeply between 1850 and 1950, then slowed somewhat during the second half of the twentieth century, leading scientists to believe that we were reaching a biologically fixed minimum age of sexual maturity. When reports of the increasing prevalence of early puberty started to appear in the late 1990s, they were greeted with a mixture of shock and skepticism. But since then multiple studies have confirmed this trend. And there are reasons to believe that we haven't seen its end.

The age at which girls go through menarche is not the age at which they begin puberty — in fact, it is closer to the age at which they reach sexual maturity. Puberty is not only finishing earlier these days, it is beginning at an incredibly young age. Studies of menarche may not even be capturing just how shocking the drop has been.

The earliest observable changes that a young girl is maturing are "breast budding" and the growth of pubic hair, each of which can occur as much as three years before she gets her first period. If girls today on average are menstruating for the first time around their twelfth birthday, this means that the average American girl is beginning puberty at around age nine.

We do not have reliable data on the average age at which breast budding occurred long ago, because doctors and scientists recorded a girl's age at menarche but little else. But we do have information on changes that have taken place in recent decades. A large survey of American children born in the early 1960s found that the average age of breast budding was close to thirteen years. By the mid-1990s, it had fallen to a little under ten.

Pediatricians today are reporting an increase in the number of girls who are showing signs of breast development as early as seven or eight years old. The most recent U.S. study, based on data from the mid-2000s, found that one-tenth of white girls and nearly a quarter of black girls had developed breasts by age seven. (That's first or second grade.) A colleague of mine in the Department of Population, Family, and Reproductive Health at Johns Hopkins University told me recently that she and her colleagues are now seeing second graders who are already *menstruating.* This means that a significant portion of girls — most typically, black girls from the inner city — are showing the first signs of sexual development in kindergarten.

Although there have been fewer recent studies of boys, similar declines in the age of onset of male puberty are being reported. In a boy, the first external sign of puberty is a change in the size of his testicles. Studies using this indicator have shown that, by 2010, 10 percent of white boys and one-fifth of African American boys were showing the first signs of puberty by age six, or first grade.

The bottom line is that for boys as well as girls, adolescence starts earlier, ends later, and lasts longer than it ever has — three times as long as it did 150 years ago, and more than twice as long as it was in the 1950s.

Why Are Children Maturing Earlier?

Scientists used to believe that the timing of puberty was largely determined by genes — if your parents were early maturers, chances are you would be, too. But we now know that the age at which someone matures is due to a mix of genetic and environmental influences.

The most forceful of these influences are health and nutrition. On average, children whose mothers are well-nourished and healthy during pregnancy, and who themselves grow up with adequate diets and in good health, are more likely to go through puberty earlier. This has been confirmed in many studies that compare children from different parts of the world or from different economic brackets within the same country. The healthier and better fed you are, the more likely you are to mature earlier. The substantial drop in the age of puberty between 1850 and 1950 was due mainly to improvements in maternal and child health.

The continuing decline in the age of puberty in recent decades is thought to have different, and more troubling, causes. In the United States, maternal and child health and diet have not improved rapidly enough in recent history to hasten the onset of puberty as much as has been the case.

In order to understand why the age of puberty has continued to drop — especially with respect to children from some of our most unhealthy and poorest populations, like inner-city black children — we need to look at how puberty is triggered. Although it ultimately affects the way we look and develop through the impact of sex hormones on the body, these are "downstream events." Sexual maturation doesn't begin in the ovaries or testicles — it begins in the brain.

How Puberty Happens

The onset of puberty is stimulated by an increase in a brain chemical called kisspeptin (so named because it was discovered in Hershey, Pennsylvania, the birthplace of chocolate kisses). Kisspeptin stimulates a cascade of neurochemical processes that culminate in signals to the ovaries or testicles to increase the production of estrogen, testosterone, and other hormones that activate our sex drive and make us capable of reproduction. These same hormones also regulate all the external changes of puberty, like breast development, the growth of pubic hair, and changes in the appearance of our sex organs. The production of kisspeptin in the brain is affected by other chemicals, most importantly leptin, which stimulates it, and melatonin, which suppresses it.

Leptin is a protein that is produced by fat cells and that exists in our body in levels proportionate to our amount of body fat. It plays a critical role in the regulation of hunger and appetite by suppressing our desire to eat when we're full. In some senses, leptin serves to signal the brain not just that we are full enough, but that we are "fat enough."

Melatonin is a hormone that helps regulate the sleep cycle. Its levels rise and fall over the course of the day. Melatonin levels rise as the day grows darker, making us sleepy. As melatonin levels continue to increase into the evening, we become drowsy enough to fall asleep. As morning approaches, melatonin levels start to fall again, and we wake up.

This cycle is directed by an internal biological clock, but it can be shifted forward by exposure to light. If you are flying to France on an overnight flight from New York City that lands at 8:00 a.m. Paris time, one way to feel less sleepy when you land is to expose yourself to a lot of light as soon as you get off the plane, which will suppress melatonin production and help shift your internal clock to the morning (instead of leaving it at 2:00 a.m., which is what it feels like when the plane touches down). Some people find it helpful to take a melatonin supplement when they travel long distances, in order to help themselves fall asleep earlier than they ordinarily would in their home time zone. The best time to take melatonin is when it is evening at your destination, regardless of what time it is in the city you're leaving.

Melatonin levels are sensitive to artificial as well as natural light. That's why people are discouraged from staring at illuminated screens (like computer monitors, smartphones, or tablets) before they go to bed — the light they give off suppresses melatonin production, which makes it harder to feel sleepy. It's little surprise that today's teenagers, nearly all of whom have 24-7 access to televisions, computers, and other devices with glowing screens, are having more sleep problems than past generations.

Your genes predispose you to go through puberty around a particular age, but the more fat cells you have, and the more light to which you have been exposed, the more likely it is that you will go through puberty on the early side of your inherited propensity. Someone with the same genes, but who is thin and doesn't get as much light exposure, will go through puberty later. This is why puberty starts earlier among obese children and among children who grow up closer to the equator. Obese children have more body fat and therefore produce a lot more leptin, which stimulates kisspeptin production. Children who live near the equator are exposed to relatively more sunlight each year, and they have lower melatonin levels as a result, so their kisspeptin production is not suppressed as much as it is among children who live closer to the poles.

The reason that body fat and light exposure affect the timing of puberty is found in our evolutionary history. Humans evolved when resources were scarce, and it was adaptive to conceive and bear as many offspring as possible, since not all of them would survive. Because women have a limited number of menstrual cycles in a lifetime, the earlier they go through puberty and start having sex, the better their chances of giving birth to more surviving children. Early puberty means more menstrual cycles, and more chances to have children.*

If the ultimate goal is to bear as many children as possible, once someone has developed enough fat and senses that the season is right for gathering food, it is time to start maturing physically. Our genes don't know that we no longer live in a resource-scarce world and can store food in our cupboards and refrigerators so that we have plenty to eat in the dark of winter. Although conditions have changed, our brains evolve much more slowly, and the timing of puberty is still affected by our brain's circulating levels of leptin and melatonin.

Understanding this aspect of our evolutionary history helps to explain why puberty occurs earlier today than it did in the recent past. Our children are fatter, and they spend more time in front of screens, especially at night, which increases their daily light exposure (it also makes them more sedentary, which further contributes to obesity). As far as the timing of puberty goes, spending additional hours in front of the computer each night, when it would otherwise be dark, is like growing up closer to the equator.

The links between obesity, light exposure, and early puberty are much more well-documented among girls than boys, which makes sense given the fact that females carry the pregnancy and are the ones who need to have enough fat and enough food to do so successfully. But boys are going through puberty earlier, too, and this can't be because it was once evolutionarily advantageous for them to weigh more or to find food when the season was right. How can we explain why boys are maturing earlier today?

The answer is that obesity and excessive light exposure are not the only causes of early puberty, and many of the other forces are affecting males as well as females.

The onset of puberty, in boys as well as girls, is being hastened by increases in our children's exposure to "endocrine disruptors" — chemicals that throw off our body's normal hormonal functioning. These chemicals influence the timing of puberty by altering the production and effects of naturally produced sex hormones and, as well, by mimicking the hormones themselves. These disruptors are found in plastics (not just those used to manufacture food containers, but also in furniture and other household

---

* In case you were wondering, how old a woman was when she went through puberty has nothing to do with her age at menopause.

items we regularly come into contact with), pesticides, hair-care products, and many meat and dairy items, which may include animal hormones as well as manmade products that affect our endocrine systems. The presence of chemicals in the environment that can accelerate puberty is so ubiquitous that children are exposed to them even when their parents are very careful about what they eat. They are nearly impossible to avoid in modern society. Children with high exposure to endocrine disruptors mature at younger ages.

Early puberty is also more common among children — regardless of sex — who were born at a low birthweight, typically because they were born premature. Low birthweight leads to the overproduction of insulin, and abnormally high levels of insulin in the blood lead to excess weight gain and, frequently, obesity. In addition to accelerating puberty through its impact on obesity, though, high insulin levels also stimulate the production of sex hormones, which can make puberty begin earlier and proceed faster. Over the past several decades, there has been a significant increase in the number of children born prematurely and in the proportion of very-low-birthweight children who survive, which very likely has contributed to an increase in the number of early-maturing adolescents.

Finally, puberty may be occurring earlier because of increases in family stress. Although the research findings on this subject are more consistent for girls than boys, numerous studies have found that puberty begins earlier among adolescents who grow up in families in which there is relatively more conflict between parents and children, in homes where there has been an absent father, and in homes in which parents and children report feeling less close to each other. The reasons for this are not exactly clear, but it is likely that the added stress of growing up amid higher-than-normal levels of family tension plays a role. In large doses, stress hormones, like cortisol, interfere with normal development, and children who have been exposed to chronic stress often suffer delayed maturation. But in small doses — like the amount of stress that results from constantly bickering with one's parents — these hormones actually stimulate physical development. Some researchers have also hypothesized that father absence stimulates earlier puberty in girls by increasing their exposure to unrelated adult males — the men their mothers date — which may trigger sexual development through pheromones, which are chemicals we secrete that affect the biology and behavior of others. Female sexual development, in particular, is highly sensitive to pheromones. Frequent exposure to the scent of unrelated, sexually mature males may stimulate puberty in girls.

The fact that early puberty is related to obesity, artificial light, endo-crine disruptors, premature births, and family stress suggests that the age at which puberty begins may well continue to decline, since there are no signs that these forces will abate (recent reports of a decline in obesity among very young children turn out to have been overly optimistic). As shocking as it may sound, soon we may be having to educate preschool teachers in the ba-sics of adolescent development.

Why Early Puberty Matters

With the exception of a small number of people with rare medical condi-tions, everyone goes through puberty sooner or later. Everyone has a growth spurt, starts looking like a sexually mature person, and becomes interested in sex. Why does it matter whether puberty comes early or late, as long as it happens at *some* point?

The timing of puberty matters for two reasons. First, early maturers are often treated differently by others, which affects the way they act and feel about themselves. Early-maturing adolescents are more likely to wish they were older, hang around with older peers, disengage from school, and be more peer-oriented. The increased time they spend with older peers often draws early maturers into behaviors they wouldn't otherwise try until a much later age, like sex, delinquency, truancy, and smoking, drinking, and using other drugs. Because these sorts of behaviors tend to cluster together, early involvement in one of them (like drinking) frequently leads to early in-volvement in another (like sex). And because early sex is often unprotected sex, early-maturing adolescents more frequently expose themselves to the risks of pregnancy and STDs.

The impact of early puberty on problem behavior is similar for both sexes, but maturing early is psychologically tougher on girls. For most boys, early maturation is a boost to their egos—they're bigger and stronger at a time when athletic prowess makes boys popular. Because of their more adult-like appearance, boys who mature early are more likely to be given re-sponsibility and asked to take on leadership positions. Perhaps because of this, early-maturing boys are, as men, more successful in the workplace.

Early maturation does not affect girls this way. Girls who go through puberty early are more likely to develop depression, anxiety, panic attacks, and eating disorders. It's not hard to imagine why. The pressure that comes from being different (because girls on average mature significantly earlier than boys, early-maturing girls really stand out from the crowd), the attention from boys, and having to make decisions about sex before they are emotionally or intellectually prepared for it, can make early adolescence an especially stressful time. At a point in development when a girl is still figuring out who she is, receiving a lot of attention in response to her physical appearance influences the way she sees herself, as well as how others see her. Not surprisingly, early-maturing girls are at elevated risk for sexual abuse.

Society is ambivalent enough about *adolescent* sexuality. Preteens who look like sexual beings evoke even more uncomfortable reactions. Sara, a young woman I first met when she was twelve, is a good example of what sometimes happens.

Sara (not her real name) was a very pretty teenager, with light brown hair and unusual blue-gray eyes, but having gone through puberty when she was ten, by the time she turned twelve it wasn't her face that drew people's attention. Sara already had the fully developed body of a young woman. Men stared at her when they passed her on the street, in all likelihood unaware that they were ogling a sixth-grader.

Sara's early physical maturation also drew the attention of older boys in school, who were attracted to her sexual appearance and eager to take advantage of her emotional immaturity. It was hard for Sara to resist their advances, and she gradually began spending more of her time with older schoolmates who, as older adolescents are likely to do, enjoyed recreational activities that are rarely on the minds of twelve-year-olds. Girls who are early maturers frequently have romantic relationships with older boys, who may put pressure on them to go further sexually than they wish or are ready for. Older boys, in fact, turn out to be a big part of the problem that early-maturing girls face. Early-maturing girls are vulnerable to emotional distress in general, but especially so when they have a lot of male friends and when they are in schools with older peers (for example, sixth-grade girls who are in a school that has seventh- and eighth-graders, too).

By the time she was in the ninth grade, Sara was drinking, smoking, and getting high regularly. Her mother, divorced and herself addicted to alcohol and tranquilizers, was oblivious to the situation. By eleventh grade, Sara had more or less stopped going to school. When she saw her friends outside of school, she'd overhear them talking about where they would apply to college. Sara began worrying about what her days would be like after all of her classmates had moved away. She fell into a deep depression, threatening suicide several times.

Today, fortunately, Sara is employed, married, and happy. Although she ended up on a timetable that was delayed relative to her classmates, she eventually graduated from community college and, after a couple of bad relationships, met a young man who treated her well and was sensitive to her personal history. But during adolescence Sara was trouble, and troubled, and it took several extra years for her to get her life in order. Sara was lucky — many early-maturing girls develop serious psychological disorders, like depression, that persist into adulthood, and some studies show that their school achievement never fully recovers from the setbacks of early adolescence.

Sara's story shows how problematic early maturation can be when it changes the dynamics of adolescents' interactions with others, which in turn affects their mental health and behavior.

Early-maturing adolescents also experience a greater gap between when they mature physically and when they mature in other ways. This discrepancy can cause problems, as when an adolescent develops an interest in sex before he can think ahead well enough to remember to carry condoms, or when a girl starts to attract boys before she has the emotional wherewithal to decline their advances.

Some aspects of brain development in adolescence are driven by puberty, but others are not. One of the most important mismatches that can take place when children go through puberty early is between brain systems that mature in response to pubertal hormones and ones that don't. Indeed, one of the reasons early-maturing adolescents tend to have more problems than their peers has nothing to do with whom they hang around with. The cause of the problem, literally, is in their head. I'll explain why in the next chapter.

Early puberty isn't just dangerous in psychological terms; it's also associated with certain types of cancer, especially in women. Menarche at twelve or earlier elevates a woman's risk of breast cancer by 50 percent compared to menarche at sixteen. There have also been studies linking early puberty in girls to adult ovarian cancer, metabolic syndrome (which increases the risk for cardiovascular disease and diabetes), and obesity. Early puberty also may be a risk factor for testicular cancer.

Because early puberty carries significant health and behavioral risks, parents ought to be doing whatever they can to diminish the chances of their children becoming early maturers. They will need to intervene long before adolescence, though — ideally in early childhood. In the final chapter, I'll explain what parents can do to delay adolescence until the time is right.

Delaying Adulthood

While parents must often intervene to delay the onset of puberty, society itself seems to be delaying adulthood. Although there are exceptions to the general pattern, official statistics and large-scale surveys show that adolescents are staying in school longer, relying more on their parents for financial support and housing, and delaying marriage and parenthood.

Although some of the generational changes have been greater for one sex than the other, the basic story for men and women is the same. A much smaller proportion of today's twenty-somethings have taken on adult roles than their parents' generation had at the same age. Consider the contrast between the high-school graduating classes of 1976 and 1977 and those of 2002 and 2003, based on large-scale surveys that have been conducted for nearly four decades.

By age twenty-three, well over 80 percent of the older generation were no longer students. The majority weren't receiving any money from their parents — no financial support whatsoever — and only 30 percent relied on their parents for one-fifth or more of their income. Two-thirds were living on their own. Three-quarters of them were working full-time (that is, more than thirty-five hours per week), and about a third were married.

When they were twenty-three, fewer members of the younger generation were finished with their schooling, employed full-time, living independently, or married. At age twenty-three, one-third were still students. Only about 60 percent were working full-time. Nearly half were living with their parents, and the proportion receiving money from their parents had climbed from fewer than one-half (in their parents' generation) to two-thirds. More than half depended on their parents for at least 20 percent of their income. Only one in six were married.

These substantial generational differences were still apparent at the age of twenty-five. In the older generation, more than 80 percent were working full-time, half were married, and a third were parents by this age. Fewer than one-fourth were still living with their parents, and only a quarter were receiving any financial assistance from them. Only 15 percent relied on their parents for at least a fifth of their income, half of what it was when they were twenty-three.

At age twenty-five, about 70 percent of the younger generation were working full-time. But more than a third were living at home, and well over a third were receiving money from their parents; for more than a fifth of them, parental assistance constituted at least 20 percent of their annual income. Only one in four were married — half the number in their parents' generation at this age. Just one-fifth had children of their own, compared to one-third of their parents' generation when they were the same age.

The shift has been striking, particularly when we focus on twenty-five-year-olds. Twice as many in the younger generation were students at that age, and only half as many were married. Fifty percent more were living with their parents, and nearly 50 percent more were getting some financial help from them.

Self-Indulgence, Rational Choices, or Arrested Development?

It's easier to assemble these statistics than it is to know what to make of them. No doubt things have changed, but the numbers don't tell us why or, more important, whether the changes matter. There are three basic takes on the situation.

One popular perspective is that young people have chosen not to take on adult roles because they're lazy, self-absorbed, and spoiled. According to this view, the parents of today's twenty-somethings coddled them, overpraised them, and raised them to believe that they were entitled to a grand life — an entitlement that included taking plenty of time to find themselves. If you have always believed that you deserve the best job, partner, or home, why would you settle for less when you can still keep on looking, especially if Mommy and Daddy will foot some of the bill? According to this theory, delaying adulthood is a result of emotional immaturity.

Another interpretation holds that the changes simply reflect rational choices. The world of work has changed, and jobs that pay well demand more education, so young people are responding by staying in school longer. Sure, college is expensive, but the economic returns on a college degree are still huge, especially in the United States. Gender roles have changed a lot in the past twenty-five years, and the ascendance of young women in higher education (where they outnumber men by a considerable margin) and in the workplace (where they are far more likely than previous generations of women to be in well-paying jobs) has made women less dependent on men to support them, and therefore less willing to get married before they've gotten their careers on track. Delaying marriage, at least for those in the middle class, tends to mean delaying parenthood as well. And for the greater proportions of people in their midtwenties who are living with their parents or relying on them for financial assistance, the economy surely bears a lot of the blame. According to this view, there's nothing wrong with today's young people — they're merely responding sensibly to changing circumstances. Had their parents been placed in similar straits, they probably would have done the same thing.

A third perspective focuses on consequences rather than causes. This "arrested development" view starts from the premise that healthy development is facilitated by the demands of adulthood — the responsibilities of marriage and parenthood, the expectations of a job, the challenges of self-sufficiency. "What Is It About 20-Somethings?" a *New York Times Magazine* cover story asked a few years ago, the author describing young people as being "untethered," "avoiding commitments," and "forestalling the beginning of adult life." The article's subhead was particularly revealing: "Why are so many people in their 20s taking so long to grow up?" According to this view, we should be worried about today's young people not because of their reasons for choosing to stay in school, remain single, and accept money from their parents, but because of what these choices might do to them.

We need a fourth perspective, which introduces and applies recent findings about brain development. Whether delaying the transition to adulthood is a good thing or a bad thing depends on how these extra adolescent years are spent. As I noted in the previous chapter, the brain remains highly plastic until we make the transition into adulthood. If this malleability is maintained by staying engaged in novel, challenging, and cognitively stimulating activity, and if entering into the repetitive and less exciting roles of worker and spouse help close the window of plasticity, delaying the entrance into adulthood is not only OK — it is potentially a boon.

The most obvious example of this beneficial activity is higher education, an experience that has been shown to stimulate brain development. Going to college isn't just a learning experience or an opportunity to acquire a degree. It actually stimulates the development of higher-order cognitive abilities and self-control in ways that simply getting older does not. Naturally, it is possible for people to go to college without exposing themselves to challenge, or, conversely, to surround themselves with novel and intellectually demanding experiences in the workplace. But generally, this is more difficult to accomplish on the job than in school, especially in entry-level positions that are less apt to require new learning beyond the initial training period. Most entry-level jobs have a learning curve that hits a plateau relatively early on. I also suspect that for many, after its initial novelty has worn off, marriage also creates a lifestyle that is more routine and predictable than singlehood. Studies find that husbands and wives both report a sharp drop in marital satisfaction during the first few years after their wedding. No matter how interesting your spouse is, there are only so many ways you can make a meatloaf or recount your day's experiences over dinner.

Delayed Adulthood Is a Double-Edged Sword

Most research on the importance of structure and supervision during adolescence has focused on high-school students, but it also applies to older adolescents, whose self-control is still developing, too. During the late teens and early twenties, self-regulation is improving, but the gains are gradual and, as anyone who spends time with college undergraduates knows, there are frequent lapses (often exacerbated by alcohol, stress, fatigue, or peer influences). Some people this age consistently demonstrate adult levels of self-regulation, and others consistently do not, but for most, self-control waxes and wanes depending on circumstances. Because the ability to rein in one's impulses is still maturing, it is easily disrupted. The combination of an easily aroused reward-seeking system and day-to-day life that is unstructured and only minimally supervised, as it is for most college undergraduates who live away from home, can be problematic. As the size of the college population has swelled, so has the magnitude of this issue.

In the past, relatively few people in their midtwenties were still in school. But the proportion of people between twenty-two and twenty-four who are enrolled in school has nearly doubled since 1980, from 16 percent to 30 percent by 2009. Compared with people in their early twenties who are not in college, students this age are a lot more likely to engage in many kinds of risky and reckless activity.

Delaying the transition into adult roles during the early and mid twenties is a double-edged sword. On the one hand, it extends the period of unstructured life, elevating the risk that the sorts of problem behavior we associate with adolescence will persist until a later age. On the other hand, too much structure in the early twenties threatens to close the window of plasticity.

What determines whether delayed adulthood is an opportunity or a risk is how the time is spent. Debating whether the current generation's longer passage into adulthood is worrisome without distinguishing between those whose delayed transition is spent constructively and those who are frittering away the time watching talking cats on YouTube is like arguing about whether TV is good or bad for you without differentiating between *Masterpiece Theatre* and *Jersey Shore*.

Rethinking Adolescence

We naturally evaluate our children relative to what we expect of people their age. But these expectations are often based on what we were like when we were younger — how we acted when we were ten years old, what we cared about when we were in high school, what we had accomplished by the time we were twenty-four.

The lengthening of adolescence, brought on by the earlier onset of puberty and the delayed transition into adult roles, requires that we change the way we think about this stage of life. Parents, schools, and society have not yet adjusted to a world in which seven-year-olds are starting to show signs of sexual maturation and twenty-seven-year-olds are still dependent on their parents for financial assistance. An eleven-year-old who wants to dress in ways that boys find attractive isn't necessarily sexually precocious, nor is a twenty-five-year-old who hasn't settled into a career automatically floundering.

We need a fresh set of standards by which to judge the behavior of pre-adolescents, teenagers, and young adults. As we'll see in the next chapter, recent revelations about how adolescents think provides a good foundation for a new way of viewing these years.

4   *How Adolescents Think*

Danny didn't think he'd had too much to drink that night. His friends agreed. According to the police reports, none of the kids who'd been at the party thought that he shouldn't have driven home. They saw him talking on his cell phone as he left, in the midst of a heated argument with his girlfriend, who kept hanging up on him. One year older than Danny, and now away at college, she wanted to end their two-year relationship and date other people. Danny was obviously upset, but he wasn't drunk. No one at the party even thought of stopping him from getting into his Accord and driving off.

He never made it home that November night.

When the ambulance arrived at the local hospital's emergency room, Danny's blood alcohol level was .06, just under the state's legal limit — the legal limit for adults, that is. But because Danny was just seventeen — old enough to drive, but young enough to be required to follow a different set of rules — he was charged with DUI. Underage drivers aren't allowed to drive with any amount of alcohol in their blood. A DUI conviction as a teenager is serious enough. But the DUI would be the least of Danny's problems.

Danny was disoriented and confused when he got to the hospital, but he wasn't seriously injured. When the doctor examined him, Danny knew he had been in a car accident, but he had no idea that he had caused a head-on collision that took the life of a sixty-year-old mother of three.*

---

* I have changed the names of the involved parties and some of the minor details of the incident.

The reconstruction of the accident by the police investigators, based on their analysis of the crash scene, revealed that Danny had been driving under the speed limit, but that he had very likely swerved across the double yellow line into the oncoming car's lane. Cell phone records indicated that during the twenty minutes between the time he left the party and the crash, Danny had called his girlfriend ten times and had texted her at least twice that often. Each unanswered call and text only provoked another infuriated attempt to reach her. The investigators concluded that the nonstop texting and calling, coupled with just enough alcohol to slow his reflexes, had probably caused Danny to temporarily lose control of the car.

George Robertson, the county prosecutor, was intent on sending a message to the teenagers in the community: his office would not take underage drinking and driving lightly. Parties like the one Danny had attended had become all too common occurrences in this affluent suburb, where parents frequently left their teenagers home alone on weekends, and where the six-packs of Sam Adams and the handles of Absolut and Jack Daniel's circulated from one family room to another each Saturday night, depending on whose parents were out of town.

Danny, an honors student and standout athlete, attended these gatherings regularly. Up until his arrest, he was heading for an Ivy League school on a baseball scholarship. Needless to say, that wasn't going to happen now.

The prosecutor didn't care about Danny's future. He believed that a well-publicized case in which an underage drinker was tried and sentenced as an adult — and sent to prison — would put the county's adolescents on high alert, and quell the weekend partying and dangerous teen driving that threatened the safety of the community. In his mind, an innocent woman lost her life because some rich high-school kid was too distracted by a quarrel with his girlfriend to pay attention to his driving.

Danny's age placed him in a legal gray area, where he was an adolescent for some purposes but an adult for others. There was no question that he'd caused the accident, but the prosecutor had several charging options. The most lenient alternative would be to charge Danny in juvenile court with "death by auto," an offense that would send him to a facility for delinquents for a maximum of three years.

A second possibility would be to bring the same charge, but to prosecute Danny as an adult in criminal court. If convicted, he would receive a sentence of a minimum of five years in the county jail. Not only would this be a longer sentence, but Danny would serve it in a far more unpleasant facility, alongside adults who had been convicted of crimes like robbery or rape. In juvenile facilities, where the focus is on rehabilitation, adolescents receive counseling and go to school. It's no picnic, but it is much more forgiving than jail. In jail, the sole emphasis is on punishment.

The most serious step the prosecutor could take would be to charge Danny in criminal court with aggravated manslaughter, a first-degree offense characterized by "reckless disregard for human life." The prosecutor would have to prove that Danny knew exactly what he was doing, was fully aware that his actions had a very good chance of killing someone, but knowingly did it anyway. If convicted, Danny could go to state prison for thirty years. His cellmates would make the ones in county jail seem like boy scouts.

As far as George Robertson was concerned, the fact that Danny hadn't been drunk made the situation even worse. The seventeen-year-old had known exactly what he was doing when he left the party and continued to call and text while he drove. The prosecutor was leaning toward aggravated manslaughter. A front-page story in the local paper about a high-school junior being hauled off to prison might prevent some other teenager from doing what Danny did, and prevent another innocent person from dying. Although the prosecutor wouldn't admit it, the publicity wouldn't hurt his career, either. There was a lot of support in the community for cracking down on underage drinking, and everyone was worried about the growing epidemic of texting while driving.

It's hard to fathom how an Ivy League–bound honors student would do something so obviously reckless as Danny had done that night. Nor was he a bad kid who routinely thumbed his nose at the law. In addition to being a standout student and athlete, he volunteered in the community and coached younger kids in the town's youth baseball league. He'd never been in trouble before, and having two beers on a Saturday night was hardly a sign of moral depravity.

How can we explain what happened that night?

Danny's lawyer asked me to serve as an expert in the case, help make the argument that it should be heard in juvenile court, and persuade the prosecution that Danny's age should be taken into account in deciding what a fair punishment should be. She thought that introducing brain science into the discussion would help. After all, she argued, Danny was a seventeen-year-old whose bad judgment was at least partly due to something he had no control over: an immature brain. I agreed to do what I could.

Cases like Danny's are all too common—I know, because I receive calls from attorneys at least once a month. Some represent teenagers who have caused serious car crashes, like Danny, and are hoping for leniency. Some have clients who have committed violent crimes, like robbery or murder, and believe that their clients' immaturity should mitigate their punishment. One attorney who called was defending a teenager who was stung by the FBI when he downloaded pornography that contained images of younger adolescents. Others are lawyers for the parents of teenagers who have seriously injured themselves, or even died, doing foolish things—like trying to balance on a deck railing while urinating in a snowstorm, or jumping into the deep end of a swimming pool without knowing how to swim. (The parents usually are seeking damages from the people they believe should have been supervising their teenager more closely.) In all these cases, the attorneys, like Danny's, were hoping to convince the court that their clients' poor judgment was a consequence of the way their brains work.

We were only partly successful in Danny's case. The prosecutor agreed to charge him with the lesser crime, but only if he would plead guilty as an adult. In return, the prosecutor would agree to recommend the minimum jail sentence—five years. Danny took the deal. The possibility of spending the next thirty years in prison, surrounded by the state's most violent criminals, was just too frightening to contemplate. The mere thought of it had turned him suicidal during the weeks prior to reaching the plea agreement.

His lawyer told me that she would never forget the terrified look on Danny's face when they handcuffed him and took him off to jail. I can only imagine what his face would have looked like had he been going to prison, knowing that he would be held there until he was nearly fifty years old.

Risky Business

Danny's poor judgment that night is not unusual for someone his age. What's particularly striking about adolescent risk-taking is that the same age pattern is seen across an incredibly varied group of reckless behaviors. In virtually all arenas, adolescents take more risks than either children or adults, and the incidence of risky behavior usually peaks somewhere during the late teens. Violence peaks at this age. So do self-inflicted injuries, unintentional drownings, experimentation with drugs, accidental pregnancies, property crime, and fatal automobile crashes. These are very different sorts of behavior, but what they have in common is that they all involve risk taking.

One of the most puzzling things about this pattern is that by the time people have reached their late teens, they're just as smart as adults. Their memories are excellent. Their ability to reason is just as good as it will be in their twenties or thirties. Performance on standardized tests of cognitive ability improves from birth onward and plateaus around age sixteen, when it remains remarkably stable for at least thirty years, before it starts to decline. According to surveys in which people are asked about risky behavior, adolescents are just as knowledgeable as adults about the dangers associated with various types of reckless acts. And contrary to stereotype, they are no more likely than adults to suffer from delusions of invulnerability. They know what can happen to you if you have unprotected sex, drive after drinking, or take up smoking.

If adolescents are so smart, why do they do such stupid things?

The answer has to do with how their brains develop.

Phases in the Development of the Adolescent Brain

The brain reaches its full, adult size by around age ten. The changes that take place in the brain during adolescence are not so much about *growth* as they are about *reorganization.*

The reorganization of the brain's neural network is like the reorganization of the adolescent's social network. Early in adolescence, as children move from elementary school into middle school, there is an explosion in the number of new friendships. Many of these new relationships don't survive for very long, however — they fade away, as the adolescent begins concentrating her time in activities with a subset of the most important new people in her life. Relationships with this smaller group of friends become stronger as a result of their repeated activity together. Cliques form, patterns of friendship begin to solidify, and these impermeable social networks become more insulated. Toward the end of adolescence, even though people often relocate, many of the friendships formed during high school and college have grown so strong that people continue to communicate, often over a great distance.

By the early twenties, the adolescent's neural network, like her social network, is more deeply entrenched, more insulated, and better able to communicate over long distances. Yes, there will be changes in the brain after adolescence — just as there will be changes in the person's peer group. But the transformation and reorganization that take place in the brain during adolescence, like those that take place in the young person's social world, will never reach this level again.

What distinguishes adolescence from other periods in brain development is not the fact that remodeling is taking place, but *where* it is happening. It occurs primarily in two regions — the prefrontal cortex and the limbic system. The prefrontal cortex sits immediately behind your forehead, and it is the main brain area responsible for self-regulation — it makes us rational. The limbic system is deep in the center of the brain, beneath the cortex. The limbic system plays an especially important role in generating emotions.

The story of adolescence is the story of how these regions learn to work together. It is a tale that unfolds in three overlapping phases.

Phase One: Starting the Engines. Around the time of puberty, the limbic system becomes more easily aroused. This is the phase that has been described as "starting the engines." During this time teenagers become more emotional (experiencing and displaying higher "highs" and lower "lows"), more sensitive to the opinions and evaluations of others (especially peers), and more determined to have exciting and intense experiences — something psychologists refer to as "sensation seeking." In most families, bickering and squabbling become commonplace between parents and children in early adolescence. Because this aspect of brain maturation is driven mainly by the hormonal changes of puberty, the start and end of this phase will be determined by the ages at which the teenager starts and finishes maturing physically. Parents of early maturers are often taken by surprise because their children enter this phase before they've formally begun the teen years. Parents of late maturers won't see these psychological changes until much later.

Phase Two: Developing a Better Braking System. The second phase of brain development is gradual, actually starting in preadolescence, but not complete until age sixteen or so. During this segment, the prefrontal cortex slowly becomes better organized, a consequence of synaptic pruning and myelination. As information begins to flow more rapidly across longer distances in the brain, advanced thinking abilities — so-called "executive functions" — strengthen, which improves decision making, problem solving, and planning ahead. In the second phase, adolescents' thinking becomes much more adult-like. During middle adolescence — say, from fourteen to seventeen — parents often find that their children become much more reasonable and easier to discuss things with. A lot of the drama that had characterized the early adolescent years fades.

Phase Three: Putting a Skilled Driver Behind the Wheel. Although a fine-tuned braking system is in place by the end of the second phase, the teenager can't always use the brakes effectively and consistently. In the third phase, which is not finished until the early twenties, the brain becomes more interconnected. This is especially true with respect to the connections between the prefrontal cortex and the limbic system. This increase in connectivity results in mature and more dependable self-regulation. During the late teens and early twenties, adolescents get better at controlling their impulses, thinking about the long-term consequences of their decisions, and resisting peer pressure. Their rational thought processes are less easily disrupted by fatigue, stress, or emotional arousal. Young people still have much to learn about life, but for all intents and purposes, the intellectual machinery of adulthood is now fully in place.

In some respects, brain maturation in adolescence is mainly a continuation of processes that began much earlier in life. Improvements in the prefrontal cortex, for instance, have been ongoing since birth, although they are far more extensive in adolescence than before. In other respects, though, the brain changes during adolescence in ways that are unique to this period of development. This is especially true with respect to some of the first changes to occur in adolescence, which take place within the limbic system — the brain's sentry.

The Brain's Sentry

The limbic system is a collection of neighboring brain structures that serve somewhat different functions. One thing these structures have in common, though, is their role in detecting elements of the immediate environment that are important to pay attention to — together, they serve as the brain's sentry. The limbic system is especially important for detecting rewards and threats in the immediate environment—things to approach and things to avoid. Being able to do this is what drives us to act on a moment-to-moment basis.

The chief task of the limbic system is to create an emotion that motivates us to act in response to what's going on in the environment. Whether and how we act is not determined by the limbic system alone, though. The limbic system and the prefrontal cortex are in constant communication. Once an emotion is generated, a "report" is sent up to the prefrontal cortex, which evaluates and interprets the emotion and makes a decision about what to do in response to it.

The prefrontal cortex is what prevents us from blindly following our feelings all the time. Despite what our limbic system signals, we don't eat every time we see our favorite foods, slap someone any time we are annoyed, flirt whenever we're attracted to someone, or shriek every time we're frightened. Our ultimate actions depend on two things: the strength of the emotion and our ability to manage it. This is why some temptations are easier to resist than others (the ones that generate stronger feelings are harder to withstand), why we are more likely to give in to the same temptations under certain conditions than under others (when we are stressed or tired, for example, our ability to control ourselves is compromised), and why some people have more trouble regulating their behavior than others do (they have a stronger limbic-system response, weaker self-control, or both).

The Pursuit of Pleasure

As I explained in an earlier chapter, puberty remodels the brain and makes it more plastic. Puberty also changes the brain's chemistry, especially in the limbic system. This remodeling makes the system much more easily aroused, especially in response to rewards, because sex hormones have a particularly powerful impact on brain circuits that rely on dopamine.

Dopamine serves many purposes in the brain, but one of its most important is to signal the experience of pleasure and motivate us to go after it. When we see cues that make us feel good—pictures of happy faces, piles of coins, plates of chocolate cake, erotic photos—an increase in brain activity in circuits that rely on dopamine is what makes us crave company, money, sweets, or sex.

Some writers have described this feeling as a "dopamine squirt." When we anticipate receiving a reward — watching a roulette wheel spin after we've placed a bet, or watching the waiter wheel over the dessert cart — dopamine is what excites us. And when we finally receive the reward we've been thinking about — taste the cake, feel the kiss, hit the jackpot — dopamine creates the sensation of delight. The reason that drugs like cocaine or alcohol make us feel so good is that their molecules are structurally similar to dopamine. These molecules fit into the receptors within the brain that are designed for dopamine, and they make us feel the same pleasure that natural dopamine does, because they enable electrical impulses to jump across the same synapses and activate the same brain circuits that make us feel pleasure.

Puberty triggers a dramatic increase in the concentration of dopamine receptors, especially in the circuits that carry messages about rewards from the limbic system, which generates the feeling of pleasure, to the prefrontal cortex, which decides what to do with this information. This increase in receptors for dopamine makes these pathways much more easily activated, because it is easier for electrical impulses to travel across the synapses when there are more receptors to receive the dopamine molecules.

Do you remember how good your first passionate kiss felt? How much you loved the music that was popular when you were a teenager? How hard you laughed with your high-school friends? Things that feel good, feel better during adolescence. A small structure inside the limbic system (called the nucleus accumbens) is the most active part of the brain for the experience of pleasure — it's the center of the reward center — and it actually gets bigger as we grow from childhood into adolescence, but, alas, smaller as we age from adolescence to adulthood.

This is why nothing — whether it's being with your friends, having sex, licking an ice-cream cone, zipping along in a convertible on a warm summer evening, hearing your favorite music — will ever feel as good as it did when you were a teenager. Adolescents actually show a stronger preference for sweet things than adults do because sweetness is, as it were, sweeter to them. (If you've ever wondered why the perfumes young teenage girls like often smell like candy, there's your answer.)

Unfortunately, the teen's reward centers are also more sensitive to the chemical pleasures of alcohol, nicotine, and cocaine. This is one reason why adolescents are especially drawn to these substances. It's also why experimentation at this age so often leads to regular use, and why regular use at this age can lead to addiction. If the brain first tastes these substances in adulthood, the dopamine squirt they produce is not as intense — and not as addictive.

Because things feel especially pleasurable during the first half of adolescence — between puberty and age sixteen or so — kids this age go out of their way to seek rewarding experiences. At all ages we seek out things that make us feel good, of course. But adolescents will even put themselves in situations that are potentially dangerous, simply in pursuit of a potential reward. Like dopamine activity in the brain's reward centers, sensation seeking — which really is nothing more than a search for the dopamine squirt — also rises and falls during adolescence, peaking around age sixteen.

This isn't just true regarding physical rewards, like food, drugs, or money. It's also true for social rewards, like praise and attention from other people. This is one reason that adolescents are so sensitive to their friends' opinions about them.

Although adolescents are relatively more attentive and responsive to rewards than adults, they're actually *less* sensitive to losses. As a result, compared to children and adults, adolescents are more likely to approach situations in which they think a reward may be likely, but they are less likely to avoid situations in which they think they may have something to lose. This bias is something that parents and teachers should keep in mind: it's easier to change an adolescent's behavior by motivating him with the prospect of a reward than by threatening him with a potential punishment.

The Point of Adolescence

It makes perfect sense that adolescence is a time of heightened sensitivity to rewards. Think about what the "point" of adolescence is. It's all about mating — the ultimate pleasure.

Mating requires several things, some of which are obvious: the physical equipment necessary to reproduce, a sex drive to motivate us to do it, and a willing partner to mate with, preferably someone outside our own family, so that we don't inbreed. Puberty ensures that these things happen. It makes us mature sexually, become horny, and seek out comparably aroused (or at least arousable) partners.

One other thing that puberty does is not as immediately obvious, but it also makes perfect sense, in light of what we know about the adolescent years of other animals. In the wild, when an animal goes through puberty, it starts to seek out potential mates and, depending on the species, may even venture out into unfamiliar environments in pursuit of them. This is potentially very dangerous. A juvenile animal has to vie for the most desirable sex partners with older and stronger competitors. Juveniles need to be willing to take risks in order to get the job done. The rapid increase in dopamine activity shortly after puberty ensures that humans will do whatever it takes to reproduce at a time when fertility is especially high. A young woman reaches her maximum fertility in the late teen years. At this age, a well-timed act of intercourse (that is, when a woman is ovulating) will result in pregnancy about one out of every three times, but the odds of getting pregnant start to decline as you mature into adulthood, dropping to about one in four by the end of the twenties. It is no coincidence that the peak in adolescent risk-taking occurs around the same age that its potential payoff — successful reproduction — is greatest.

In today's world, where we don't worry about predators and are more likely to meet potential mates on the Internet than in the wild, it may strike you as far-fetched to view the heightened reward sensitivity of adolescence as having anything to do with the search for a reproductive partner. After all, nowadays most people don't start trying to have children until their thirties, long after puberty. But many traits that developed when humans were evolving have remained with us, even ones that no longer serve the same adaptive function they once did. Teenage risk-taking is one such vestige.

We generally think of puberty as something that ignites our libido — which indeed it does. But we now know that sex hormones make us more sensitive to rewards in general, and not merely interested in the pleasures of sex. As a result, puberty provokes all sorts of reward-seeking behaviors, some of which are perfectly fine, but others of which are dangerous — it's a package deal where the "bad" risk-taking comes with the "good." The problem is that we want adolescents to take some risks — try out for the school play, take an AP course rather than the standard fare, run into a scrum of players chasing a soccer ball — but we don't want them to try drugs, break into buildings, or drive through yellow traffic lights.

Fortunately, our ancestors also evolved a brain system that can regulate the passions stimulated by puberty.

The Brain's CEO

The prefrontal cortex is the brain's chief executive officer, responsible for higher-level cognitive skills, like thinking ahead, evaluating the costs and benefits of different choices, and coordinating emotions and thoughts. Connections between neurons in the prefrontal cortex proliferate from birth until around age ten, and are then gradually pruned, a long process that continues through about age twenty-five. During this same period, there is a steady increase in white matter in the prefrontal cortex, as more of the circuits that survive the pruning process become myelinated.

Before preadolescence, children aren't very good at thinking ahead. They have trouble controlling themselves. Teachers spend a lot of time asking them to sit still or raise their hands rather than blurting out the answer. Even in middle school, students find it difficult to stop talking to each other and fooling around when asked to do so. They can control themselves when forced to, but it's difficult.

All of this changes gradually by midadolescence. In fMRI experiments that use relatively easy self-control tasks, such as those that present participants with a rapid succession of letters and ask them to press a button each time a specific letter is capitalized but hold back when it is not, scientists see a more diffuse pattern of prefrontal activation in children than in teenagers, even when the age groups perform similarly. Regions that are not really needed to perform the task are more likely to light up in younger brains, whereas the pattern is more focused in the adolescent's brain. Imagine heading over to your favorite chair after dinner with a book you've been looking forward to reading. The difference between preadolescence and adolescence is the difference between turning on all the overhead lights in the room versus using the reading lamp next to the chair. Both approaches will get the job done, but the latter uses a lot less energy.

The brain doesn't mature overnight, however. As a result, during middle adolescence, mature self-control has a "now you see it, now you don't" quality. Scientists have studied this by administering the same self-control tasks to adolescents and adults under very different conditions. When the circumstances are ideal — no distractions, no strong emotions — a sixteen-year-old performs just as well as an adult. In fact, adolescents can exercise self-control just as well as, or even better than, adults when they know they will be rewarded for success. But being upset, excited, or tired interferes more with prefrontal functioning during adolescence than during adulthood, because the relevant brain circuits aren't fully mature. Fatigue and stress can interfere with self-control at any age, but they have a particularly powerful impact when the skills they disrupt are still somewhat tenuous.

These studies demonstrate just how important it is for parents and teachers to understand that teenagers' capacities for self-control and good judgment can be bolstered or undermined by circumstances. High-school-aged adolescents make better decisions when they're calm, well rested, and aware that they'll be rewarded for making good choices. When they're emotionally or socially aroused, their judgment deteriorates. In the next chapter, for example, I explain how the mere presence of other adolescents can make teenagers more likely to take risks.

As we mature into adulthood, the prefrontal cortex not only becomes more efficient. It also gets better at recruiting additional resources when a task demands more than this region can handle on its own. Compared to adolescents, adults are more likely to use multiple parts of the brain simultaneously. On very challenging tasks of self-control, adults, like children, often show more widespread activation than that seen in adolescents, but unlike the diffuse and scattershot pattern seen among children, the activity in different parts of the adult brain is highly coordinated — like the movements of experienced soccer players rather than the disorganized play of kids who know the basic rules but haven't yet figured out the intricacies of team play.

This kind of teamwork is made possible by an increase in actual physical connections between nonneighboring brain regions. Compared to a child's brain, an adult's has many more thick white "cables" connecting widely dispersed brain regions. Generally speaking, children's brains have a lot of relatively "local" connections — links between nearby brain regions. As we mature through adolescence and into adulthood, more distant regions become wired together. The brain continues to grow more interconnected until age twenty-two or so.

During the first half of adolescence, then, the prefrontal cortex improves by becoming more focused, which works fine as long as the challenges encountered are relatively simple and the environment doesn't weaken the ad-olescent's concentration (by fatigue or stress, for example). Self-regulation in early adolescence is stronger than it had been in childhood, but it is still somewhat tenuous and easily disrupted. During the second half of adoles-cence, self-control gradually becomes governed by a well-coordinated net-work of brain regions, which is helpful when we face a demanding task or distracting background conditions and we need additional brainpower. Part of becoming an adult is learning when we can do things on our own and when we need to ask for help. Brain maturation during this stage of life fol-lows a parallel course.

Teacher Sux

The combination of heightened sensitivity to rewards and immature self-control helps explain why otherwise intelligent adolescents, like Danny, do such obviously reckless things. Fortunately, not all instances of adolescents' poor judgment have fatal results. But many nevertheless have serious, and potentially life-altering, consequences.

Justin Swidler was an excellent student, but he and his math teacher, Kathleen Fulmer, had developed an intense dislike for each other. It was never clear just what it was about the fourteen-year-old boy that bothered his teacher, but according to him, she had singled him out, harassing him in class, calling him names, and insinuating in front of other students that he was gay. Once, when Justin had leaned over to pick up a piece of paper he tossed that had missed the trashcan, she remarked to the class that he appeared to be getting ready for his likely future as a garbage collector. Ac-cording to Justin, his teacher had sprayed him with a water bottle, hit him with a pillow, and deliberately flicked his ears with her finger as she walked down the aisle alongside his seat, just to annoy him.

A bright student with excellent computer skills and a squeaky-clean disciplinary history, Justin created a website to retaliate. If his teacher was going to make fun of him, he'd do the same to her. He showed his creation, "Welcome to Teacher Sux," to a classmate at his Bethlehem, Pennsylvania, middle school. Within a few days, a few other students had learned how to access the site.

The website's programming was sophisticated for an eighth-grader, but its content was quintessentially juvenile. It contained a top ten list of reasons that Mrs. Fulmer deserved to die, among them her body odor, her "fat fucking legs," and her incompetence as a math teacher. It featured a page on which a photo of her face morphed into a picture of Adolph Hitler and back again, over and over. On another page was an image in which the teacher's neck was cut, with blood spurting out. The site included a plea to send Justin twenty dollars so that the fourteen-year-old could hire a "hit man."

Soon after Justin's friends found out about the website, word began to spread among the students. A teacher received an anonymous email about its existence. The teacher looked into it and reported the website to the school's principal. As it turned out, Kathleen Fulmer was not the only member of the school staff who was being mocked. The principal, Thomas Kartsotis, was an object of Justin's antipathy, too. A crudely rendered video game invited visitors to the site to shoot out the eye of a cartoon figure of his likeness. A list of reasons that the principal "sucked" insinuated that he was having an affair with the principal of another school in the district.

Justin's website reflected the judgment of an eighth-grader who wasn't thinking about the possible consequences of his behavior. And his timing could not have been worse. School shootings were beginning to receive national attention. The widely publicized fatal shooting near Jonesboro, Arkansas, where an eleven-year-old and a thirteen-year-old had killed four students and a teacher, had occurred just two months earlier, in March 1998. The following month, a fourteen-year-old in Edinboro, Pennsylvania, had shot and killed a teacher at a middle-school dance. Just one week after Thomas Kartsotis first learned of Teacher Sux, a fifteen-year-old named Kip Kinkel killed his parents and two schoolmates, and wounded twenty-five others, in a shooting in Springfield, Oregon.

Kartsotis reported the website to the local police and the FBI. He also showed it to Kathleen Fulmer. She was terrified. According to her reports, she became anxious, started to have trouble sleeping, and lost her appetite.

About a week after the school principal had reported the website to the authorities, Justin voluntarily took Teacher Sux down. The FBI conducted an investigation, but declined to pursue the matter further, determining that Justin was not a "credible threat." Thomas Kartsotis was nevertheless concerned about the morale of his staff. The crisis was occupying too much of everyone's time and energy. It was exhausting.

The end of the school year brought a welcome respite from the matter, but questions remained about what to do. After holding a few hearings over the summer, the district decided to expel Justin and prohibit him from returning in the fall. His family sued the school district, contending that Justin's expulsion violated his First Amendment right to free speech.

The case had received so much attention in the local press that even before Justin was formally expelled, his parents decided to send him to a boarding school in Colorado. As word about Justin's case spread through the media, the incident started to generate attention outside Bethlehem. Justin was called out by the conservative talk-show host Laura Schlessinger ("Dr. Laura"), who described the incident and called him a "little creep." She urged listeners to send the school district money to help cover the costs of its legal defense against the Swidlers' suit. The district prevailed, both in the lower court and, as well, after the Swidlers appealed the initial ruling to a higher court. In both rulings, the judges found that although the satirical and sophomoric content of the website did not pose a credible danger, it was nevertheless disruptive to the school. That was enough to justify Justin's expulsion.*

The affair didn't end there, though. Parents of Justin's new classmates complained to the Colorado school. Justin was asked to leave. He returned to Pennsylvania, where he was homeschooled for several years before completing his high-school requirements and enrolling in college in Florida. Justin would eventually graduate and go on to receive a law degree from Duke University. He now practices law at a small firm.

The Swidlers' lawsuit against the school district wasn't the only legal matter prompted by Teacher Sux. In 1999 I was contacted by an attorney representing Justin in a civil suit brought by Kathleen Fulmer against Justin and his parents. In it, she alleged that the eighth-grader's misbehavior had defamed her character, invaded her privacy, and caused her so much emotional distress that she had to end her twenty-eight-year teaching career. She was seeking damages for her pain and suffering and lost future income.

From the moment I had first spoken with Justin's attorney, I was certain

---

* In previous cases, courts have held that a school's need to carry out its educational mission trumps students' First Amendment rights to free speech. Students are welcome to express their opinions, but the expression can't get in the way of the school carrying out the business of education.

that the civil suit would never come to trial. I understood why the school district had won the suit over Justin's expulsion, because the case *had* become a disruptive distraction. There probably would have been better ways to handle the situation than proceeding so quickly to expulsion hearings, but it was certainly plausible that the district had no choice but to force Justin to go to school somewhere else in order to restore order to the school. But a teacher suing a fourteen-year-old for defamation of character? It struck me as preposterous.

To my surprise, the judge permitted the suit to go forward, but I was absolutely sure the jury would take Justin's side. Even the judges who had previously sided with the school noted that the website, while tasteless, rude, and disruptive, wasn't dangerous. I started to get a little nervous, though, as I drove to the Northampton County courthouse on the day I was to testify on Justin's behalf. It was a few days before the 2000 presidential election. As I got farther away from my home in Philadelphia and closer to the court, the placards for Al Gore, which blanketed my neighborhood, progressively vanished. By the time I arrived, the only visible signs of the upcoming election broadcast support for George W. Bush. This was going to be a tough jury to sway, especially after the publicity generated by the shootings in Jonesboro, Edinboro, and Springfield. But still I thought that common sense would prevail.

On the witness stand I testified that Justin's behavior struck me as wrong, but nonetheless pretty typical for an eighth-grade boy who had a beef with a teacher, and that both the district and the teacher had overreacted. I urged the jury not to confuse the medium with the message. Had Justin written his top ten list in a notebook and circulated it around school, rather than constructing an elaborate and graphic website, I said, I doubted that we would be sitting in court. The website clearly indicated poor judgment, but it was obviously a parody that hardly constituted a real threat. As one of the dissenting judges in the Swidlers' unsuccessful lawsuit wrote, this type of sick humor was regularly seen in popular television shows like *South Park*. If every teacher who was made fun of by a fourteen-year-old student became upset enough to quit the profession, we'd have to close down our junior high schools. If each one decided to bring a lawsuit, we'd have to shut down our courts.

Boy, was I wrong. The jury ruled in Kathleen Fulmer's favor and awarded her $500,000 in damages.

Is This Portrait of Adolescence Universal?

Observing adolescents taking risks in their day-to-day lives tells us *what* they do. But it doesn't tell us *why*. If we want to really understand how adolescents make decisions—like Justin's decision to create his website, or Danny's decision to text his girlfriend while driving—it is also important to understand how they think. We don't know if Danny's accident was really caused by nonchalance about texting while driving, which is what the prosecutor contended. Perhaps he really hadn't realized just how risky it was. Or maybe the accident had nothing to do with texting at all. Maybe Danny drifted into the oncoming car's lane because he was busy fiddling with the radio, or because he dozed off for a short time. In order to prevent tragedies like adolescent driving fatalities, we need to understand how adolescents make decisions.

Unfortunately, we can't do this simply by asking teenagers to explain their actions. Adolescents, like adults, don't always know why they behave as they do. Sometimes the best way to understand how people make decisions is to test them under controlled conditions and see how their thought processes change when the conditions are altered. In experiments, we can induce different sorts of mental states, like distraction or fatigue, or change the incentives for making safe or risky decisions, or the amount of knowledge people have about the potential consequences of their choices, and see what happens.

Over the past fifteen years, my colleagues and I have tested thousands of adolescents and adults in our research laboratories in order to understand the underlying causes of adolescent risk-taking. We study whether adolescents take more risks than adults simply because they are willing to put themselves in situations they know are dangerous, because they are unaware of what is risky, or because they are so fixed on how taking a risk might be fun that they don't pay close attention to how a decision might go wrong. Each of these accounts of adolescent risk-taking is plausible, but each has potentially different implications for what we might do to deter adolescents from behaving recklessly. It would be pointless to spend a lot of time educating adolescents about what is risky, for example, if ignorance isn't the underlying problem.

Our experiments have consistently documented two important differences between children, adolescents, and adults. First, people's sensitivity to the potential rewards of a risky choice—like the possibility of winning a low-probability bet—peaks around age sixteen or so. Compared to children or adults, it is easier to get adolescents to gamble even when their odds of winning are small or uncertain. Second, children make more impulsive decisions than teenagers, and teenagers make more impulsive ones than adults. This combination of reward sensitivity and impulsivity makes middle adolescence—from about fourteen to eighteen—a very vulnerable and dangerous time. Teenagers' attraction to rewards impels them to do exciting things, even when they might be risky. But their poor self-control makes it hard for them to slow down and think before they act.

The picture of adolescence painted by this research is now widely accepted by scientists. One limitation of most research on adolescent decision making, though, is that it has been conducted mainly in the United States. Perhaps the portrait of the sensation-seeking teenager with poor impulse control isn't a hardwired feature of adolescence, but just a consequence of the way Americans raise their kids. Of course teenagers in the United States are out of control, some have said—that's because their parents aren't strict enough.

There is good reason to think that this basic pattern should be seen in other parts of the world, however. All children (or virtually all of them) go through puberty, and all of their brains are basted with sex hormones. The impact of these hormones on dopamine receptors is a basic biochemical process that has been demonstrated in numerous studies. So it's highly likely that the adolescent spike in reward sensitivity occurs around the world. And as we saw in the previous chapter, other consequences of puberty, like the accident hump, are universal across time and place.

It is harder to make predictions about self-control, which is less influenced by sex hormones. On the one hand, we would expect to see improvements in self-control during adolescence pretty much everywhere, since all societies ask teenagers to take some responsibility for their own behavior, and the more that people practice self-control, the better they should become at it. On the other hand, the maturation of the prefrontal cortex seems to be more sensitive to experience than the development of the limbic system. This would make us think that teenagers in cultures that demand a lot of self-control—as in Asia—should develop this capacity faster.

In 2010, with support from the Zurich-based Jacobs Foundation, I launched a study to see if what we had observed about American adolescents was true in other parts of the world. We administered a battery of tests identical to those we'd previously run on nearly one thousand Americans aged ten to thirty to samples of about five hundred people of the same age in China, Colombia, Cyprus, India, Italy, Jordan, Kenya, the Philippines, Sweden, and Thailand. (We also tested about five hundred new people of similar ages from the United States.)

My colleagues and I were stunned at how similar the results were across these very different places. The same age patterns in reward sensitivity and self-control that we had seen in our earlier study of Americans are also evident in these very different countries.

That said, there are cross-cultural differences in how this heightened reward sensitivity is *expressed*. In our study, for example, we saw a sharp increase in drinking during early adolescence in the United States, Sweden, and Italy, where alcohol is widely used by adults and readily available to teenagers. We saw no such increase in Jordan, though, where drinking is strongly discouraged, even among adults, and where opportunities for adolescents to obtain alcohol are scarce. Although rates of adolescent drinking are very low in Jordan, smoking, however, increases sharply around age thirteen in that country, just as it does in the United States, Sweden, and Italy. That's because smoking is socially acceptable in Jordan and it is easy for adolescents to get cigarettes.

The bottom line is that in places that are very different from the United States, and from each other, adolescence is characterized by heightened sensation seeking and still-maturing impulse control, as well as a greater willingness to take risks. Whether and in what form these inclinations manifest themselves in the real world may be culturally dependent, because different countries give young people differing levels of opportunity to try risky behaviors. We don't see high rates of teenage binge drinking in places where teenagers have a hard time obtaining alcohol. Nor do we find much unprotected sex among teenagers in societies where *any* sex before marriage is frowned upon. And we see little teenage gun violence in countries with strict gun-control laws. But the underlying inclinations that lead adolescents to take risks appear to be universal.

In other words, the reason that rates of adolescent risk-taking differ around the globe is not because adolescents are fundamentally different from one country to the next, but because the contexts in which they live are. This realization has important implications for how we should try to prevent adolescent risk-taking in the United States. It suggests that we should pay less attention to trying to change teenagers and more to trying to change the settings in which they spend time. I'll have much more to say about this in the next chapter.

The hallmarks of adolescence aren't just evident in humans; we see them in all mammals. The density of dopamine receptors in the limbic system peaks during puberty in mice, rats, and other primates. Like human adolescents, adolescents in other species show a sharp increase in the pleasure they get from drugs like alcohol, cocaine, nicotine, and methamphetamine. Interest in socializing with others the same age, experimenting with the unfamiliar, and taking risks all rise dramatically when mice go through puberty, just as they do in humans.

The fact that adolescence is beginning at a younger age now than ever before adds an interesting wrinkle to this story. Because the age of puberty is continuing to fall, so is the age at which the brain's reward system becomes so easily aroused. The maturation of the brain's self-control system is not driven by puberty, however. This means that the development of self-control has not been affected by the fact that children go through puberty earlier. Adolescents' abilities to plan, think ahead, and control their impulses probably don't develop along a more accelerated pace today than they did a hundred years ago.

When adolescence was only five years long, the age at which the brain became easily aroused as a consequence of puberty coincided with when we become able to effectively deal with this arousal. Because the age at which people develop mature self-control has not declined, but the age at which their passions are ignited has, the gap in years between these occurrences has widened. And with it, so has the length of the period during which young people are vulnerable to the consequences of having a mismatch between the power of their accelerator and the strength of their braking system.

Adolescence today is not only longer than it's ever been — it's also much more perilous.

5 *Protecting Adolescents from Themselves*

W hen our son, Ben, was fourteen, he and a bunch of friends from his suburban Philadelphia high school often spent Friday or Saturday nights hanging out together at one of their homes. They'd do just what you might expect teenage boys to do: stay up late, watch movies, eat junk food, and play video games. At around 2:00 a.m. on one of these nights, after they had finished watching *Happy Gilmore,* a movie they probably had seen about a dozen times, Ben, Josh, Steve, and Jason decided to sneak out of Jason's house and pay a surprise visit to Lindsay Hillman, a girl who lived a few blocks away. (Except for Ben's, all of those names are pseudonyms.) Jason was interested in her, and all of them were in one of those euphoric moods that Mountain Dew, Ruffles, and two hours of laughing at Adam Sandler can induce in fourteen-year-old boys.

I should make clear that they were very good kids. My wife and I knew them well. They all were good students, got along with their parents, and usually showed very good judgment. They were typical middle-class suburban boys growing up in the late 1990s—by no means angels, but far from being troublemakers. Before sneaking out of the house that night, in fact, they left a note on the kitchen table for Jason's parents, letting them know where they were going so that they wouldn't worry if they woke up and discovered the boys were gone.

When they arrived at Lindsay's house, Ben and his friends tossed some pebbles at her bedroom window, *Romeo and Juliet* style, to wake her up. Instead, they woke up the entire block. They'd accidentally set off the house's burglar alarm, which began to shriek. Unbeknownst to the boys, the Hillman's security system sent a call to the local police department, which immediately dispatched a patrol car to the house.

When the alarm went off, the boys ran away from Lindsay's house, down the dark, tree-lined street — and right into the police car, which had stopped when the officers saw the oncoming boys in their headlights. It would have been easy enough for the boys to tell the officers what had happened. There was no curfew in our town, and although the officers would likely have asked where they lived and what they were doing out at that hour, Ben and his friends knew that they weren't in serious trouble. Instead of explaining themselves, though, they scattered, and each went his own way, cutting through neighbors' yards on the way back to Jason's house. The police were able to follow only one of them, whom they apprehended and escorted back to his own home, where he received a stern lecture from his parents. The other three quietly snuck back into Jason's bedroom, where they recounted their adventure with much laughter and a fair amount of embellishment. I found out about this early the next morning, when Lindsay's mother called. Did I know where Ben had been last night? Yes, I said, at Jason's house. Ah, but did I know what he and his friends had been doing at two in the morning?

After I apologized to Lindsay's mother and hung up the phone, I called Ben on his cell phone. Get your things together and meet me outside of Jason's house, I told him. He was too groggy to ask why.

When I pulled up, Ben was sitting on the curb, zombie-like, his hair still uncombed and his eyes bleary. After he got into the car, I launched into a lecture. "Do you realize how insane it was to run from the police? It was dark, they have guns, and they might have thought they were interrupting a burglary. What were you thinking?"

Ben paused. "That's the problem," he replied. "I wasn't."

At the time, neither Ben nor I had any idea just how insightful his pithy diagnosis was.

Another kid, another story:

A fifteen-year-old boy I know well who was taking high-school chemistry figured out how to use supplies that he pilfered from the classroom supply closet to make small crystals that exploded and emitted puffs of violet smoke when they were touched. The explosions weren't loud — more like crackles than booms — but the noise and smoke were enough to startle the unwary.

This boy decided to play a practical joke on his chemistry teacher, an easygoing middle-aged former pharmaceutical scientist named Art Silverman, who had started teaching just a few years earlier, after retiring from a successful career with a big drug company. He enjoyed being around teenagers, and his relaxed manner made him one of the school's favorites.

Before class began, the practical joker sprinkled a handful of the crystals on one of the lab tables and gently placed a piece of loose-leaf paper on some of them, leaving others in plain sight. It looked like someone had left Oreo crumbs amidst the beakers and Bunsen burners. When the teacher entered the classroom, he saw the mess, casually picked up the piece of paper, smiled at the room full of students, and in mock anger asked, "Who left this *schmutz* on my desk?"

Using the paper as an impromptu sponge, he started to gather up the crystals. As soon as he crumpled the paper and pressed down on the pile, though, they crackled loudly, and a billow of purple smoke rose from the table. "What the hell?" he muttered. The other students, who were in on the joke, burst out in hysterics. The chemistry teacher was stunned for a moment, then joined in the laughter.

This incident happened in 1967, long before school shootings and terrorist threats were on anyone's mind. Had I done something this stupid today, I'd probably be arrested.

Deterring Risky Behavior

My high-school chemistry prank and my son's early-morning brush with the police luckily didn't have any unfortunate consequences, but that isn't the case for many of the reckless things that teenagers do. According to statistics from the FBI, most crimes are committed by adolescents. Arrests increase dramatically from age ten until eighteen, when they reach their peak, and then they decline precipitously between ages eighteen and twenty-five, gradually diminishing until age thirty, after which very few people commit serious crimes. This so-called age-crime curve is seen wherever crime statistics are recorded, and has been found decade after decade in the United States and Great Britain, where criminologists have done the most extensive work on the topic. Although social scientists continue to argue about the causes of crime, no one contests this trendline. It's true for violent crimes like robbery, rape, and assault, and it's true for nonviolent crimes like burglary, drug possession, and auto theft. The age-crime curve is not a function of police picking on this age group. It's there regardless of whether the data come from official arrest records or from anonymous surveys in which people disclose their wrongdoings with the promise of confidentiality. Either way, adolescents break the law more than children or adults.

Many different theories have been advanced to explain why crime rises during adolescence and then falls during the twenties. It's been attributed to the marginalization of youth, poverty, and intergenerational conflict, among other things. Criminologists would do well to look outside their field, though, because it's not just crime that follows this pattern. Almost all forms of risky, dangerous, and reckless behavior do. People become more reckless as they go through their adolescent years, and less reckless as they mature into their twenties. The fact that crime rises and falls during this same fifteen-year period actually may have nothing to do with crime per se.

Consider the statistics on accidental drowning, for example. According to the Centers for Disease Control and Prevention, drowning is more common during midadolescence than any other period of life except infancy. The high rate during adolescence is surprising, because we tend to think of drowning as something that is caused by physical weakness — problems in endurance, a lack of arm or leg strength, difficulty breathing, and so forth. By these measures, teenagers should be among the *least* likely to drown, not the most. In all likelihood, they drown more than other age groups because they're more likely to put themselves in situations in which swimming is more perilous — not from a lack of stamina, but from poor judgment.

Adolescents are also more likely than other age groups to experiment with alcohol, cigarettes, and illicit drugs. They are more likely to have unprotected sex, which explains why adolescents are more likely than adults to have unintended pregnancies and account for nearly half of all new STDs each year. They are less likely to wear bicycle helmets or seat belts. They are more likely to binge drink, engage in cutting and other forms of deliberate self-injury, and attempt suicide.*

Risky driving is especially common during adolescence. Adolescents are more likely to speed behind the wheel, get impatient with others who drive

---

* Adults are more "successful" at killing themselves, but adolescents try more frequently.

slowly, and say they like the sensation of driving fast. Adolescents have more car crashes, and not just because they're less experienced drivers. Studies that take this into account — that compare inexperienced teen drivers with equally inexperienced adults — find higher crash rates among teenagers, despite the fact that people in their teens and early twenties have quicker reaction times than adults in their thirties or forties.

The high rate of recklessness in adolescence, along with the consequences that it often leads to, creates a paradox as far as adolescent health is concerned. Adolescence is one of the healthiest periods in human development — very few people, relatively speaking, suffer from physical illness or disease at this age. Yet despite the fact that adolescents are healthier, stronger, and smarter than children, morbidity and mortality both increase between 200 and 300 percent between childhood and adolescence. Nearly half of all deaths during adolescence are due to accidents — and while motor vehicle crashes account for three-fourths of these fatalities, one-quarter of them are due to things like accidents involving swimming, poisonings, and guns. The second- and third-most-common causes of death in adolescence also have nothing to do with illness or disease — homicide and suicide. Similarly, the major causes of morbidity in adolescence — health problems that are serious but that don't necessarily lead to death — are behavioral: alcohol and drug use, unprotected sex, and obesity. The elevated rates of risk taking in adolescence create a massive public health problem, because many have consequences that persist long after adolescence ends.

Over the years, many explanations for adolescents' heightened risk-taking have been offered, among them, that people this age are irrational, lack the intellectual abilities to make good decisions, suffer from delusions of invulnerability, underestimate the riskiness of various dangerous activities, or are just plain ignorant about what is risky and what is not.

These assumptions have guided our approach to preventing adolescent risk-taking for decades. The basic idea has been to make adolescents more rational, more knowledgeable, and more realistic.

We spend hundreds of millions of dollars each year trying to increase adolescents' knowledge about various risky activities, improve their decision-making skills, and convince them that they're not indestructible. School-based health education is nearly universal in the United States. According to national surveys, more than 90 percent of American adolescents have taken classes in which they've been warned about the dangers of smoking, drinking, and using illegal drugs, and about 95 percent have had some sort of sex education.

Unfortunately, the whole premise on which most health education is based is just plain wrong. Adolescents are just as likely as adults to know what's risky and what isn't, and no worse than adults at estimating whether doing something risky will lead to a bad consequence. Nor does it seem that adolescents are any worse than adults in how they make decisions. Studies of people's intellectual capabilities and their ability to reason logically show that by the time they're sixteen, teenagers are just as good at these things as adults. Research on delusions of invulnerability similarly finds that adults are just as likely as adolescents to endorse these sorts of fables. When it comes to their health, people of all ages often act as if they can get away with things that others can't.

Much attention has been paid to adolescents' immature prefrontal cortex and poor impulse control as the cause of their reckless behavior. And in many instances, that attention is well placed, as we've discussed. But this is only half the story. After all, I wasn't acting impulsively when I planned my chemistry class prank well in advance of pulling it off. It took preparation and patience to make those crystals. More important, I didn't put them on Mr. Silverman's lab table because I wasn't thinking about the consequences. I did it precisely because I *was* thinking ahead. The thought of making my classmates laugh — and the chance to bask in their admiration of my cleverness and audacity — was too much to resist.

In other words, adolescent risk-taking is not just about the prefrontal cortex. Adolescents are far more sensitive to rewards than adults are — compared to life as an adolescent, life for an adult is like walking past a plate of warm chocolate-chip cookies with cotton in your nose, or running your fingers over an angora sweater with surgical gloves on. In either case, you can smell the cookies and feel the soft wool, but the scent and sensation are dulled. And as a result, you don't feel as strong a desire to eat one of the cookies or buy the sweater.

This supersensitivity to rewards makes adolescents naturally more attentive to the good things that might arise from their risky behavior. In our research, when we ask people to rate risky activities in terms of how dangerous they are, or how likely they are to lead to negative consequences, we don't see big differences between teenagers and adults. Everyone agrees that things like driving drunk or venturing into a dangerous neighborhood are risky. The notion that adolescents take risks because they don't know any better is ludicrous.

Where we see the most reliable differences between adolescents and adults is in how people view the relative costs and benefits of risky behavior. When asked how the potential upside of things like having unprotected sex or smoking compares to the potential downside, adolescents assess the potential costs just as well as children and adults do, but they place a lot more emphasis on the potential rewards. In other words, sometimes adolescents' apparent failure to delay gratification is not due to an inability to control themselves, but to a stronger preference for the immediate reward.

Intellectually, adolescents can understand consequences, but emotionally they are less sensitive to them than are other age groups. One of my favorite illustrations of this comes from a brain-imaging study in which adolescents and adults were presented with a series of statements, each briefly describing an activity, and asked to push a button to indicate whether the activity was a good idea or a bad idea. Some of the activities were obviously good ("eat a salad"); others were obviously bad ("light your hair on fire"). As you'd expect, everyone, regardless of age, indicated that the good activities were fine and the bad ones weren't. But adolescents took a little bit longer before making their decisions, even when the suggestions were as crazy as "swimming with sharks" or "drinking a can of Drano." Parts of the brain that are activated when we are shown something scary or disgusting — that create that visceral feeling of dread or revulsion we feel in our gut — were more likely to light up in adults' brains. Surprisingly, though, the parts of the brain that are engaged when we are deliberating were *more* likely to be activated in the adolescents' brains. As this research shows, teenagers are fully capable of identifying risks; they're just drawn more strongly to rewards.

The Peer Effect

For a long time, I puzzled over Ben's response that he hadn't been thinking when he ran from the cops that night. He was, and still is, someone who thinks about things a lot. He'd be the first to admit that he is more likely to obsess over a decision than to act rashly. The more I thought about it, the more I came to wonder if it was something about being with his friends that temporarily turned an otherwise levelheaded teenager into a reckless one.

Ben's behavior that night wasn't unusual for someone his age. Adolescents do far more foolish and reckless things when they are with their friends than when they are by themselves (most of us can recall crazy escapades with our friends that wouldn't have happened had we not been part of a group). Official statistics provide plenty of confirmation for our personal recollections: the presence of a group of teenage passengers in a car when a teenager is behind the wheel more than quadruples the chance of a crash (and the risks of a crash increase sharply with each additional teen who is in the car), but adults driving with passengers are no more likely to crash than when they're driving alone. When adolescents commit crimes, they're far more likely to offend in groups than adults, who are far more likely to be alone when they break the law. Most initial experimentation with alcohol and illicit drugs takes place when kids are with their friends. Even in Italy, where it's acceptable for adolescents to drink in the presence of family members, they're seven times more likely to drink for the first time with their friends than with their family, and they almost never drink for the first time by themselves.

Most people think that adolescents are more reckless with their friends because of peer pressure — that teenagers actively encourage each other to take chances, or at least ostracize the ones who don't. As one of my colleagues used to say, the fear of being called "chicken" has caused a lot of dangerous and foolish adolescent behavior.

As it turns out, peer pressure isn't necessarily the culprit that most people think it is.

My colleagues and I have been studying the effect of peers on adolescent risk-taking for ten years, motivated in part by my son's fateful nighttime visit to Lindsay Hillman's house. Some of our findings have surprised us. Even when we make it impossible for teenagers to communicate with each other — that is, impossible to pressure each other into taking risks — simply knowing that their friends are nearby makes them take more chances. They don't even have to know the kids who are watching. In fact, the presence of peers is so powerful during adolescence that it can even make mice misbehave. But I'm getting ahead of myself.

We first discovered this "peer effect" in a study of risky driving. We invited people of different ages to come with two friends to our research office, where we then randomly assigned them to play a video driving game, either alone or with their friends in the room, watching.

The game puts players in a situation familiar to anyone who drives — deciding whether to run a yellow light in order to get someplace in a hurry. The player is asked to navigate, as quickly as possible, a series of intersections with traffic lights that unexpectedly change from green to yellow. Participants are all paid for being in the study, but we tell them that the faster they complete the route, the more money they'll receive. That's the incentive to run the yellow lights rather than stopping and waiting for them to cycle from yellow, to red, to green.

You're told in advance that sometimes a car will come through the intersection just as you enter it, and if you are unlucky enough to crash, you lose a lot of time. That's your incentive to play it safe and put the brakes on when the light turns yellow. If you wait for the traffic signal to cycle back to green, you lose a little time, but not as much as you lose if you crash.

The problem is that you don't know beforehand which intersections are dangerous and which are not. Each time you reach an intersection, you have to balance your desire to get to the end of the course as quickly as possible and take home a bonus payment, against the knowledge that you might crash and risk losing the chance to earn extra money. In the real world, as in our driving game, decisions often involve choices between a sure, safe thing and a risky but more attractive one.

Adolescents take more chances when they play this game in front of their friends than when they play it alone — even when their friends aren't allowed to communicate with them. They run more yellow lights and they crash more often. Adults, on the other hand, play the game exactly the same way when they are being observed by their friends as when they are alone. They take risks every so often, but they aren't more likely to do this when their friends are watching them than when they are by themselves. These results parallel what we know about real-world driving — adolescents crash more often when other teens are in the car; adults drive the same way with or without passengers. Interestingly, the effect of passengers on real-world teen driving is only seen when the passengers are other teenagers. When adolescents drive with their parents in the car, they drive even more cautiously than they do when they're by themselves.

Why does the mere presence of friends make teenagers take more chances? We found the answer inside the adolescent's brain.

The Social Brain

In addition to firing up the brain's reward center, puberty also seems to cause changes in regions that oversee our reactions to other people. These regions, which together are sometimes referred to as "the social brain," are activated when teenagers are shown pictures of others' emotional expressions, when they are asked to think about their friendships, when they are asked to judge whether other people's feelings have been hurt, or when they're made to feel socially accepted or rejected. We all pay attention to other people's expressions, thoughts, feelings, and opinions of us. Adolescents just do it more than adults do. (Many autism researchers believe that problems in the social brain may be the root cause of this illness.)

The social brain is still changing in adolescence, and these changes help explain why young peoples' concerns about what their peers think increase during this time. It's the perfect neurobiological storm, at least if you'd like to make someone painfully self-conscious: improvements in brain functioning in areas important for figuring out what other people are thinking, the heightened arousal of regions that are sensitive to social acceptance and social rejection, and the greater responsiveness to other people's emotional cues, like facial expressions. Given all of this, it is easy to see why changes in these parts of the brain increase adolescents' sensitivity to their status within their peer group, make them more susceptible to peer pressure, and make them more interested in gossiping (and more anxious about becoming the subject of other people's gossip). Brain scientists have discovered the neurobiological underpinning of all of that social drama.

It hurts to be rejected at any age, but it's actually more painful during adolescence than at any other time. (In fact, the pain of social rejection so closely resembles physical pain in neurobiological terms that taking acetaminophen, the active ingredient in Tylenol, actually can help alleviate it.) This supersensitivity to the opinions of others can have serious consequences. Many experts think that this may cause the spike in depression in adolescence and explain why it is so much greater among girls than boys.

From an early age, girls are more sensitive to interpersonal events. Being female confers an advantage when it comes to empathy, but it raises the risk of depression in the face of social rejection.

No matter what gender they are, adolescents' fixation on others' emotions can dull their perception of potentially important information elsewhere in their environment. In a series of experiments, researchers conducted brain scans of adolescents and adults while they were viewing an intermingled sequence of four types of images — red circles, scrambled images, neutral faces, and emotional faces. The participants were instructed to indicate whenever they saw a red circle. Unlike adults, adolescents showed heightened brain activation whenever the emotional faces appeared, which interfered with their ability to note the appearance of subsequent red circles. This helps explain why yelling at a teenager in an angry voice can be a poor way of conveying your message, because she may pay more attention to your anger than to the content of your words. I always advise parents who are angry about something their adolescent did to come right out and say, "I'm too angry to discuss this with you right now, but we need to talk later, when I've calmed down." This strategy will improve the odds of having a more effective conversation.

The Folly of Crowds

It has become axiomatic in the business world that groups of people make better decisions than individuals, a phenomenon referred to as the "wisdom of crowds." How can we square this with the finding that adolescents do more foolish things in groups than when they are alone?

It turns out that even among adults, wise choices don't always result from group decision making. Studies find that groups work best when the people in them feel free to give their own opinions. When members of the group are too concerned about how other members perceive them, and conformity takes over, the quality of decision making is actually worse than when decisions are made by individuals. Given adolescents' heightened concern about what their peers think of them, their recklessness in group situations is perfectly understandable.

Decision making is the product of two competing brain systems — a reward system that is on the lookout for immediate stimulation, and a self-regulation system that keeps impulses in check and encourages us to think ahead. Before adolescence, self-control is still very immature, but by the middle of elementary school, that part of the brain is powerful enough to keep the reward system in check. If we think of the brain as a seesaw, we can say that it is well balanced during preadolescence.

With puberty, weight is added to the reward system's side of the seesaw. There simply isn't enough weight on the self-regulation side of the plank to balance this added force, which grows heavier until about age sixteen or so. Fortunately, as the prefrontal cortex matures, ballast is gradually added to the self-regulation side of the seesaw, offsetting the power of the reward-seeking system. As reward seeking declines, and self-control strengthens, the seesaw becomes balanced again.

But this balance can be easily upset during middle adolescence. Emotional arousal, fatigue, and stress can strain the self-regulatory system, diverting energy away from the challenge of keeping reward seeking in check, and tipping the balance in favor of arousal.

Introducing recreational drugs into the mix, for example, increases the brain's craving for dopamine, stimulating an even more intense search for sensation and novelty, either in the form of more or different drugs, or in other activities that further fuel the search for excitement. Rather than sate our need for rewards, exposure to one sort of rewarding stimulus tends to stimulate a desire for others. In other words, the brain's reward center is primed by pleasure from one source to unconsciously seek pleasure from others, the way a drink before dinner stimulates the appetite, or the way a cup of coffee or a glass of wine will often incite craving for nicotine in a smoker. Obese adolescents, for example, show hyperresponsivity not only to images of food, but to nonfood rewards as well.

There's a reason that retailers strive to put us in good moods when we're in their stores — positive feelings derived from one source, like pleasing music or free snacks, stimulate more reward seeking (otherwise known as shopping). Casino owners don't hand out free drinks to gamblers to get them drunk — if that were their goal, they wouldn't water the drinks down so much. They understand that priming the brain's reward centers a little bit with one source of pleasure — diluted liquor — induces us to seek out others (the sound of the slot machine going off). This is why we tend to eat and drink more when we are enjoying ourselves with other people than when we aren't having a good time. Feeling good makes us want to feel even better.

This explains why teenagers are more reckless when they are with their friends. During adolescence, peers light up the same reward centers that are aroused by drugs, sex, food, and money. Adolescents get a dopamine squirt from being with their friends, just as they do from other things that make them feel good. It's true in adolescent rodents as well as human adolescents. Being around animals the same age is so rewarding during adolescence that socializing with peers provokes chemical changes in the adolescent rodent's brain — but not the adult's brain — that are similar to those seen when the animals are given alcohol!

Just by being around their friends, adolescents' heightened sensitivity to social rewards makes them more sensitive to *all* kinds of rewards, including the potential rewards of a risky activity. When we conduct our risk-taking experiments in conjunction with brain imaging, letting the adolescent know that his or her friends are watching from the next room activates adolescents' reward centers — but not adults'. And the more these centers are activated, the more risks adolescents take. If we show adolescents pictures of rewarding stimuli — big piles of coins — while their friends are watching, their reward centers light up more than if we show them the same pictures without observers present. And, again, we don't see this peer effect when we test adults.

The impact of peers seems to make immediate rewards especially compelling. We've done several experiments in which we ask people which is more appealing, a small immediate reward ($200 today) or a larger delayed one ($1,000 in a year). Adolescents' preference for immediate rewards is intensified by the presence of their peers. It doesn't even have to be an actual friend — or an actual person, for that matter. We can make adolescents more reward sensitive in our experiments just by leading them to think another student is in the next room, watching them on a computer screen.

In other words, it's not necessarily overt peer pressure that leads adolescents to do more reckless things with their friends. It's that being around friends when you are a teenager makes everything feel so good that you become even more sensitive to rewards than you ordinarily are, which leads you to take chances you wouldn't otherwise take. Think back to Stacie's arrest, which I discussed at the beginning of the book. Put concretely, when adolescents are with their friends, things like shoplifting, experimenting with drugs, driving fast, or sneaking out to visit a friend at two in the morning actually feel more appealing than when they're alone.

In fact, the recklessness-enhancing effect of being around peers is strongest when adolescents actually know that there is a high probability of something bad happening. Vulnerability to this peer effect is still strong when people are in their early twenties — which goes a long way toward explaining some of the surprisingly juvenile behavior of otherwise mature college undergraduates when they're with their friends. One important implication of this research for parents is that they should try to minimize the amount of time their teenagers spend in unsupervised groups, because even adolescents who ordinarily are well behaved will be more likely to misbehave when they are with friends.

Because the increased sensitivity to social relationships in adolescence is triggered by puberty, we would expect to see similar patterns of behavior in other mammals — and this is the case. Adolescent mice are far more social than adult mice, and in studies that use different sorts of rewards to get mice to learn things, like finding their way around mazes, adolescent mice are more responsive to social rewards than adult mice are. If adolescent mice learn something in a social setting, the learning is more likely to be retained; this doesn't happen for adult mice. Many studies have found that human adolescents also learn more from group projects than from working alone, which is why discouraging collaboration in classrooms, out of an interest in evaluating individuals independently, may limit what adolescents gain from their time in school.

My colleagues and I wondered whether the effect of peers on human adolescents' risk-taking and sensitivity to rewards would be evident in mice as well. We did an experiment in which we raised mice in groups of three and then tested the effects of having peers present on their alcohol consumption. Half of the mice were tested shortly after puberty, and half were tested when they were fully grown adults. Amazingly, adolescent mice drank more alcohol when they were tested with their "friends" in the cage than when they were tested alone, but adult mice drank the same amount regardless.

The bottom line is that peers affect the adolescent brain in different ways than they do the adult brain. This discovery is important to parents — who need to be aware that adolescents exercise poorer judgment when they are in groups than when they are alone. This is one reason that passenger-restriction laws that prohibit adolescent drivers from having teenage passengers until they have accumulated a certain amount of experience driving alone have been so effective in reducing automobile deaths — far more effective than driver education. This is also why working parents who can't supervise their teens after school shouldn't let them have other adolescents over or let their kids spend their afternoons at the homes of other adolescents whose parents are absent. Countless studies have shown that, during adolescence, unstructured, unsupervised time with peers is a recipe for trouble. The prime time for adolescents' initial experimentation with alcohol, drugs, sex, and delinquent behavior is not on Friday or Saturday nights, but weekday afternoons.

Parents aren't the only ones who need to contend with this risky dynamic. I was once chatting with a retired U.S. Army general who was trained as a psychiatrist. I was describing our research on peer influences on risky decision making and asked him whether the Army took into account how it grouped soldiers when sending them out on combat missions. Few of us stop to think about it, but an enormous number of people serving in our armed forces, especially on the front lines, are adolescents; approximately 20 percent of active-duty military personnel (and more than a third of all Marines) are twenty-one or younger. The Department of Defense is the largest employer of people this age in the United States.

When soldiers are sent out on combat missions, they're often divided into fireteams composed of four warfighters. These foursomes must constantly make difficult decisions, frequently under conditions of fatigue, stress, and emotional arousal — the very circumstances that can impair adolescents' judgment. If these teams are exclusively composed of adolescents, especially adolescents under age twenty-two, they may make riskier decisions than teams that contain a mix of adolescents and adults. My colleagues and I have received a grant to study whether small groups that contain both adolescents and adults make better decisions than ones that include only adolescents. We hope that when the research is complete, we'll be able to guide the military on how best to compose teams of soldiers to optimize their judgment in combat and better protect them from harm.

Our research on how adolescents behave in groups may also be useful to employers of teenagers. I'll bet that few supervisors think about the age composition of work teams when they assign employees to shifts. They may well find that their younger employees are better behaved, and make better decisions, when adolescents and adults are mixed together than when adolescents work in groups composed exclusively of people their own age.

Protecting Adolescents When They Can't Help Themselves

In early 2013, the City of New York announced that it was going to attack the problem of teen pregnancy by putting posters on the city's subways alerting adolescents to the fact that studies have found that the children born to teen parents complete fewer years of schooling. In one, a tearful toddler explains, "I'm twice as likely not to graduate high school because you had me as a teen," demonstrating a command of the sociological literature that is absolutely remarkable for a two-year-old, let alone one born to a teenager.*

After the plan was publicized, controversy broke out over whether the $400,000 campaign unfairly stigmatized teen parents and, as representatives from Planned Parenthood put it, created "negative public opinions about teen pregnancy and parenthood," as if the public's view of teen parents could possibly be more disapproving than it already is. Richard Reeves, a fellow at the Brookings Institution, fired back at critics of the program, arguing in an op-ed in the *New York Times* that shaming teens into abstinence or safe sex was "a powerful weapon to reduce teen pregnancy."

I shook my head in astonishment at this debate. I couldn't decide which was more out of touch with reality, the city's campaign, Planned Parenthood's response, or Mr. Reeves's rejoinder. Put yourself in the position of a teenager for a moment. Imagine that you are a sixteen-year-old, cuddling on the couch after school with your boyfriend or girlfriend while your parents are at work. Imagine that one thing leads to the inevitable other, and that you are both now nearly unclothed. Imagine that you hadn't expected to go this far, and that neither of you is prepared with a condom. And now, imagine that one of you says, "Let's not — our baby's educational attainment may be compromised."

Whoever dreamed up the subway campaign simply doesn't understand how adolescents think. The main reason teenagers don't use contraception regularly isn't that they are unaware of the future consequences of having a child. It's that they often don't plan on having sex and, as a consequence,

---

*Apparently, the child wasn't aware that correlation is not necessarily causation. Teen parents are also, by and large, poorer than people who don't have children until they are adults, and children born into poverty are relatively less likely to succeed in school, regardless of how old their parents were when they were born.

start fooling around when they are unprepared. Just about anyone who was a sexually active teenager knows how hard it is to jump off *that* runaway train.

New York's subway campaign against teen pregnancy is but one of many examples of poorly conceived attempts to change adolescents' behavior. Many of these efforts are based on faulty premises, such as assuming that teenagers think about the future consequences of their acts when they are emotionally aroused (they don't), or that they take risks because they are ill-informed about what might happen to them if they do (they are well aware). Even if teenagers found the antipregnancy subway posters persuasive on an abstract level, the odds are slim that they would call up this knowledge in the throes of passion. Although the study of adolescent brain development has revolutionized our understanding of this stage of life, many of the policies and practices aimed at young people have not been influenced by these discoveries, and they remain grounded in old, antiquated, and erroneous views of the period. As a consequence, we waste hundreds of millions of dollars every year on programs whose failure could be easily predicted by anyone familiar with the science of adolescence.

We've made considerable progress in the prevention and treatment of disease and chronic illness in this age group, but haven't made similar gains in reducing the suffering and fatalities that result from risky and reckless behavior. Although rates of certain types of adolescent risk-taking, such as driving under the influence of alcohol or having unprotected sex, have dropped, the prevalence of risky behavior among teenagers remains high, and there has been no decline in adolescents' risky behavior in several years. Because many forms of unhealthy behavior initiated in adolescence, like smoking or drinking, elevate the risk for the behavior in adulthood, and because some forms of risk taking by adolescents, like reckless driving or crime, put all of us at risk, reducing risk taking among young people would substantially improve *everyone's* well-being.

For decades, the primary approach to doing this has been through educational programs, most of them school-based. There is good reason to be skeptical about the effectiveness of these programs. Despite the near-universal implementation of sex education, 40 percent of high-school students didn't use a condom the last time they had sex. And even though we require almost all adolescents to take courses in alcohol and drug education, nearly one-half of American adolescents have tried cigarettes, and nearly

20 percent are regular smokers. About 40 percent of American high-school students drink monthly, and nearly one-fifth *binge drink* each month. Each year, nearly 25 percent of adolescents ride in a car driven by someone who had been drinking. Almost 25 percent smoke marijuana monthly. Given the near-universal provision of health education, not to mention the coverage of the obesity epidemic in the press, it is hard to imagine that adolescents are ignorant of the risks of being overweight. Yet almost one-third of American high-school students are overweight or obese. We have made some progress in reducing a few forms of risky behavior, but in the last few years there has been no change in condom use, obesity, or cigarette use, and there actually has been an increase in suicide and marijuana use.

Long-term trends in many types of drug use do not inspire confidence that health education has had much of an effect on this activity. Adolescent substance use has been tracked very carefully in the United States since 1975. Forty years ago, about one-fourth of high-school seniors smoked marijuana monthly. That's about what it is today. Twenty years ago, about a third of high-school seniors got drunk regularly. That's about what it is today. I think most people would be stunned to learn that slightly more eighth graders use illicit drugs today than twenty years ago. Clearly, whatever we are doing has not been very effective.

The only place where we've made substantial and sustained progress has been in reducing teen smoking—but most experts agree that this has had almost nothing to do with health education. Fewer teens are smoking today than in the past mainly because the price of cigarettes has increased at more than twice the rate of inflation. A pack of cigarettes cost an average of sixty-three cents in 1980. Today the average is seven dollars. It's little wonder that fewer adolescents are smoking.

Correlational studies that track changes in risky behavior over time are subject to all sorts of problems of interpretation—among them, that lots of things can change over a time period that affect trends in behavior. An ineffective program may appear to work if it is in place during a time when opportunities to engage in the targeted behavior decline—a drop in cocaine use, for instance, might have nothing to do with drug education, but be due to more interdiction by law enforcement. Conversely, a program that actually works may look as if it doesn't if it is implemented at a time when the behavior it is supposed to reduce is increasing for other reasons. An antidelinquency program is far less likely to succeed if the economy crashes and fewer adolescents are able to get jobs. It could be that things would be even worse without these efforts.

For these reasons, it is important to look at the results of controlled experiments, in which adolescents are randomly assigned to programs designed to change their behavior and compared with matched groups of adolescents who have been assigned to control groups. Such "randomized trials" are the gold standard by which programs can really be judged.

Unfortunately, these evaluations are just as discouraging as the correlational studies. Most systematic research on health education indicates that even the best programs are successful at changing adolescents' knowledge but not in altering their behavior. Indeed, well over a billion dollars is spent each year in the United States on programs that educate adolescents about the dangers of smoking, drinking, drug use, unprotected sex, and reckless driving — all with surprisingly little impact on how adolescents actually behave. Most taxpayers would be surprised — and rightly angry — to learn that vast expenditures of their dollars are invested in health-, sex-, and driver-education programs that either do not work, such as DARE, abstinence education, and driver training, or are at best of unproven or unstudied effectiveness.

Given what we know about the root causes of adolescent risk-taking, the ineffectiveness of programs designed to educate kids about the dangers of different types of risky activity is predictable. The programs change what they know, but not how they act. Information is not enough to deter risky behavior, though, when the risk-taker is at a point in development where it is easy to become aroused and hard to control the impulses that this arousal generates.

It's as if the people who design health-education programs are not only clueless about adolescents, but are amnesiac about their own teen years. Many of us were in these very situations as adolescents and made the same bad choices. And if we think back to these times, we know that no amount of education would have stopped us from having unprotected intercourse when sex had passed the point of no return, from sharing a joint even though we promised ourselves that we weren't going to get high that night, from testing the limits of our driving ability, or from having another beer when we were already drunk.

Programs aimed at enhancing adolescents' general capacity for self-regulation are far more likely to be effective in reducing risky behavior than are those that are limited to providing them with information about risky activities. Such programs, which I describe in chapter 8, focus on generic skills that enable adolescents to exercise self-control rather than teaching them about the dangers of specific types of risky activity.

We need a new approach to public health interventions aimed at reducing adolescent risk-taking. Adolescents need protection when they are on their own, especially during the vulnerable period of mismatch between an easily aroused reward system and a still-developing self-regulatory one. Risk taking is a natural, hardwired, and evolutionarily understandable feature of adolescence. It may no longer be especially adaptive in the world in which we live, but it is in our genes, and there isn't much we can do to change that. Heightened risk taking during adolescence is normal and, to some extent, inevitable.

We should devote fewer resources to trying to change how adolescents think, and focus instead on limiting opportunities for their inherently immature judgment to hurt them or others. There is probably very little we can or should do to limit the increase in reward sensitivity that takes place at puberty, although there are steps we can take that may delay its onset, so that less time elapses between this shift and the maturation of self-control. As I discuss in the next two chapters, we can encourage the maturation of self-control, but doing this on a large scale would require significant changes in the ways in which we raise and educate adolescents. While I hope that this book will inspire parents and educators to consider this approach, I am realistic enough to know that there are limits to how widespread any change of this sort will be. There is an alternative, though.

Instead of trying to change adolescents into something they aren't—which is an uphill battle against evolution and endocrinology—we should try to change the context in which their natural inclinations for risk taking are played out. We do this already, but we need to do more of it, and we need to do it better. Parents can monitor and supervise their adolescents more consistently, and be especially watchful when they are going to be in groups. Communities can provide more and better afterschool programming that provides structure and adult supervision. Strategies such as raising the price and minimum purchase age of cigarettes, more vigilantly enforcing laws governing the sale of alcohol to minors, expanding adolescents' access to mental health and contraceptive services, and raising the driving age would likely be more effective in limiting adolescent smoking, substance abuse, pregnancy, and automobile fatalities than attempts to make adolescents wiser, less impulsive, or less shortsighted.

Some things just take time to develop, and mature judgment is one of them. While our kids are maturing, we must protect them from themselves, both by limiting their access to dangerous activities and by helping to foster their powers of self-regulation. In the short term, we might save to lives, and in the long term, we can help ensure that they live better lives for decades to come.

6   The Importance of Self-Regulation

One of the most famous studies in the history of psychology is widely known as the "marshmallow test." A preschooler is seated at a table, and a small treat that the child enjoys, like a marshmallow, pretzel, or cookie, is placed on a plate directly in front of the youngster. The experimenter then explains that he or she is going to leave the room and that the child has a choice: "You can have this treat whenever you want, but if you wait until I return, you'll get two of them, not just one." The experimenter turns, walks out, and goes into a room with a one-way mirror, to watch what happens. The test measures what psychologists call "delay of gratification," an important aspect of self-control.

A few kids give in right away. About a third are able to wait until the experimenter returns, which can take up to fifteen minutes. Most hold on as long as they can, but end up eating the treat before the experimenter returns. (If you search for "marshmallow test" on YouTube, you can watch some hysterical videos of kids' strategies for resisting temptation: some close their eyes, some sit on their hands, others place something over the marshmallow so that they can't see it.) Researchers use the marshmallow test to classify children either as "delayers" — the ones who wait the full fifteen minutes — or "nondelayers" — the ones who don't.

The original marshmallow study was done nearly fifty years ago. Follow-up studies that have tracked the children as they have grown up have found significant differences between the delayers and the nondelayers at all ages; the delayers consistently perform better on tests of self-control.

More remarkably, the people who were delayers when they were four years old turned out to be more successful in life as well as in the lab. As teenagers, the delayers had higher SAT scores and better coping abilities. As young adults, they had completed more years of schooling, were better at dealing with stress, and had higher self-esteem. The adults who had problems delaying gratification when they were preschoolers were more likely to be overweight and to have developed all sorts of behavioral problems, including drug abuse. The marshmallow test seems to gauge something about people that stays with them as they grow up.

A few years ago, researchers located some of the people who had been given the original marshmallow test, and conducted brain scans of them in their forties as they took new tests of self-control. Even in middle age, those who had been delayers when they were four showed more effective functioning of brain regions important for self-regulation and less arousal in regions that light up in the presence of rewards. In other words, people who could exercise self-restraint when they were very young had less easily activated "accelerators" and better "brakes," even as adults.

The marshmallow test may seem contrived, but it measures a skill we must use all the time in the real world. Life is constantly presenting us with choices between smaller immediate rewards and larger delayed ones—between spending money today versus saving it for retirement, going out with friends the night before an exam or staying home to study, breaking a diet because of a tempting dessert or forgoing it in order to look better at the beach in a couple of weeks. Although all of us succumb at some moments and resist at others, people have general inclinations that surface and resurface. Some of us are delayers, others not.

Now or Later?

In our lab, where we study adolescents and adults, we use a test we call "now or later" that's more appropriate for them than the marshmallow test. We present people with a series of hypothetical choices between two amounts of money and ask them which they would take—a smaller amount delivered sooner ($200 tomorrow) or a larger amount at a later date ($1,000 in a year). If the participant chooses the larger amount, we counter with a new amount for the more immediate offer that is midway between the original two ($600 tomorrow versus $1,000 in a year), to see what happens when we increase the desirability of the immediate reward. If this new offer is accepted, we counter again, this time with a smaller amount that is midway between the first immediate offer, which was declined, and the one that was just accepted ($400 tomorrow versus $1,000 in a year).

We keep adjusting these alternatives until we push people to the point where the immediate and delayed offers feel equivalent — their so-called "indifference point." Everyone has an indifference point. A person's indifference point reflects a preference more than an ability, because unlike the marshmallow test, our test doesn't really involve self-control. We're simply measuring how willing someone is to settle for less in order to get it sooner.

In our lab, we test participants using hypothetical money, but many studies have found that people who have a lower indifference point when the choices they are offered are theoretical also show a stronger preference for immediate rewards when the choices are real. Nor does the experiment have to involve money. If thirsty people are given the choice between a couple of drops of orange juice now or a full sip in ten minutes, some people go for the drops, and others wait for the sip.

There are two interesting observations that have been made using this sort of task, whose formal name is "delay discounting" (because it measures how much people devalue, or "discount," a reward because they have to wait for it). First, people's indifference point typically increases between childhood and adulthood. On average, children are more attracted to immediate rewards than teenagers, who are more attracted to them than adults.

There is an especially sharp drop in preference for immediate rewards during the first part of adolescence. Up until they are twelve, adolescents' preferences resemble those of children. By the time they are sixteen, they look just like adults'. Something important happens during the first part of adolescence that makes people less drawn to immediate rewards, and more willing to squelch this desire in exchange for a bigger prize down the road. This parallels what we know about the development of the brain's reward centers, which are easily aroused during the first half of adolescence but less intensely activated as people mature toward adulthood.

This pattern describes an average, of course. We all know adults whose ability to resist temptation is about as strong as a preschooler's. Which leads to the second important observation from studies of delay discounting: people who show a stronger preference for immediate rewards on tests like "now or later" actually have a lot more problems in life. They show higher rates of compulsive gambling, obesity, substance abuse, alcoholism, low school achievement, criminal behavior, and poor hygiene. It isn't clear whether these are consequences of being especially reward sensitive (drinking just feels better to them than to the rest of us), being particularly impulsive (they can't stop themselves when they see a bottle), or simply caring more about the present than the future (they figure they'll deal with the hangover tomorrow). But the inability or unwillingness to delay gratification — to decline an immediate reward in order to wait for a larger one — is a huge, lifelong liability.

The Ultimate Marshmallow Test

A friend of mine told me that when her ten-year-old daughter complained that doing homework wasn't fun, she turned to her daughter and asked, "Where did you ever get the idea that it was supposed to be?"

Like it or not, that's a lesson that all children need to learn: to succeed in life, you have to be able to force yourself to do plenty of things that you'd rather not be doing at the time in order to collect a larger payoff later. American parents worry too much about whether their children have fun in school. Students in countries that score highest on tests of achievement typically report enjoying school *less*. That's because their schools demand more hard work from them.

Doing what it takes to succeed in school frequently taxes children's ability to delay gratification. Most kids report that sitting in class every day is about as much fun as doing homework was for my friend's ten-year-old. By age eighteen, an adolescent has done this about three hundred times a year, year in and year out, for thirteen years — nearly four thousand times. College adds four, five, or, increasingly, even six more years to what already feels interminable. Business school, law school, grad school, and med school delay the prize even more. Let's not even talk about internships, clerkships, or assistantships. In a world that now demands so much formal education, good things come mainly to those who can wait.

Waiting for Marshmallows During the Longest Decade

The original marshmallow study was conducted in the late 1960s. The participants, who were four years old when they were tested, entered young adulthood in the early 1980s, when lots of people — not just poor people, but middle-class people — were getting married well before they were twenty-five, and when it was still possible for high-school graduates without college degrees to find jobs that paid living wages. The wage gap between those with high-school diplomas and those with college degrees was substantial then (adults who were college grads averaged about $20,000 annually, compared to high-school grads, who earned around $13,000), but the gap had been about that size for some time, and lots of people who weren't crazy about school were willing to tolerate it. In the early 1980s, though, the wage gap between those with just a diploma and those with a college degree began to widen. Few would have imagined how much it would grow over the next twenty years.

Success in the labor force has always been linked to how many years of schooling one has completed, but the prolongation of adolescence has intensified this relationship. As the educational requirements for a well-paying job have increased, those who lack the wherewithal to stay in school through college graduation have suffered disproportionately. In the early 1980s, adults who had graduated from college earned about 60 percent more than those who had taken college courses but not finished. By 2000, the average college graduate was earning almost twice as much as the average high-school grad.

From an earnings standpoint, going to college without getting a bachelor's degree is now pretty much a complete waste of time. In 2011, someone with a couple of years of college — even with an associate's degree — earned just 10 percent more than a high-school graduate with no college at all. In 2012, the unemployment rate of those with a few years of college was hardly above that of those who had never taken a class beyond high school. In other words, if you want to earn more than someone with just a high-school diploma, nowadays it is essential not only to go to college, but to actually get a bachelor's degree. For many people, that's a lot of gratification to delay.

As adolescence has been elongated, life's marshmallow test has gotten a lot harder. The arousal of the reward system, driven by puberty, occurs earlier and earlier. But it takes more and more time to start adulthood and earn a decent living.

In the twenty-first century, if you aren't a "delayer," you are in for a very tough time. On life's ultimate delay-discounting test, people who have strong self-control or a less sensitive reward system — or better yet, both — are the ones who are going to succeed. In the original marshmallow study, the experimenter with the promise of two marshmallows stepped out of the room for just fifteen minutes. Today, it's as if he's stepped out for fifteen years.

Angelica's Story

Discussions of how to fix what ails our labor force often focus on getting more people more education. But this has proven difficult to accomplish, in part because succeeding in school doesn't just depend on academic skills. This was illustrated perfectly in a 2012 front-page story in the *New York Times*. The story concerned the plight of three economically disadvantaged teenagers from Galveston, Texas, whose attempt to make a better life for themselves by going to college was derailed, despite their having been enrolled in a weekend and summer program designed to improve college readiness.

One of the girls, Angelica, had been admitted to Emory University, one of the nation's top schools and an institution that is extremely generous with its financial aid for needy students. Angelica had completed a college-prep program and was offered a free ride at Emory. Four years after graduating from high school, though, when she should have been marching at her college commencement, Angelica was back home, working as a clerk in a furniture store and $60,000 in debt. The other girls profiled in the article fared equally poorly.

The richly detailed story told in the article is a bit of a Rorschach — as the reporter notes, the links between social class and educational attainment are complicated. So many obstacles got in the way of these girls' success — family dysfunction, filial obligations, financial strain, a lack of familiarity with the world of higher education — that it is difficult to know just where to begin to formulate an explanation. The reporter wrote that "the tale could be cast as an elite school failing a needy student or a student unwilling to be helped," but I have a different take on it altogether. One factor that cut across the girls' stories was their incredibly poor judgment, which was tainted by their tendency to focus on the immediate and their difficulty in delaying gratification. This was not a central point of the article, but it's what jumped out at me when I read it.

Consider these details: Angelica was eligible for full financial aid from Emory but failed to fill out the necessary forms on time, despite repeated attempts by the university to remind her to complete them. She remained involved with a deadbeat high-school boyfriend whom she knew was a bad influence, and whose joblessness and financial reliance on her saddled Angelica with credit card debt and the need to take on a job while in school (which would not have been necessary had she filled out the financial-aid forms). Distressed and depressed by her situation, Angelica reacted by partying, increasing her work hours, and skipping classes. Not surprisingly, she spiraled downward.

There are many reasons to feel sympathy toward Angelica and her situation, much of which was out of her control. But when she could have acted in her own best interest, she was easily distracted by immediate rewards (like her boyfriend) and inattentive to the long-term consequences of her decisions (and indecisions). My point is not that Angelica was responsible for the obstacles she encountered, or that we should overlook the genuine difficulties that beset young people from poor families. It's that Angelica's problems had nothing to do with her academic preparation (she had good grades, high test scores, and college-readiness preparation) or a lack of money (Emory would have given her a free ride, had she only applied for financial aid). Indeed, a recent assessment of federal programs designed to prepare low-income students for college found that the only intervention whose evaluation was scientifically credible — a program called Upward Bound — didn't work. Moreover, and contrary to widespread belief that most students who drop out of college do so for financial reasons, studies of financial-aid and student-loan programs show that they have no impact on college completion.

The United States is facing a shortage of highly educated workers. People who think we can fix this problem merely by expanding college-prep courses and increasing financial aid are deluding themselves. So are those who believe that we can address our labor-force problem by convincing more students to enroll in college. If doing so just creates more Angelicas, we will have accomplished nothing and saddled a lot of poor people with a lot of debt.

Angelica's story certainly doesn't suggest that we shouldn't lower the barriers faced by the underprivileged, but it shows us that expanding opportunities to go to school without ensuring that people have the determination necessary to take advantage of them is unlikely to succeed. Encouraging more people to stay in school longer, without giving them the psychological capacities they need to succeed, is a fool's errand.

Unfortunately, Angelica's story is all too common. Today in the United States, nearly one-third of students who enter a full-time, two-year college program drop out after just one year, as do about one-fifth of students who enter a four-year college. The United States spends more money, in absolute and relative dollars, on postsecondary education than nearly any other country. It has one of the highest rates of college *entry* in the industrialized world. Yet it is tied for last in the rate of college *completion*. Getting our adolescents to go to college isn't the problem. It's getting them to graduate.

What Lucy Lacked

Nondelaying is hardly limited to the underprivileged. Not long ago, I was having lunch with a close friend, whining about my inability to predict which applicants to our graduate program would develop into first-rate students and successful scholars.

I had been describing the object of my latest frustration — a student whose standardized test scores and grades were off the chart, but who had proven disappointingly unproductive in her first three years of our doctoral program. Lucy (not the student's real name) and I would meet, discuss an idea that intrigued her, and I would ask her to write a short thought piece — no more than a couple of pages — that developed the idea and explained why it was interesting. I have found that asking beginning students to put their initial ideas on paper is a good way to help them clarify their thinking. In order to keep the exercise informal, I always tell them not to worry about using fancy prose, but to describe the idea as if they were explaining it to a family member or friend who knew nothing about psychology.

Lucy's pattern was always the same. She would leave our meeting inspired, and then she would disappear for weeks, avoiding any contact with me. After I would track her down and ask what had happened to the thought piece, she would just shrug and smile sheepishly. I would suggest that we schedule another meeting, which we would do, but the same scenario would inevitably unfold again. This had gone on for several years, and I was now ready to suggest that she consider a different career — or at the very least, changing advisors.

Some professors would have been more assertive in trying to address the underlying problem, but that isn't my style — something I make clear whenever a student expresses an interest in working with me. Success in our field requires self-direction and initiative — when you're a faculty member, no one harangues you about getting your research done. If you want to be a productive scholar and have any hope of someday being granted tenure, you have to put pressure on yourself. I want my students to get used to this as soon as they start graduate school. My chasing after them to see that they get their work done wouldn't do anybody any good.

I had been thinking about my initial decision to take Lucy on as a student and what I must have missed in my assessment. In my mind, I ran through the list of the thirty or so doctoral students I had mentored over the years and thought about what it was that consistently differentiated those who had been successful from those who hadn't. It certainly wasn't any of the factors that graduate programs base their admissions decisions on — GRE scores, undergraduate GPA, letters of recommendation, past research experience, a personal statement, or a brief interview. As I took myself through this exercise, matching former students and their careers with my recollection of their credentials at the time they applied, it struck me that the things we asked about on our admissions application were more or less useless in predicting future success in the field.

The friend I was sharing sushi with that afternoon is the founder of an internationally renowned investment firm that handles billions and billions of dollars for institutional investors — it manages the endowments of private foundations, nonprofit organizations, major universities, large corporations' retirement accounts, and the pension funds of state employee associations. His thoughts on the market are routinely quoted in the *Wall Street Journal*, *Barron's*, the *Financial Times*, and other top publications in the world of finance. Needless to say, when his firm hires new analysts, he can choose from among the top graduates of the world's best business schools. I was curious about how he did this, and whether he was any good at it.

My friend's firm is famous for its rigorous, quantitative, data-driven approach to investing. As opposed to investment houses that rely on a mix of hard data, general impressions, and educated hunches, his analysts build elaborate statistical models that are based on mountains of data. The quality of the firm's investment decisions depends entirely on the pinpoint accuracy of these models.

Given my friend's data-driven philosophy, and in view of the fact that he is in the prediction business, I figured he must be exceptional at using data to identify which job applicants would make the best analysts. I was surprised to hear him confess that he was pretty bad at picking analysts. We traded stories about some of our best (and worst) people-picking experiences. He agreed that the ones who became his firm's best analysts were not necessarily the smartest ones or from the most prestigious finance programs, but that they shared in common something that wasn't discernible until after they had been working for a while. Plain and simple, they worked harder. Like his other analysts, they built statistical models based on hundreds of pieces of data. But when they searched for data, they dug deeper. They read more reports, interviewed more experts, collected information on more indicators of a company's performance. Contrary to popular wisdom, they *did* sweat the small stuff.

It boiled down to the same thing my successful students all had, and what Lucy lacked. It has nothing to do with intelligence. It's all about the capacity to stay focused on a task and see it through to completion. Tenacity is more important than talent.

Determined to Succeed

If you had asked experts several decades ago what distinguishes young people who do well in school from those who do not, they would have answered that success is closely tied to intelligence. It was seen as self-evident that the students who succeeded in school were, well, smarter. Experts debated how best to assess intelligence, which aspects of it were most important, whether there were different kinds of intelligence or learning styles, and whether various types of intelligence tests were valid, but the assumption was that intellectual ability — however it was measured — determined who did well in the classroom.

As obvious as this may seem, when social scientists looked at the evidence, it turned out to be only partially true. Performance on IQ tests is highly correlated with how people do on other standardized tests, like the SAT, but this is largely because many of the items on these tests are similar, and because some people are just good test-takers. Only about 25 percent of school performance is accounted for by intelligence. The remaining 75 percent is due to something else.

Scores on other measures of intellectual ability aren't very predictive, either. As with IQ tests, performance on these tests predicts the grades that students earn, but the correlations are small. If you had to determine which first-graders would have successful scholastic careers, and you relied solely on standardized tests, you'd be wrong more often than not.

It's also true at the other end of the scholastic spectrum. Standardized test scores, like the GRE (taken by applicants to graduate school), LSAT (law school), and GMAT (business school), are correlated with grades, but the correlations are again very small, and once you start trying to predict success beyond grades in first-year classes, these tests don't perform very well at all — probably because the further you go in postgraduate school, the less your performance depends on taking tests. And as with intelligence tests and the prediction of success in elementary school, the standardized tests used for admission to graduate and professional programs are only marginally predictive of who succeeds in the real world. The tests aren't worthless — they just aren't all that helpful.

One of the reasons tests of intelligence, talent, or ability don't predict much in school, work, or life is that they don't measure characteristics like determination, persistence, or "grit." By determination, I mean more than the willingness or ability to work hard — although that is surely a part of it. People who are determined are also dedicated enough to maintain their focus and persevere even when the going gets tough. Determination involves conscientiousness, stamina, and sustained commitment. It requires delay of gratification — investing time and effort in an activity that may not have an immediate payoff, putting work in now for a reward that won't come until much later, and that may not come at all. Surprisingly, there is no correlation between determination and intelligence, ability, or talent.

Obviously, determination alone won't guarantee success. If you lack the basic skills of carpentry, no amount of perseverance will enable you to build a sturdy house. But talent without determination won't produce success either. We all know plenty of talented people who simply can't or won't work hard. A skilled carpenter who has difficulty completing projects is not going to build sturdy homes — or at least not habitable ones.

Noncognitive Skills

Determination is part of what education experts refer to as "noncognitive skills." The current revolution taking place in the study of school achievement focuses on these contributors to students' accomplishment, rather than on academic ability. Many experts now believe that it is these noncognitive factors that really distinguish children who succeed from those who don't.

Although I wholeheartedly agree with this reorientation, I think that "noncognitive skills" is a misnomer. The distinction isn't really between thinking and nonthinking. It's the difference between factors that are *intellectual* and those that are *motivational*.

The derivation of these two words makes this distinction clear. "Intellectual" comes from the Latin word for "understand." "Motivational" comes from the Latin word for "move." The current revolution involves a shift in focus from how to get kids to understand things to how to encourage them to use what they understand.

I also object to the "skills" portion of "noncognitive skills." Determination, perseverance, and tenacity aren't skills, like riding a bike, using a word processing program, or playing a G-major scale on the violin. Determination, perseverance, and tenacity are capacities that are nourished, rather than skills that are acquired.

This distinction between skills and capacities is vital, because intellectual abilities and the drive to succeed are cultivated through entirely different processes.

With a piece of chalk and a blackboard, I can teach you how to diagram the parts of speech in a sentence or calculate the area of a rectangle. I can help you understand the causes of the Civil War or the portrayal of women in early American literature by lecturing you on these topics. You can learn the symbols in the periodic table or the rivers of South America by reading a chemistry or geography textbook. But no amount of chalk, lecturing, or reading will help you develop the determination to sit at your desk and study for a grammar or geometry exam when you could be playing video games, or spend your spring break doing extra research for a term paper rather than going to Jamaica with your roommates.

Nearly twenty years ago, my colleagues and I described the results of a massive study of high-school achievement in a book called *Beyond the Classroom.* Of all the findings we presented, none received more attention than those concerning ethnic differences in school performance. Across the nine very different schools and twenty thousand students we studied, Asian American adolescents consistently performed better than any other group. Being Asian was more predictive of success than coming from a wealthy family or a two-parent household — two demographic variables consistently associated with school success in hundreds of other studies.

When we delved into this "mystery," we found that Asian students were more likely to believe that sustained effort paid off. As a consequence, they spent twice as much time studying, were less likely to cut school, were more likely to concentrate when they were in class, and were more likely to do their homework. They got better grades for the same reason that my friend's best analysts are more successful: they worked harder.

The determination to succeed is not cultivated through conventional academic instruction. Understanding what actually fosters it is crucial to helping children and adolescents do well in school, at work, and in life.

Why Do We Neglect Motivation?

The notion that perseverance pays off is hardly a revelation. It is a recurrent theme in the stories we read to our children (*The Little Engine That Could*), in classic works of literature (*I Know Why the Caged Bird Sings*), in popular movies depicting comebacks against all odds (*Rocky*), and in our cultural lore (Washington's troops at Valley Forge). We certainly recognize that motivation is critical for success. I'm not sure whether we think it just develops naturally and can't be cultivated, or that some people have it and others don't. But tenacity can be fostered, and psychologists know exactly how to cultivate it.

For whatever reason, this knowledge simply hasn't spread to most parents — or to our educational system. Helping children develop the capacity to persevere is not in the curriculum. Given that America leads the world in college dropout rates, it clearly should be.

How Much Does Motivation Matter?

It's not surprising that people who work hard are more successful than those who don't. What is surprising (at least to some) is that determination is more predictive of real-world success than intellect or talent. Adolescents who score high on measures of perseverance but only average on measures of intelligence are more successful than those who score high on measures of intelligence but only average on measures of perseverance.

Success in the world of work — how much money one earns, for example — is also more strongly correlated with effort than ability. The difference between a salesperson who accrues a lot of commissions and one who doesn't is persistence. No amount of smarts will make up for an unwillingness to keep pounding the pavement, even in the face of rejection.

In my field, over 80 percent of scientific papers and grant proposals are rejected. The researchers who get their papers published and their studies funded are the ones who revise and revise again, not the ones with brilliant ideas. Certainly brilliance doesn't hurt, but in my experience it matters less than persistence.

The abilities needed in most jobs can often be acquired after one is hired, but capacities like perseverance and conscientiousness must be nurtured before adulthood. Employers typically say that they prefer to hire hard workers than those who have specific skills. We shouldn't be surprised that ten thousand hours of practice predicts success in a given activity. It's not just that practice helps one develop skills; anyone who is willing to devote that much time to becoming better at something has what it takes to succeed — at anything.

Self-Regulation Is at the Heart of Determination

Determination demands many things — a strong motivation to succeed, self-confidence, commitment to completing a task, a belief in the power of hard work, and a focus on the future rather than the present. But at its core, more than any other capacity, determination requires self-regulation. The ability to control our emotions, thoughts, and behaviors is what enables us to stay focused, especially when things get difficult, unpleasant, or tedious. We rely on self-regulation to stop our minds from wandering, to force ourselves to push a little more even though we're tired, and to keep still when we'd rather be moving around. Self-regulation is what separates the determined — and the successful — from the insecure, the distractible, and the easily discouraged.

Self-regulation and the traits it influences, like determination, comprise one of the strongest predictors of many different types of success: achievement in school, success at work, more satisfying friendships and romantic relationships, and better physical and mental health. People who score high on measures of self-regulation complete more years of school, earn more money and have higher-status jobs, and are more likely to stay happily married. People who score low on these measures are more likely to get into trouble with the law and to suffer from a range of medical and psychological problems, including heart disease, obesity, depression, anxiety, and substance abuse.

People who can control their feelings are less likely to fly off the handle, which makes them less inclined to get into fights and arguments, less prone to emotional meltdowns, and easier to get along with — all good qualities to have in school, on the job, and at home. This, in turn, gets them better grades, bigger promotions, and more smiles from family members. Good self-regulators are also less likely to give in to temptation, and are therefore less likely to overeat, develop addictions, commit crimes, and spend beyond their means. As a consequence, they are less likely to become ill, be arrested, or fall into financial difficulty. And they're better at resisting distraction, focusing attention, and stopping themselves from obsessing over things they can't do anything about. This allows them to be more productive, more able to make and carry out plans, and less likely to fall into a funk they can't pull themselves out of.

The teenage years are a crucial time for developing self-regulation and for putting it into practice, since secondary schooling demands more independence, initiative, and self-reliance — when students are expected to work by themselves on assignments that take a long time to complete, like a term paper that's due at the end of a semester. In the primary grades, teachers and parents often help students who have weaker self-control stay focused. This support wanes as students get older, because we expect older children to be more independent.

Several findings from studies of self-regulation are especially relevant to this discussion. First, we've learned that self-regulation contributes just as much to health, happiness, and success as intelligence and socioeconomic status (SES), which themselves are well-established and robust predictors of positive life outcomes. Most people are aware of the huge advantages that intelligence and wealth confer. Fewer realize that it is just as advantageous to have strong self-control.

Adolescence is a key time to develop self-regulation. As we know from the marshmallow test, young children already have widely divergent levels of self-regulation. But the brain systems that govern this capacity remain highly plastic throughout adolescence. What's crucial to note in this regard is that after adolescence, many basic intellectual capacities are not plastic in the same way.

The Cultivation of Self-Control

Intelligence, as measured on most standardized tests of ability, is highly determined by genes—neuroscientists have even demonstrated that patterns of neural architecture in brain regions that regulate our performance on items that comprise intelligence tests are highly heritable. From about age six on, scores on tests of intelligence are remarkably stable. This doesn't mean that we don't become smarter as we get older, only that people who are relatively intelligent for their age as first-graders are likely to be relatively intelligent for their age when they're high-school seniors. Moreover, intelligence is even more stable over the course of adolescence than childhood.

Intelligence isn't as determined by one's genes as is a physical trait like height, but it is more strongly determined by genetics than most other psychological traits. Extreme deprivation, especially early in life, will compromise intellectual development, but small variations within the typical range of environments that children are exposed to don't matter very much.

Because we can measure levels of self-regulation so early in life with the marshmallow test, and because those early levels are so predictive of future success, it's tempting to conclude that problems in self-regulation must have strong genetic underpinnings that are engraved into the brain's circuitry. Not so. Like all psychological traits, self-control has a substantial genetic component, but the influence of genes on self-control is only about half that of intelligence. Even at a neural level, patterns of development in regions of the brain responsible for self-control are less genetically determined than those in regions that govern basic intellectual abilities.

On average, children who are relatively more impulsive when they are young are also relatively more impulsive when they are older, but the correlation between early and later impulsivity is surprisingly modest. This means that it is harder to predict adolescent impulsivity from measures of childhood impulsivity than it is to predict adolescent intelligence from childhood intelligence, in part because changes in self-control during adolescence are more influenced by the environment.

Changing the environment of an infant can have a profound effect on many aspects of the baby's development, including his intelligence. Unfortunately, taking an intellectually dull adolescent and moving him into a stimulating environment will do little, if anything, to alter how smart he is. But moving an adolescent with poor impulse control into an environment that encourages better self-regulation can make a real difference. Studies show that even the most impulsive, aggressive juvenile delinquents can be helped to develop better self-regulation.

Until the last decade or so, it was believed that if you had a particular genetic vulnerability (like a tendency toward depression) and were exposed to certain environmental conditions (like stress), you were destined to develop the problem. New research in genetics indicates that the story is more complicated than this.

It turns out that one of the most important tendencies we inherit is plasticity—how susceptible we are to the influence of the environment. Thus, what had been thought of as a genetic vulnerability to specific problems may really be a more general plasticity-proneness, which can work in either a positive or negative fashion. The very same genes that make us become depressed if we grow up in a bad environment, make us become psychologically stronger if we grow up in a really good one. There are several of these all-purpose plasticity genes, and adolescents who have a lot of them appear to be particularly susceptible to the influence of environmental forces that affect self-regulation. In other words, although genes contribute to self-control, whether these genes help it or hurt it depends on the environment. And the most important environmental contributor to self-regulation is the family.

7 How Parents Can Make a Difference

Infants come into the world with very poor abilities to regulate themselves. This is why parents have to help babies do this—rocking them into relaxation before putting them to sleep, calming them when they are having trouble feeding, holding them when they are on the verge of an emotional meltdown.

Helping a child develop self-control is a gradual exchange of the external regulation provided by parents (or some other source) for the internal regulation the child provides himself. The transition is so gradual that it's hard to connect the first dot of infancy with the endpoint of young adulthood. But the connection is there. The young adult who can control her thoughts, emotions, and behavior was once an infant who could barely do any of this, and who needed her parents to do it for her.

Three factors govern this transition. First, children must be emotionally secure enough to make the movement from external control to self-management. Second, they must be behaviorally skilled enough to know how to act when they're on their own. And third, children must be self-assured enough to seek and take responsibility for their own behavior. In other words, in order to develop adequate self-control, a child needs to be calm, competent, and confident.

Psychologists now know that parents whose children are good at self-regulation lay this foundation by doing three things very well from the start. They are *warm,* they are *firm,* and they are *supportive* of their child's growing sense of self-reliance. If you are a parent and you do these three things from the time your child is an infant, your adolescent will be better able to develop the ability to regulate his feelings, thoughts, and behaviors. If a parent hasn't done these all along, it is still possible (although more difficult) to stimulate security, competence, and self-assurance during adolescence itself.

Here, then, is a scientifically proven prescription for helping a child develop self-regulation.

Be Warm

Warm parents are affectionate, generous with praise, and responsive to their children's emotional needs. This contributes to self-regulation, because when children feel loved, they develop a strong sense that the world is a safe and benevolent place. This allows them to function away from their parents without worrying that trouble lurks around every corner. It's what allows a securely attached infant to crawl away from his mother's leg and explore the environment, a kindergartner to say goodbye to his parents the first time he goes off to school, or a seventh-grader to move from a familiar and intimate elementary school into a new, bigger, and more intimidating middle school.

Parents who are cold, aloof, or inconsistent in their warmth make their children feel insecure. Far from toughening a child's character, this type of parenting produces a veneer of strength that is actually brittle — like the thin shell of hardened chocolate sauce on a scoop of ice cream. The coating controls the shape of the ice cream for a while, but the least little disturbance will crack the shell and let the ice cream leak out. Children whose parents are not warm seem strong on the outside, but their trust of themselves, like their trust of others, is fragile.

As with all aspects of parenting, the ways in which good parents express warmth will vary from family to family and change as their child develops. The key is not so much how a parent expresses warmth, but the child's sense that he or she is loved, valued, and protected. Parental warmth makes children feel calmer when they are on their own, which is essential for the development of self-regulation.

There are several specific points to keep in mind when it comes to fostering a child's sense of security:

- *You cannot love your child too much.* Your child will not be harmed by being told every single day that you love him. Your child will not be harmed by being reminded that she is a source of endless happiness for you. Your child will not be hurt by being showered with physical affection, with care, and with praise when it's heartfelt and well deserved. Don't hold back affection or act aloof because you think your child will become spoiled by too much attention. Some parents believe that holding back love helps develop a child's character. In fact, just the opposite is true. When children feel genuinely loved, they're almost always less needy.

- *Be physically affectionate.* Children need plenty of physical affection from their parents, not just during infancy, but throughout childhood and adolescence. Parents don't always realize that children need physical affection even after they have reached a stage where they may seem too grown up for overt displays of it. Sometimes you just have to be a little subtle in when and how you express it. There is no reason to make a big deal about it — in fact, expressing your affection for your child physically probably is more satisfying for your child when it is a natural, day-to-day part of your relationship. In other words, learn to express physical affection toward your child without making a big show of it — with a quick kiss before she leaves for school in the morning, a hug when she returns in the afternoon, a shoulder rub when she is leaning over the kitchen table doing her homework, or a back massage while you tuck her in for the night. All of this physical contact, however subtle and low-key, reinforces and strengthens your emotional connection to each other.

- *Try to understand and respond to your child's emotional needs.* By this, I don't simply mean comforting your child when he's crying or reassuring her when she's afraid. It also entails observing your child's moods carefully and reacting in ways that help his emotional development. Children's emotional needs change as they develop. During infancy, parents must instill a sense of safety and trust by soothing their baby when she is upset. During early childhood, parents must help a child feel in control and more grown up by rewarding mature behavior with praise. During elementary school, when kids are often insecure about their abilities, responsive parents help them feel more capable by setting up situations so that their child can succeed. And during adolescence, being responsive means helping to foster your teenager's confidence in his or her ability to function independently by providing opportunities for meaningful decision making.

- *Provide a safe haven.* Children need to feel that their home is a place where they can retreat from the tensions and pressures of everyday life. Create the sort of atmosphere in your home that allows your child to really relax and escape from his problems, by limiting his exposure to stress, upsetting arguments, and out-of-control displays of emotion. Children need this peace of mind whether they've had a tough day at school, an awful experience on the playground, a day of heartless rejection at the hands of their friends, or an argument with a boyfriend or girlfriend. You can't make these problems go away, but a safe haven at home will provide some necessary respite and distraction.

- *Be involved in your child's life.* The strongest and most consistent predictor of children's mental health, adjustment, happiness, and well-being is the degree to which their parents are involved in their lives. Children with involved parents who attend school functions do better in school. Those whose parents spend casual time just talking to them feel better about themselves and are less likely to develop emotional problems. When parents know their children's friends, their children are less likely to take risks or get into trouble. There is nothing more important to your child's psychological development than your deep and sustained involvement. Being an involved parent takes time and hard work, and it often means rethinking and rearranging your priorities. It frequently means sacrificing what you want to do for what your child needs you to do. It may mean skipping an unnecessary meeting at work or arranging an out-of-town business trip to be as brief as you can afford it to be. But it's worth it. It will give him a legacy of psychological well-being that will last him his entire life. And it is absolutely crucial for the development of self-regulation.

Be Firm

Firmness refers to the degree and consistency of limits that parents impose on their child's behavior. Firm parents have clearly articulated the rules they expect their child to follow, and they make demands on the child to behave in a mature and responsible fashion. Children raised in this way know what their parents expect of them and understand that there are consequences for violating their expectations. In contrast, lenient parents have few rules or standards for their child's behavior, or have rules but enforce them lackadaisically or inconsistently. In the absence of sufficient guidance, children come to feel that anything goes or, alternatively, that it is impossible to know what is, or is not, acceptable behavior.

Some parents are reluctant to be firm because they don't want to make their children feel controlled or pressured. They put themselves in their child's position and imagine what it must feel like to have other people tell you what to do all the time. And because feeling constrained by others feels bad to adults, they figure that it must feel bad to kids, too. But kids aren't adults, and they react differently to limitations than we do. The structure imposed by rules and limits doesn't make children feel bad. Quite the contrary. Structure makes children feel safe.

We learn how to regulate ourselves by being regulated. Children acquire self-control by taking the rules that their parents have imposed on them and imposing them on themselves. When the external control isn't there to begin with, the internal control won't develop. If you don't brush your child's teeth for him when he's young, he won't know how to brush them himself when he gets older. Parental firmness contributes to children's ultimate ability to manage themselves.

Naturally, parents' specific rules and expectations should change as their child matures and displays an increasing capacity for self-regulation. A parent's job is to pay attention to these signs and to adjust the rules accordingly. Children of all ages need limits, but these should gradually become relaxed as children show they can impose limits on themselves. This is an important part of the gradual transition from external control to self-control.

Here are some tips on how to be a firm parent:

- *Make your expectations clear.* Sometimes parents' expectations are not clear because they're left unstated. You assume he knows that he's not supposed to leave wet towels on his bed. Or that he's supposed to call you when he's going to be late for dinner. Or that when he sees you shoveling snow off the front walk or weeding the garden, he's to come out and lend a hand. But what seems to you like something that ought to be a given may not be a given in the mind of a teenager. He may look like an adult, but that doesn't mean that he thinks like one. Sometimes parents' expectations aren't clear because they're stated too vaguely. It's not enough to tell your twelve-year-old that you expect her to keep her room clean. She may think that this means straightening up her desk. You need to explain that cleaning her room also includes putting clothes away if they're clean and in the hamper if not, dusting off her dresser, and vacuuming once a week. When you tell your adolescent what you expect, make sure you spell it out in detail. If it is possible to use a specific number when describing an expectation — the time your teenager is supposed to be home from a concert, the number of minutes you expect her to practice her instrument, and so forth — use one. Finally, your expectations may not be clear to your child because they're not entirely clear to you. When your teenager asked if she could take on a part-time job to earn extra spending money, you told her that she could work, but only if she did well enough in school. But what does "well enough" mean to you? Trying her hardest? Earning straight As? Doing better than her classmates? Doing better than she did last year? All of these are different things, even though each could be construed as an indicator of doing "well enough." If you're not sure, your child can't possibly be.
- *Explain your rules and decisions.* When children understand the logic behind their parents' expectations, it is much easier for them to figure out how to behave on their own. There is no point in having expectations if your child is confused about what they are. Don't hesitate to ask your child's opinion about a rule you have made or

an expectation you've expressed. Soliciting your child's opinion tells her that you value her point of view and are willing to look at things from her perspective; it makes her a part of the decision-making process. It may be an inconvenient irritant that your child has his own opinions about matters you believe are a parent's business, but this is a small price to pay for having a child who won't be shy about asserting his opinion in other situations when he doesn't think he's getting a fair shake. Remember, the lessons your child learns in his relationship with you are going to shape the way he behaves when he is with other people.

- *Be consistent.* The single greatest parental contributor to poor self-control in children is inconsistent parenting. If your rules vary unpredictably from day to day, or if you only enforce them inter-mittently, your child's misbehavior is your fault, not his. The easi-est way to teach a child how to behave appropriately is to make her good behavior a habit that she doesn't even have to think about, and you do this by being consistent. Establish routines that regu-late the daily rhythms of your household. As much as possible, your family should eat meals at regular times; follow the same routines for recurring tasks, like getting your children dressed, to and from school, and ready for bed; and go to sleep and wake up at more or less the same time each day.

- *Be fair.* Establish rules that make sense, that are appropriate to your child's age, and that are flexible enough to be modified as your child matures. The rules you make for your child should be ones that you've thought out; they should have some logic and pur-pose behind them. When you notice that your child has started to act more maturely and demonstrate more responsibility and self-reliance, it's a good idea to reexamine your rules. If their logic still makes sense, and their purpose is still valid, there's no reason to change them. If your spouse or your child points out that a rule no longer serves the purpose that it once did, however, and this is the case, there's no sense in being inflexible. For example, you used to make your daughter finish all her homework before she went out to play, but now that she's better at managing her time, it makes more sense to simply insist that her homework be completed before bed-time, and let her choose when she does it. Changing rules when they need changing shows your child that your rules are grounded in logic, rather than merely your authority. Consistency is not the same as rigidity. Good parents are flexible without being inconsistent.

- *Avoid harsh punishment.* All children have to be punished sometimes, but the kind of punishment affects the development of self-control. Children whose parents use physical punishment, are nasty and demeaning toward them, or who express a lot of anger when they punish are more likely to develop problems regulating their own behavior and emotions. Effective punishment needs to include five things: identify the specific act that was wrong ("We agreed that you would be home by midnight, but I didn't hear you come in until two"); describe the impact of the misbehavior ("I can't fall asleep if I'm worrying about where you are, and I need to get to bed by midnight to get enough sleep"); suggest one or more alternatives for the undesirable behavior ("Your curfew is still midnight, but if for some unavoidable reason you're going to be late, please call as soon as you find this out, and explain why"); clearly state what the punishment is going to be ("You are not allowed out next Saturday night because of this. You can have friends over, but I want you home"); and explain that you expect your child to do better the next time ("You're usually so good about everything — please remember to call the next time you are out and are going to be late").

Be Supportive

Supportiveness refers to how much parents tolerate and encourage their child's growing capacity for self-management. Parents who do this well use a technique that psychologists call "scaffolding." Scaffolding is just what it sounds like — it's support for kids as they develop the abilities they need to manage themselves. As a child's self-management structure becomes stronger, the scaffolding can be gradually dismantled.

Scaffolding entails giving kids slightly more responsibility or autonomy than they're used to — just enough so that they'll feel the benefits if they succeed but not suffer dire consequences should they fail. For example, it's letting an eleven-year-old who's never been left home alone spend an hour by herself while her parents are visiting the next-door neighbors. This is a good way for the child to practice regulating her emotions (staying calm), thoughts (not worrying about when you'll return), and behavior (not trying anything she wouldn't try if you were home).

The hour may seem like an eternity to both parent and child, but once it's over, both will have developed the confidence that the child can handle this new level of self-management. But if the new expectation is too demanding a challenge (having to manage four hours alone the first time, and putting herself to bed), there is a risk that the experiment will backfire, undermining the child's self-assurance.

An analogous situation for an older adolescent might be one in which you phase in driving privileges for a newly licensed teenager, permitting him to drive by himself during daylight hours for a few months before you allow him to drive alone at night, and not allowing him to drive at all with his friends in the car until he has been driving, accident- and citation-free, for six months.

Scaffolding strikes the right balance between what the child can already handle and what she will soon be ready to handle. At a neurobiological level, the brain circuits that regulate self-control have been engaged and sufficiently strengthened to make self-regulation easier and more automatic.

Remembering these principles will help you be a more supportive parent:

- *Set your child up to succeed.* Create expectations that help him demonstrate just how mature he is. Your expectations should be set so that meeting them will require a level of maturity that slightly exceeds what your child has shown up until that point, but that is still within your child's reach. This way, when your child succeeds, he will gain confidence in his abilities to do things well and on his own. When he is not successful, don't make him feel like he failed. Focus instead on what went right, and if possible, help him figure out what he might have done differently or better.

- *Praise your child's accomplishments, but focus on the effort, not the outcome.* Praising children not only makes them feel good about themselves, but when done correctly, it helps them learn important lessons about the value of working hard to achieve a goal. Saying, "You did a great job on your book report," is better than saying

"I love how smart you are." Focus your praise on the link between the accomplishment and the effort your child made, rather than attributing your child's achievement to some "natural" or innate characteristic. Tie your praise to the quality of the accomplishment, not to the grade or rating it has received from someone else. Saying "I'm really proud of how well you spell," is far better than saying "I'm really proud of the A you got on your spelling test."

- *Don't be overly intrusive.* Part of what makes a child healthy, happy, and successful is developing a sense of mastery and self-sufficiency. It's certainly true that your child needs to know that you're there for her, but she also needs to know that there are plenty of situations that she can handle without you. If you micromanage her life in a way that never gives her a chance to do anything on her own, she won't develop confidence in her own competence. Ultimately, the only way your child can develop a strong sense of self-regulation is if you give him the freedom to venture out and make some of his own decisions, even if this exposes him to hurt or disappointment. Good parenting requires a balance between involvement and independence. At either extreme — when parents are disengaged or when they are intrusive — children's mental health suffers. But in any situation, you must weigh the trade-off between the benefits of intervening to protect or help your child and the costs of denying him opportunities for personal growth that come from independence. Resist the temptation to rewrite your fifteen-year-old's history paper because you are worried about the grade he might receive, or call his basketball coach because he is unhappy with the amount of playing time he's getting. It is fine to read a first draft and offer suggestions for improvement, or to rehearse how best to approach his coach, but he needs to learn how to manage his schoolwork and speak up for himself when he believes he's been treated unfairly. Even the best-intentioned actions on your part can stifle your child's development if you are too intrusive.

- *Relinquish control gradually, as your child gets better at managing her own life.* Remember that the development of self-regulation depends on the progressive exchange of external control (imposed by a parent or other adult) for self-control. There should never be a point during your child's development where you don't impose *some* limits and structure. But, as your child gets older, ease up on your restrictions as he demonstrates more responsibility. Changing the rules is like driving on an icy road — you want to avoid speeding up, hitting the brakes, or changing directions abruptly. Each time you ease a restriction, you should watch and see how your child responds. If he handles the additional freedom responsibly, you made the right decision. (If not, you should reinstate the previous limit.) Leave things in their new, less restrictive state until you are completely satisfied that the new, more independent arrangement is working. Suppose you regularly monitor the amount of time your twelve-year-old spends on homework. You might cut back on this for one grading period and see how she does. If her grades remain good, you can leave the new arrangement in place.

- *Help your child think through decisions rather than making them for him.* Sometimes what seems like the obvious choice to you isn't so obvious to your adolescent. Helping him see why one choice is better than another is better than simply making the correct choice for him. Suggest what he might consider when making an important decision, without actually making the decision for him. If he is trying to decide between several different summer jobs, for example, you can help him see that salary is only one factor to consider and that it may be worth taking a slightly lower-paying job that will teach him skills he's interested in acquiring, or look more impressive on a college application, over one that pays more but is inherently less interesting.

- *Protect when you must, but permit when you can.* In order to develop competence, children need to learn from their mistakes. Many parents have trouble letting this happen, because our natural inclination is to protect our children from harm, failure, or disappointment. In situations where your decision about an activity your child wants to engage in can easily go one way or the other, try to maximize your child's autonomy so long as doing so doesn't jeopardize his health, well-being, or future. Ask yourself whether the activity is dangerous, unhealthy, illegal, unethical, or likely to close some doors that are better left open (like failing to take the courses he needs in order to apply to a highly selective college). If your child wants to do something that doesn't fall into any of these categories, I'd say, let him. Of course, if you believe his action could have bad consequences, don't allow it, but do explain why you reached that conclusion.

Styles of Parenting

Parents must strive to excel at all three components — being warm, fair, and supportive — not just one or two of them. The impact of any one of the three elements of effective parenting is amplified when it occurs in conjunction with the other two. In other words, although all children benefit from parental warmth, children with warm parents who are also firm and supportive profit more from their parents' warmth than do children whose parents are equally loving, but overly permissive or excessively controlling.

The link between warmth and firmness is especially crucial. Many parents understand the need to be firm, to impose standards for their child's behavior, and to enforce rules consistently. But research shows that in order for discipline to be effective, children need to feel that their parents are loving and nurturing as well. Without warmth, a child will likely perceive firmness as harsh, unfair, and overly punitive, and these perceptions may provoke disobedience, defiance, or feelings of helplessness.

Although in theory one could imagine many permutations of warmth, firmness, and support, in reality this isn't the case. Extensive research has found that three parenting styles predominate.

One style, called "autocratic," describes relatively cold, firm, and psychologically controlling parents. Autocratic parents have adopted a "Do it because I say so" attitude toward their child, and they discipline by asserting their power and control, often in cold and punitive ways. Autocratic parents are frequently rigid in their approach to child rearing, preferring consistency (even when they know they're wrong) over compromise or flexibility. "Tiger mothering," at least as it is described in the best-selling book *Battle Hymn of the Tiger Mother,* is autocratic parenting. Research clearly shows that autocratic parenting does not foster healthy development, and psychologists, myself included, have roundly criticized so-called tiger parenting. Plenty of studies show that children — including Asian American children —

have better mental health *and* fare better in school when their parents are warm and supportive.

Another common parenting style, called "permissive," is the opposite of tiger parenting. Permissive parents are warm and supportive, but very lenient, too often indulging their kids' whims and letting them have their way. These parents adopt a laissez-faire attitude, typically striving to keep their child happy by avoiding setting limits and steering clear of conflicts.

The third common style — "authoritative" parenting — is the ideal; it is high in warmth, firmness, and support. Unlike permissive parents, authoritative parents don't hesitate to set limits on their child's behavior or maintain standards the child must adhere to. But unlike autocratic parents, who also have limits and standards for the child, authoritative parents discipline from a position of warmth rather than power, in ways that support, rather than squelch, the child's growing sense of autonomy. In other words, authoritative parents are firm without being harsh, strict without being stifling. Authoritative parents are usually experts at scaffolding.

These three different approaches to parenting reflect very different values and beliefs about what is best for the child. Autocratic parents view their main responsibility as controlling the child's impulses. They believe obedience and respect for authority are the most important traits a child can learn. Generally, they love their kids just as much as any other kind of parents, but they may appear aloof or cold (either to an outside observer or to their kids), because they believe that displays of affection undermine discipline.

Permissive parents approach child rearing from a completely different perspective. They view their main responsibility as making their child happy by fulfilling all his needs and desires. Unlike autocratic parents, permissive parents believe that children are basically good, and that parents should allow their natural inclinations to blossom. Permissive parents are not there to control the child, but to facilitate growth by staying out of the way as much as possible. In fact, these parents worry about the risk of excessive control — that the child's natural creativity, curiosity, and inquisitiveness will be squelched by too much overt authority. They acknowledge that children can make bad choices, but they believe that mistakes impart valuable lessons that outweigh the negative consequences of these errors.

If autocratic parents place a premium on obedience, and permissive ones on happiness, authoritative parents emphasize self-direction. To authoritative parents, the primary issue isn't whether a child is obedient or happy, but whether the child is mature — capable of self-regulation. For authoritative parents, the most important goal is orchestrating a smooth transition from external control to internal control.

Each of these goals — obedience, happiness, and maturity — is laudable, and virtually every parent desires all three to some extent. The question isn't really whether a parent values one of these traits rather than the others, but which trait they emphasize.

The emphasis makes a huge difference in the development of self-regulation.

The Power of Authoritative Parenting

The notion that authoritative parenting is superior to other styles of parenting now enjoys widespread acceptance among social scientists, and for good reason. Virtually without exception, research shows that children and adolescents who come from authoritative households are more self-reliant and more self-controlled than their peers from autocratic or permissive homes.

The benefits of authoritative parenting accrue regardless of the child's age, sex, birth order, or ethnic background. These benefits have been found in studies from all around the world, in poor families and rich ones, and in families with divorced, separated, and married parents. The power of authoritative parenting is so strong that its basic tenets even apply to people who aren't parents — to teachers, coaches, and work supervisors. An authoritative approach to dealing with adolescents in the classroom, on the playing field, and in the workplace helps students learn, athletes excel, and employees succeed.

Authoritatively reared adolescents are more confident, more poised, more determined, and more self-reliant. This, in turn, makes them less susceptible to peer pressure, less likely to use or abuse drugs or alcohol, and less likely to commit serious crimes or more minor offenses, such as cheating on school tests or cutting classes. Because they're better at regulating their emotions, adolescents from authoritative homes report less anxiety, less depression, and fewer psychosomatic problems, such as insomnia or excessive appetite. And because they're better at delaying gratification, adolescents from authoritative homes do best in school, as measured by their grades, their attitudes toward schoolwork, the time they invest in their studies, and how many years of school they complete.

Teenagers from autocratic homes, in contrast, have been overpowered into obedience. If all a parent cares about is making sure his or her children don't misbehave, autocratic parenting will work just fine. Because they have been exposed to extreme parental firmness, teenagers from autocratic homes are less likely than other youngsters to use drugs and alcohol or get into other types of trouble. But when it comes to measures of psychological well-being, the disadvantages associated with autocratic rearing are readily apparent. Teenagers from autocratic homes have lower self-esteem than other youngsters, and are less socially poised. They are less self-reliant and less persistent, and as a consequence they give up more easily in the face of obstacles. When the going is easy, they do just fine. But when the going gets tough, adolescents from autocratic homes can't muster the necessary fortitude. Autocratic parenting makes adolescents toe the line, but it prevents them from becoming self-assured or psychologically mature.

Adolescents from permissive homes are in some ways a mirror image of those from autocratic homes. They generally report levels of self-assurance, confidence, and social poise comparable to those seen in teenagers from authoritative households. On measures of misbehavior, though, permissively raised adolescents fare worse than their peers. Their drug and alcohol use is higher than other adolescents, their school performance is lower, and their motivation to achieve is weaker. Teens from permissive homes are more comfortable than other kids in social situations, but more susceptible to their friends' influence. All in all, it appears as if parental permissiveness leads teenagers to be more oriented toward their peers and less oriented toward their parents and other adults, such as teachers.

Helping Adolescents Develop Mature Self-Regulation

The fact that prefrontal development is both preprogrammed into our genes and dependent on experience helps explain why just about all adolescents improve in their abilities to engage in higher-order thinking and self-regulation (which are governed by the prefrontal cortex), but why some improve more than others. Puberty may open the window of plasticity in the prefrontal cortex, but how the plastic brain is molded depends largely on the environment.

Adolescents who are fortunate enough to have warm, firm, and support- ive parents will enjoy a huge advantage when it comes to the development of advanced thinking abilities and self-regulation. These capabilities, in turn, will increase their chances of excelling in school, completing more years of education, and avoiding problems like addiction, delinquency, obesity, and premarital pregnancy.

Because brain systems that govern self-regulation are developing from birth through early adulthood, there is a vast window of opportunity for parents to help their children acquire the capacity for self-control (and, un- fortunately, an equally long period during which parents can derail the pro- cess). The size of this window makes this particular brain system one of the most sensitive to environmental influence, because there are repeated op- portunities to stimulate positive development, but just as many chances to do harm.

The single most important thing parents can do to raise healthy, happy, and successful kids is to practice authoritative parenting. My advice to par- ents, then, is straightforward: Be warm. Be firm. And be supportive.

In the next chapter, we'll see how schools can embrace these same prin- ciples and take advantage of the opportunities that adolescent brain plastic- ity provides.

8 Reimagining High School

For more than three decades, we've been told repeatedly that American students fare poorly in international achievement comparisons, that a shocking proportion of them lack basic skills in reading, mathematics, and science, and that student achievement is no better today than when the infamous blue-ribbon commission report, *A Nation at Risk,* sounded an alarm over the "rising tide of mediocrity" in 1983.

The wake-up calls come several times every year as another report confirms the all-too-familiar findings. Each time, education experts, politicians, and pundits all pontificate about the "true" source of the problem—inadequate teacher compensation, growing diversity in the student population, the poor quality of graduates from our teacher-training programs, too little funding, too much testing, disengaged parents, income inequality, take your pick—and the issue receives media attention for a day or so.

Soon afterward, the president or the secretary of education visits a school district that has defied the odds, singles out one or two students for their extraordinary accomplishments, and delivers a nationally publicized speech that announces a plan that is certain to turn things around. Within less than a week, the "crisis" fades into memory, until it is revived by the next disheartening report, press release about the latest round of substandard test scores, or revelation that an education hero or heroine had all along been faking the data.

Amid all this noise, one vitally important signal almost never gets picked up: these problems exist primarily in America's high schools. In international assessments, our elementary-school students generally score toward the top of the distribution, and our middle-school students usually place somewhat above the average. But our high-school students score well below the international average, and they fare especially badly in math and science compared to the country's chief economic rivals.

It's important to make clear that our poor showing is not a function of anomalies in the measurement process. Though many other countries group their students differently than we do (placing some in vocational tracks and others in college-preparatory programs), the organizations that administer the surveys are very careful to ensure that every country gives a representative sample that includes students at every level of ability. Nor do we fall behind because our teachers must deal with a greater diversity of skills in the classroom (which might make it harder for teachers to target their curricula effectively). In general, there is more intellectual diversity within a typical American high-school class than in other countries, but overall the disparity between our best and worst performers is comparable with other countries, indicating that the numbers aren't skewed by this diversity. So what's holding back our high-school kids?

One clue comes from a little-known study that compared the world's fifteen-year-olds on two measures of student engagement: participation and "belongingness." The measure of participation was based on how often students attended school, arrived on time, and showed up for class. The measure of belongingness was based on how much students felt they fit in to the student body, were liked by their schoolmates, and had friends in school. We might think of the first measure as an index of academic engagement and the second as a measure of social engagement.

On the measure of academic engagement, the United States scored only at the international average, and far lower than our chief economic rivals: China, Korea, Japan, and Germany. In these countries, students show up for school and attend their classes more reliably than anywhere else in the world.

On the measure of social engagement, the United States topped all four of these economic competitors except Germany.

In America, high school is for socializing. It's a country club for kids, where the really important activities are interrupted by all those annoying classes. Pity the poor Chinese, Korean, and Japanese students, in their all-work-and-no-fun schools. You might be surprised to learn that, despite the stereotype of the pressure-cooked Asian student, the teen-suicide rate is higher in the United States than in China, Korea, Japan — or, for that matter, Germany.

For all but the very best American students — the ones in AP classes who are bound for the nation's most selective colleges and universities — high school is tedious and unchallenging. Studies that have tracked American children's moods over the course of the day find that levels of boredom are highest during their time in school, especially among adolescents, and that their moods improve dramatically around 3:00 p.m. and toward the end of the week, as the weekend approaches. (The emotional low point in the life of an American adolescent is Wednesday morning.) The majority of American high-school students say they are just going through the motions at school, calibrating their level of effort to ensure that they do well enough to stay out of academic trouble. One-third of American high-school students report that they have little interest in school and get through the day by fooling around with their friends. And keep in mind that these surveys don't include the 20 percent or so of students who have dropped out. If they were included, the proportion of disengaged teenagers would be considerably higher.

One might be tempted to write these findings off as mere confirmation of the well-known fact that adolescents find *everything* boring. But American high schools are more boring than schools in other countries. Surveys of exchange students who have studied in America, as well as surveys of American adolescents who have studied abroad, confirm this. More than 80 percent of foreign students who have attended American high schools report that their home schools are more challenging. More than half of American high-school students who have studied in another country agree that our schools are easier. Objectively, they are probably correct: American high-school students spend far less time on schoolwork than their counterparts in the rest of the world.

Trends in achievement within the United States reveal just how bad our high schools are relative to our schools for younger students. The National Assessment of Educational Progress (NAEP), administered by the U.S. Department of Education, routinely tests three age groups: elementary-school students (nine-year-olds), middle-school students (thirteen-year-olds), and high-school students (seventeen-year-olds).

Over the past forty years, reading scores rose by 6 percent among nine-year-olds and 3 percent among thirteen-year-olds — small but statistically significant improvements over the four decades at both age levels. Math scores rose by 11 percent among nine-year-olds and 7 percent among thirteen-year-olds — again, small but statistically significant increases at both ages.

By contrast, high-school students haven't made any progress at all. Reading and math scores have remained flat among seventeen-year-olds during this period. High-school students' scores on subject-area tests in science, writing, geography, and history, which have been tracked only for the last two decades, haven't changed either. And by absolute rather than relative standards, American high-school students' achievement is scandalous. In 2012, only 6 percent of seventeen-year-olds scored at the highest level of reading proficiency for their age, compared to 15 percent of thirteen-year-olds and 22 percent of nine-year-olds. Just 7 percent of seventeen-year-olds scored at the highest level of proficiency in math that year, compared to 34 percent of thirteen-year-olds and 47 percent of nine-year-olds.

In other words, over the past forty years, despite all of the debates about curricula, testing, teacher training, teachers' salaries, and performance standards, and despite billions of dollars invested in school reform, there has been no improvement — none — in the academic proficiency of American high-school students.

It's not just No Child Left Behind that has failed our adolescents — *it's every single thing we have tried.* The list of unsuccessful experiments is long and dispiriting. Charter schools aren't any better than standard public schools. Students whose teachers "Teach for America" don't achieve any more than those whose teachers came out of conventional teacher-certification programs. Once one accounts for differences in the family backgrounds of students who attend public and private schools, there is no advantage to going to private school, either. Vouchers make no difference in student outcomes. No wonder school administrators and teachers from Atlanta to Chicago to Philadelphia have been caught fudging data on student performance. It's the only education strategy that consistently gets results.

If anything, logic would suggest that the test results for seventeen-year-olds would be better than those for younger kids. Hardly any students drop out of elementary or middle school, but many seventeen-year-olds have dropped out by the time the NAEP rolls around. With this academically challenged group no longer being measured, the seventeen-year-olds'

NAEP scores should be somewhat better than the nine- and thirteen-year-olds' scores. But of course the opposite is true.

This shortfall is perplexing. It has nothing to do with high schools having a more ethnically diverse population than elementary schools. In fact, elementary-school-age children are *more* ethnically diverse than high-school kids. Nor do high schools have more poor students. Elementary schools in America are more than twice as likely as secondary schools to be classified as "high poverty" based on their students' family incomes.

And it's not because high-school teachers are paid less; salaries are about the same for secondary- and elementary-school teachers. It's not because high-school teachers are less qualified; secondary-school and elementary-school teachers have comparable years of education and similar years of experience. Student-teacher ratios are the same in our elementary and high schools. So are the amounts of time that students spend in the classroom. We don't shortchange high schools financially, either; American school districts actually spend a little more per capita on high-school students than on elementary-school students.

Nor are our high-school classrooms understaffed, underfunded, or underutilized by international standards: only Switzerland, Norway, and Luxembourg spend more per high-school student than the United States. We also spend about the same proportion of money on core educational activities in relation to ancillary funding for things like meals and transportation. Contrary to widespread belief, American high-school teachers aren't underpaid; their salaries are comparable to those in most European and Asian countries. American class sizes and student-teacher ratios are also about average relative to other nations. And American high-school students actually spend more hours in the classroom each year than their counterparts in other countries.

The bottom line is that it is hard to point to anything about American high schools themselves that explain why they perform so poorly, both in comparison to high schools around the world and in comparison to elementary and middle schools in the United States. Some commentators have argued for lengthening the school year or the school day. It's hard to argue that high-school students should spend *more* time in school, though, given the fact that they already spend more time there than students in many other countries with higher achievement-test scores.

Maybe our high-school teachers are less qualified or more poorly trained than those in other countries, but it's unlikely that our teacher-training pro-grams are worse at admitting and training high-school teachers than ones bound for elementary- or middle-school classrooms. In fact, the reverse may be true: a recent report from the National Council on Teacher Quality found that only one in nine programs for future elementary-school teachers adequately prepared them, compared to one in three programs for future high-school teachers. Many more training programs for secondary-school teachers received high marks than did programs for elementary-school students.

Using School to Build Self-Control

Most discussions of school reform focus, not surprisingly, on schools and teachers. They typically call for changes in the curriculum, in instructional methods, or in the selection, training, or compensation of teachers. Nearly twenty years ago, I noted that no school-reform effort would have any im-pact if students didn't come to school ready and able to learn. The funda-mental problem with American high-school achievement is not our schools. If parents don't raise their children in ways that enable them to maintain in-terest in what their teachers are teaching, it doesn't much matter who the teachers are, how they teach, what they teach, or how much they're paid. Without changing the culture of student achievement, changes in instruc-tors or instruction won't, and can't, make a difference.

All of this was true when I first pointed it out, and it only seems truer now as two decades' worth of flatlining high-school achievement has ac-crued.

High-school students from many Asian and European countries outper-form their American counterparts mainly because the cultures of achieve-ment are very different in these other countries. These cultures give rise to higher expectations at home and more support for achievement within the adolescent peer group. In addition, in many other countries, especially in Asia, parents demand much more self-control from their children at much younger ages. By the time children in other cultures have matured into adulthood, they have much stronger self-control than Americans do.

Cultural differences also explain why children from families who have recently immigrated to the United States achieve more in school than their peers from similar ethnic backgrounds, but whose families have been living in America longer; this phenomenon is known as the "immigrant paradox." Immigrant children attend the same schools as children from families who have been living in the United States for generations. They have the same teachers and are exposed to the same curricula.

The superior performance of immigrant children—despite the enormous obstacles that their families face and the fact that their parents may not even speak the language of school instruction at home—can't possibly be due to the fact that their teachers are better prepared than those of non-immigrants. The fact that Asian American children in particular do so well in our putatively terrible schools and with our ostensibly terrible teachers has nothing to do with what goes on in the classroom. It has everything to do with how they are raised and what their parents expect of them.

In our international study, which I described in chapter 4, we tested people's impulse control at different ages, ranging from ten years old to thirty.* At age ten, there were very few differences in self-control between Chinese and American children—the Chinese children scored about 10 percent higher. This gap widened little by little each year; by fourteen, the Chinese scored 20 percent higher, and by eighteen, they scored 45 percent higher. In their twenties, the Chinese demonstrated 50 percent more self-control than the Americans. This advantage is unlikely to be due to cultural differences in temperament, since we would expect to have seen the self-control gap at the younger ages as well as the older ones. It is likely a consequence of how adolescents are raised.

If all of this is true, why have we been able to make inroads into improving student achievement in elementary schools? The answer is that the non-cognitive skills that have been shown to be so fundamental for success in school become more important as students get older. As students progress from elementary to middle to high school, the work becomes more challenging, and the demands for self-reliance intensify. Adults provide less supervision and assistance—students are expected to work more independently. High-school assignments take longer to complete; exams take longer to study for. The work is harder. Students who have strong self-restraint and the capacity to delay gratification have a greater advantage in high school

---

* The measure was how long people waited before making their first move on a task that required planning out a strategy.

than they do in elementary school. A child doesn't need much perseverance to succeed in second grade. In other words, it is easier to improve elementary schools without paying attention to noncognitive skills.

There are also fewer distractions in elementary school — or, more accurately, elementary-school students are less likely to be distracted in school by things like gossip, social status, attention from peers, and, of course, sex. Adolescence, as we have seen, is a time during which brain systems that process social information become more easily aroused, which is an especially strong liability in a school environment that places undue emphasis on peer relations, as is the case in the United States. At an age when the admiration of one's peers takes on special salience, students in other countries benefit from a peer culture that respects academic achievement, rather than one that derides it, like that in most American high schools.

Rethinking Secondary Education

There is growing interest in the idea of rethinking secondary education in ways that focus not only on the usual academic skills for which schools have been responsible (but which they have not been very successful in imparting), but on the development of adolescents' healthy psychological functioning. The basic premise behind this movement is that success in life is only partially determined by mastery of the conventional academic skills taught in school. As I explained in a previous chapter, success is also influenced by things like perseverance, determination, and self-control.

There are many reasons to be enthusiastic about incorporating deliberate efforts to improve psychological health into our high-school curricula. In the rapidly changing world in which we now live, schools cannot possibly anticipate the specific skills that will be needed to navigate the ever-evolving labor force. Many experts agree that schools should focus on fostering more general competencies that have value in many different work settings. These include, but are not limited to, being able to work effectively with others, being able to develop and carry out long-term strategic plans, knowing how to acquire and use new information, being able to think flexibly and creatively, and, of course, self-regulation. Most employers agree that these qualities are among the most important competencies they are looking for when they hire new employees.

These skills have always been valued and valuable within middle-class and professional occupations. Historically, they were less desired (and perhaps even undesirable) in blue-collar jobs, where good employees were expected to be obedient, not creative, and to focus on the immediate tasks in front of them, rather than thinking long-term. The successful employee was one who was able to follow and execute the specific instructions he or she was given by a supervisor. The last thing a factory owner wanted in someone on the assembly line was the inclination to "think outside the box."

The styles of child rearing I described in the previous chapter — authoritative, autocratic, and permissive — differ tremendously in popularity among people from different socioeconomic backgrounds. It is easy to see why. Working-class parents, who tend to favor an autocratic approach, emphasize in their children the very traits that they, as adults, have found useful. A father or mother whose job necessitates listening to supervisors and following instructions without questioning them will be inclined to raise children in a way that emphasizes these qualities. "Do it because I said so" is simply a parent's way of saying that it is important to follow what the boss says. (In this instance, the "worker" is the child, and the "boss" is the parent.) In the mind of a working-class parent, learning to obey someone in a position of authority leads to success in life.

Middle-class and professional parents, in contrast, tend to work in occupations that reward initiative, self-direction, and flexibility. This is why they're more likely to adopt an authoritative approach to child rearing, because it promotes these qualities. When middle-class parents engage their teenage kids in dinnertime discussions about expectations and consequences, in which the kids are encouraged to express their viewpoints, the family is holding a "meeting" not unlike that which might take place in a corporate office. An adolescent who raises questions about the wisdom of a given rule is not punished for questioning authority but praised for "thinking for himself." The same behavior in a working-class household would probably be seen as disrespectful.

As blue-collar jobs — like those in the auto industry — have dwindled, so has the value of the skills that facilitate success in these occupations. Gone are the well-paying jobs where following orders is the way to get ahead. The jobs that have replaced them require the skills that middle-class parents have emphasized for generations. In the past, children who grew up in autocratic households emerged with a marketable set of noncognitive skills, chief among them being able to listen to a supervisor and follow instructions, rather than work independently or think creatively. Today, there are few opportunities to use the capacities fostered by autocratic parenting.

The psychological outcomes of authoritative child-rearing are also the competencies that are required for success in institutions of higher education, and especially so in colleges that cater to the relatively more privileged, where students are expected to show initiative, challenge their professors' thinking, and carry out projects that take several months or more to complete. These are the very talents that they will need to be successful in today's workplace, and even more so in the workplace of the future. Students who attend schools that do not provide these opportunities will graduate at a disadvantage — perhaps one reason that completing a two-year program at a community college, which is unlikely to nourish these capacities, no longer yields any economic or occupational benefit.

This is also why the notion that we will be able to prepare the next generation of thinkers through a university education that is composed entirely of online courses is doubtful. These computer-based courses may be effective for the transfer of information. They may contribute to the acquisition of some of the skills that will assist in obtaining an entry-level job. But they will do little to cultivate the capacities that are necessary to rise to the top. And to the extent that adolescents from different backgrounds are differentially tracked into online versus in-person education — as they surely will be because of the price differential — the growth of online-only education will widen, not shrink, the occupational and earnings gap between children from families of modest means and those who grew up in affluence.

Before going any further, let me be clear that I am not suggesting that we abandon the conventional academic goals of formal education or lose sight of the fact that at least some of what schools should be doing is teaching specific skills and transferring certain bodies of knowledge. There are many academic skills and a great deal of information that students need to acquire during the secondary-school years.

My point, though, is that the list of competencies we focus on developing through schooling is presently incomplete, because it largely ignores noncognitive skills. The need for schools to foster the development of capacities like perseverance and determination is especially great for socioeconomically disadvantaged adolescents, who are less likely to grow up in home environments that contribute to their growth.

Fostering these capacities is not only important for success in higher education or the labor force, though. This supplement to conventional education would have the added advantage of cultivating the sorts of inner strengths that help protect against the development of problems such as depression, obesity, delinquency, and substance use. These problems stem in part from deficiencies in self-regulation, so anything schools can do to strengthen this capacity will have benefits that are likely to be far-reaching. Reorienting schools to help strengthen self-regulation in addition to teaching academic skills will not simply prevent problems from developing — it will actually help promote adolescents' physical and psychological well-being.

There is growing consensus that schools need to pay more attention to strengthening students' noncognitive skills. The question is: how can we do that?

Is Character Education the Answer?

Over the last few years, there has been a growing awareness of the need to incorporate character development into school curricula, and various efforts to do so have received wide attention. Perhaps the best-known effort is the Knowledge Is Power Program, or KIPP, which has been implemented in close to 150 charter schools across the country.

KIPP is aimed at children and teenagers from low-income families. Its explicit goal is increasing college enrollment by combining an emphasis on factors proven to bolster academic success (high expectations, parental involvement, time spent on instruction) with a novel focus on developing seven character strengths — zest, grit, self-control, optimism, curiosity, gratitude, and social intelligence. These strengths are tracked on a "character growth card" and encouraged through classroom discussions and assignments that incorporate lessons about character into more conventional academic activities. Teachers also go out of their way to both model and praise displays of good character.

KIPP has a long record of impressive accomplishments, which have garnered much media attention, including a best-selling book called *How Children Succeed*. Students attending schools that use the KIPP approach have higher rates of high-school graduation, college enrollment, and college completion than students from similarly disadvantaged backgrounds who attend other types of schools. Numerous evaluations of KIPP schools have found that students show larger-than-expected gains on various measures of achievement.

However, because KIPP schools are charter schools, the students who attend them have parents who have chosen this option. Parents who go out of their way to enroll their children in academically rigorous programs are atypical. Most studies of KIPP schools therefore can't rule out the possibility that their students' success has nothing to do with the KIPP program itself. The sorts of families that enroll their kids in KIPP schools are different from those who send their kids to conventional schools in ways that might well lead KIPP students to succeed regardless of where they went to school. These parents value academic achievement and want to get involved in their children's education, two factors that have been shown time and again to contribute to scholastic success.

With this parental predisposition in mind, a recent evaluation of KIPP middle schools by an independent evaluator is particularly intriguing. This evaluation drew its comparison group from a sample of children whose families had entered, but didn't win, a lottery to gain admission to the local KIPP school. Comparing children from this group with those who'd won the lottery controls for whatever unique factors may characterize families who choose to enroll their kids in KIPP — since *both* groups had tried to get their kids into KIPP.

The study assessed performance on standardized achievement tests as well as measures of various character strengths. Consistent with the prior studies, in this objective evaluation, KIPP students outperformed the comparison children on numerous measures of achievement, across a range of subject areas. KIPP students also spent more time on homework. The differences were not only statistically significant, but substantial. This is the stuff of headlines, and rightly so.

However, some of this study's findings were not so widely broadcast. The KIPP children showed no advantage on any of the measures of character strengths. They weren't more effortful or persistent. They didn't have more favorable academic self-conceptions or stronger school engagement. They didn't score higher than the comparison group in self-control. In fact, they were more likely to engage in "undesirable behavior," including losing their temper, lying to and arguing with their parents, and giving teachers a hard time. They were more likely to get into trouble at school. Despite the program's emphasis on character development, the KIPP students were no less likely to smoke, drink, get high, or break the law. Nor were their hopes for their educational futures any higher or their plans any more ambitious. A different study found that rates of college graduation among KIPP graduates, while far better than those of students from comparably disadvantaged backgrounds, were disappointing: nearly 90 percent of the KIPP students enrolled in college, but only a third graduated—less than half the proportion the program's developers had hoped for.*

These findings don't necessarily show that schools cannot play a role in strengthening self-regulation and other noncognitive skills. They may simply indicate that the approach taken by KIPP, while effective at boosting academic performance, doesn't really have an impact on kids' character. In some ways, these findings are reminiscent of the evaluations of classroom-based health-education programs discussed in chapter 5. Informing kids about health issues or character traits in school will increase their knowledge of these subjects, but it won't change their behavior.

I don't mean to minimize the impressive impact that KIPP appears to have on academic success—and in all fairness, this is the developers' primary objective. The KIPP schools have dramatically improved scholastic achievement in a demographic where any improvement in this area has historically been difficult to accomplish.

But developing teenagers' self-regulation may require something other than parables, slogans, inspirational banners, and encouragement from compassionate teachers.

Looking to Neuroscience for an Alternative

The systematic study of techniques for improving higher-order cognitive skills—what psychologists call "executive functions"—is relatively recent, with most studies conducted during the past five years. So any conclusions we draw about the best methods for improving self-regulation are, by neces-

---

* I have since learned from KIPP's founders that college-graduation rates have improved a bit in several KIPP schools, but that they are still far behind KIPP's expectations.

sity, somewhat provisional. As in many new areas of work, the findings in this field are sometimes exaggerated — as are criticisms of them.

At this point, no single approach warrants unequivocal endorsement. Few programs have undergone the kind of rigorous laboratory testing and retesting that are needed to draw reliable conclusions. Fewer still have been evaluated outside university settings, where virtually all approaches to improving executive functions are more successful than they are in the field, where it's harder to control the conditions under which the training is conducted.

Some programs designed to stimulate self-regulation and other aspects of executive functioning during childhood and adolescence are encouraging but not yet ready for prime time, and others have sizable but statistically unreliable effects — when they work they work well, but they fail as often as they succeed. There are programs that work for some people but not for others, or at one age but not others, or in some settings but not others. Sometimes the reasons for these varying results are known, but usually they're anyone's guess. Many important details have not yet been worked out — not only the nature of the training, but important specifics of implementation, such as how long the training should last, the number of sessions it should be divided into, and the length of each session. Not knowing how best to structure an encouraging approach to training executive functioning is like having a promising new anticancer drug but not yet knowing how much to prescribe or how often to administer it.

There are dozens — perhaps hundreds — of programs being peddled to consumers that purport to "strengthen" the brain, but very little hard evidence on their effectiveness. Such products are rarely studied using techniques accepted within the scientific community. The outcomes of this sort of training must be studied over months or even years to verify that they are more than fleeting. These sorts of studies take time and cost money, and the people who are in a hurry to get rich typically don't have much of either. I typed "brain training" into the application search window of my iPhone and retrieved dozens of programs that purport to be able to improve my brain's functioning. Television infomercials promise similar results. I can't say with any certainty that these programs aren't effective, but I am pretty sure they haven't been subject to rigorous evaluation. Downloaders and viewers, beware.

All that said, we can identify several approaches that will likely strengthen self-regulation and other aspects of executive functioning.

Most of the interventions that have been studied have relatively modest effects, but it's possible that combining these approaches would increase an adolescent's powers of self-regulation. At this point, we just don't know whether the impacts of different approaches to training are duplicative, cumulative, or even synergistic.

What we do know, and the reason I believe we should be optimistic, is that several recent studies have shown that some types of training designed to enhance executive functioning have effects that are reflected in changes in the brain's anatomy that portend broad effects on self-regulation. The finding that training can influence brain development isn't new. As I've mentioned, numerous studies have indicated that teaching specific skills results in changes in the brain in the expected regions—learning the urban geography of London changes brain regions associated with spatial memory, practicing the piano changes brain regions that govern fine motor coordination, and so forth. These are interesting results, but hardly surprising. Any type of enduring learning has to be reflected in some sort of neural change.

The recent studies are notable because they suggest that their effects extend beyond the specific skills and brain regions they target. Various types of programs—training designed to improve memory, strengthen attention, increase mindfulness, and improve reasoning—have been shown to produce changes in the brain's anatomy, especially in the degree of interconnection between different brain regions. This is because stronger connections between different parts of the brain improve executive functioning and self-regulation more generally. This raises the possibility that some sorts of training may result in changes that are more extensive than the specific capability that is being trained. It's as if a program designed to improve your eyesight not only made you see better, but improved your hearing too.

The most promising efforts to improve self-regulation fall into five categories: exercises designed to improve one or more specific aspects of executive functioning, practices devoted to increasing "mindfulness," aerobic exercise, physical regimens that require intense concentration, and specific strategies designed to boost self-control or strengthen the ability to delay gratification.

It's important to keep in mind that not all of the approaches I cata-log below have been tested in adolescents; many have been tested only in younger children or in adults. We don't know whether findings from one age group generalize to another — or, more specifically, *which* findings gen-eralize and which ones don't. But because the adolescent brain is particu-larly plastic in regions that govern self-regulation, we have good reason to suspect that such training would prove especially successful in adolescence.

Training Executive Functioning

The most widely studied and promising approaches to stimulate better ex-ecutive functioning are those that focus on training "working memory." Working memory refers to how we retain information in our minds and use it — like keeping the first part of a long sentence in mind while you fin-ish reading it, so that the end of the sentence makes sense, or holding a set of directions in your head as you drive, so that you know what landmarks to look out for. Working memory is probably the most critical component of executive functioning because it's essential to things like planning ahead, considering multiple possible actions at the same time, or comparing the short- and long-term consequences of a potential decision. Working mem-ory is critical for self-control too, because in order to stop yourself from doing something (grabbing that first marshmallow), you must be able to hold an alternative goal in mind (the prospect of getting two marshmallows if you wait).

There are many working-memory exercises, but the best-known one is something called the "*n*-back task," in which you're presented with a se-quence of items (like letters) one at a time and have to indicate whether the letter you are shown next is the same as the letter that appeared *n* let-ters ago. For example, in a 3-back task, if the sequence was *F J D U T D*, you would say no when the *U* appeared (because three letters back was *F*) and no when the *T* appeared (three letters back was *J*), but yes when the *D* ap-peared (three letters back was also *D*). The task may sound easy as it's de-scribed here, but it's very hard to actually do. There are many free versions of this task available online, and you can try it and see for yourself.

Practicing the *n*-back task has been shown to improve working memory. Whether this task affects other executive functions, such as self-regulation, is a controversial subject among psychologists. Some contend that it does, and they've shown that working-memory training improves performance on tasks that don't depend on memory, like impulse control. Others believe that the *n*-back task improves working memory but not much else. They contend that training a specific cognitive ability doesn't affect other aspects of executive functioning, and that the greater the disparity between what is trained and the actual skill one wants to improve, the less likely it is that the training will work. According to these critics, teaching someone how to play the guitar may dramatically improve his ability to play the guitar and might slightly improve his ability to play the piano (because there is some overlap in the skills needed to play any instrument), but it probably won't improve his ability to do algebra.

Other researchers point out that many brain regions frequently serve multiple purposes. If regions that are important for learning music are also important for learning math (which happens to be the case), then improving one's ability to play a musical instrument actually may have an impact on math skills, even if these skills don't seem similar on the surface. The prefrontal cortex is a reasonable target for training that one hopes will generalize across different abilities, because it is involved in many different aspects of thinking. Many studies of how narrowly or broadly working-memory training transfers to other abilities, such as impulse control, are underway, and scientists are eagerly awaiting their results. But even if the ultimate conclusion is that this training only improves working memory, it may still be worthwhile, because improvements in working memory have been shown to bolster performance on tests of reading comprehension and math.

Mindfulness Meditation

Exercises that practice mindfulness may also strengthen self-regulation. Mindfulness involves focusing one's attention on the present moment in a nonjudgmental fashion — really attending to what your senses are picking up, without trying to interpret or think about the experience. The most common of these exercises is mindfulness meditation. There are numerous guides to meditation, from mobile applications to classes and workshops taught by experts.

You can get a little taste of mindfulness by simply sitting still, with your eyes open, and focusing on your breath for a full minute. Pay attention to the sensation of air passing in and out of your nostrils, to the movement of your chest, and to the sound of air entering and leaving your body. When you feel your mind start to wander from these points of focus, bring your attention back to your breath, noting the distraction but not dwelling on it. Meditation is difficult at first, but with practice you can gradually increase the amount of time you can maintain your attention on your breathing. Because successful meditation forces us to control our breathing and attention, it may strengthen our ability to regulate our thoughts, feelings, and actions as well.

Mindfulness meditation has been shown to reduce stress and help alleviate many psychological disorders, especially those that involve anxiety, trauma, and addiction. There also is evidence that it helps strengthen self-regulation in people who don't have psychological problems. One of the advantages of using meditation to improve self-control is that it has beneficial effects beyond this specific outcome. Because mindfulness meditation helps reduce stress, it also improves sleep, cardiovascular health, and immune function.

Aerobic Exercise

Another, more active pursuit — aerobic exercise — may also improve self-regulation, although here the data are very limited. Aerobic exercise does improve brain health in general, by increasing blood flow, so it could have a positive impact on various aspects of cognitive functioning at all ages. Research on exercise and the brain, which has focused mainly on improving memory among older adults, has shown a link between working memory and working out.

A few studies have looked at the impact of exercise on adolescents' executive functioning. There is some evidence that acute exercise (single periods of intense activity, like running fast on a treadmill) may have transient positive effects on adolescents' executive functioning, but whether these effects endure has not been sufficiently studied. Ongoing exercise (multiple workouts over a period of weeks or months) also may have positive effects on executive functioning, but these effects are more likely to be seen when the exercise itself demands challenging thinking as well as physical exertion, as in team sports that combine aerobic activity with strategy. Given this, it is not surprising that participation in school-sponsored organized athletics appears to help promote the development of self-regulation and initiative. In these cases, we can't say for sure whether the positive effects are due to the exercise, the cognitive demands, or, most likely, a combination of the two.

Mindful Physical Activity

Activities that combine a challenging physical activity with mindfulness, such as yoga or certain martial arts, like tae kwon do, also appear to strengthen the development of self-regulation. To date, there have been few well-executed studies of how such activities affect adolescents' cognitive or brain development, but a few encouraging findings have emerged. As with aerobic exercise, it probably isn't the physical component of these activities alone that improves self-regulation, but the combination of exercise and the mindfulness and self-discipline required to perform these activities well.

Teaching Self-Regulation Skills and Strategies

Finally, it appears that training in specific self-regulation strategies and skills (like learning how to control anger) can also improve adolescents' capacity for self-regulation more generally. Some schools now incorporate "social and emotional learning" (SEL) into their curricula. SEL programs teach adolescents how to regulate their emotions, manage stress, and consider other peoples' feelings before acting. Although many of these programs were first intended to reduce problem behaviors like aggression or delinquency (and have been evaluated with this goal in mind), they've also been shown to improve self-regulation in teenagers who don't suffer from these problems.

There are many different programs available for schools interested in SEL to choose among — far too many to catalog here. Many of them target elementary and middle schools; a few are aimed at high-school students. A recent review of effective, school-based SEL programs, which compiled data from more than two hundred different evaluations involving 270,000 students, found that four characteristics distinguished the ones that worked from the ones that didn't. These characteristics have been abbreviated with the acronym SAFE.

First, effective programs include activities that are *sequenced;* they follow a prescribed order in which advanced skills build on more rudimentary ones. Second, effective programs are *active.* Students in these programs are not just the passive recipients of information; they have plenty of opportunities to actually practice the skills. Third, the most effective programs *focus* on SEL rather than treat this content as an afterthought or add-on; this is especially important when SEL is integrated into the regular curriculum, where it may be given short shrift, especially in schools that are preoccupied with testing students' academic skills. Finally the best programs are *explicit;* they target a specific social or emotional skill (or skill set) and concentrate on developing it.

Other interventions have sought to teach adolescents how to envision and plan long-term goals more effectively. Most of us have made a resolution — exercising every day, for instance — and stuck to it for a while, only to fall off the wagon when we encountered an obstacle, like an unforeseen emergency that stops us from going to the gym and breaks our new routine. Research has found that if we imagine these potential impediments beforehand, and make a plan for dealing with them, we're more likely to keep our resolutions.

One approach tries to firm teenagers' resolve by encouraging them to envision a goal and imagine the positive consequences of achieving it, think of a potential obstacle and a strategy for overcoming it, then make a written or verbal commitment to implementing this strategy should the need arise. Despite its cumbersome name — Mental Contrasting with Implementation Intentions (MCII) — it works. For example, students might be asked to describe a positive academic goal for the semester (getting better grades in math) and fantasize for a bit about the best thing that would result from achieving it (my parents will increase my allowance). They would then be asked to think of a potential obstacle (the problems will be too hard) and a plan for overcoming it (if I don't understand something, I will stay after class and ask my teacher for extra help).

In one recent study, students who were taught and encouraged to use MCII showed greater improvement in their grades, school attendance, and school conduct than students who were simply encouraged to think positively about an academic goal and the consequences of achieving it, without mapping out a strategy they might use if they encountered an obstacle to their goal. The next time you decide to try to lose a few pounds, before you embark on a diet, try fantasizing for a while about what the best outcome of losing weight will be, then think of what might get in the way of achieving it, and come up with a plan for what you will do if this impediment arises. You'll be more likely to succeed.

The important point is that these programs designed to train self-regulation strategies appear to have effects above and beyond the specific target of the intervention. That is, showing adolescents how to manage their emotions or envision a long-term goal may improve their self-regulation abilities in general. Helping kids regulate their emotions can lead to an improvement in their grades, for example, even though the intervention has nothing to do with academic achievement. This happens because the self-regulation skills that help control emotions are also helpful for things like studying and homework.

Sustained, Scaffolded Stimulation

As different as these kinds of exercise are, their success requires three common principles. First, the training must be *stimulating*. Adding another tedious activity to an already boring school day will only further disengage students. In order to be stimulating, the activities must be demanding and challenging. Note that I did *not* say they need to be pleasurable. Some students will enjoy being pushed to work harder; others will push back. As long as they're being challenged, they'll benefit from the activity.

Second, the training needs to be *scaffolded*. By this I mean that the activities should be demanding, but not so demanding that they overwhelm the adolescent's current capabilities. As with effective parenting, an effective school-based intervention should be calibrated to fall into the "zone," so that it's challenging but not so difficult as to frustrate or discourage the child. Once the child has mastered a particular task, the degree of difficulty should be increased, but just slightly. So, for example, a teenager should master a 2-back working-memory task before proceeding to a 3-back version. Similarly, it wouldn't be realistic to expect a teenager who has never meditated to begin with a thirty-minute session. Begin with a more reasonable period, like one minute, and then lengthen the amount of time gradually, after each previous level has been mastered.

Finally, the activities must be *sustained* over time through deliberate practice. There is no substitute for devoting time to getting better. Deliberate practice is more than mere repetition, though. It is repetition that is structured to improve performance. It is slow, methodical, and purposive. For example, the *n*-back task to strengthen working memory requires keeping a sequence of letters in mind. Practicing it might involve repeating multiple letter-sequences of the same length until this number of letters is mastered (and not increasing the length of the sequence until success at this length is routine), and then seeing if it is possible to lengthen the sequence by one letter (and practicing versions of this longer sequence with different letters until it is mastered). Schools also can encourage practice by incorporating training exercises into other classroom activities throughout the day. Working-memory training doesn't have to involve memorizing letters — you can use foreign capitals, chemical elements, or any list of items it might be useful to memorize. Adolescents can also practice various types of training at home, using computer-based exercises.

Given the need for adolescents to develop strong self-regulation skills, and evidence that this might be encouraged through activities like aerobic exercise, team sports, yoga, martial arts, and meditation, it is unfortunate that schools have cut back so much on physical education, where these activities would logically fit into the curriculum. Many schools have shortened, or even eliminated, portions of the school day that are devoted to students' physical well-being, on the assumption that exercise is a luxury that doesn't really contribute to learning or intellectual development.

We now know that this is simply not true, that physical activity is more than just recreation, and that the distinction between conventional education and physical education is a false dichotomy. The notion that things like exercise, yoga, and meditation contribute to intellectual and mental health, and not just physical health, which was once derided as some sort of New Age fad, is now treated as if it is little more than common sense. Nearly all of my friends and colleagues have incorporated one or more of these activities into their daily routines, not just because they make them feel better, but because they help them think better, too. Our schools should do the same, because not all children have the resources or opportunities to pursue these activities after school or on weekends. As I've made clear, our students spend more time in school, but achieve less, than most adolescents in the developed world. If schools devoted one hour each day to physical activity, our children and adolescents would not only be physically healthier, they would have stronger self-control as well, and that, in turn, will facilitate learning and achievement.

In this chapter on schools, and in the previous chapter on the family, I've discussed a number of ways that parents and educators can raise and teach adolescents more effectively by using a range of techniques that improve the vital skill of self-regulation. This skill is more important than ever for all adolescents, but it's especially crucial — and difficult to master — for those coming from low-income families, for whom adolescence can be particularly challenging, even dangerous. Moreover, as we'll soon see, the lengthening of adolescence hits kids from poor families hardest. Why this is so, why it's a serious problem for everyone (not just poor people), and what we can do about it are all questions we'll tackle in the next chapter.

9   *Winners and Losers*

The gap between the haves and the have-nots has been increasing not only in America, where it has grown steadily since around 1980, but in nearly every country in the developed world.

The fact that income inequality has been growing is well known. The fact that it has been exacerbated by the lengthening of adolescence is not.

The connection between the elongation of adolescence and the widening gap between rich and poor isn't obvious. But it is just a new chapter in an all-too-familiar story of the rich getting richer and the poor, poorer. The crucial difference here is that the "riches" are not only financial but psychological and neurobiological. People who can delay the transition into adulthood — because they have both the ability and the support to do so — reap the benefits of a longer period of plasticity during which higher-order brain systems continue to mature. Far from being a consequence of or contributor to immaturity, as it has been mistakenly portrayed, extending adolescence both reflects and portends advantage. It is an asset, not a liability.

As we discussed in chapter 3, people in their twenties who are delaying the transition to adulthood should hardly be ridiculed or denigrated. If brain development is facilitated by prolonging adolescence, society is benefiting, not suffering, from their choices and actions. Delaying the transition to adulthood is creating a more capable labor force, in both cognitive and noncognitive skills, like self-regulation. This benefits all of us.

If the journey toward neurobiological maturity were a boat race, we'd all agree that some people begin with a head start, better sails, the wind at their backs, and calmer waters. Since this race is longer than it's ever been before, these advantages favor those who have them more than ever—and leave everyone else even further behind.

Entering Adolescence at a Disadvantage

The neurobiological advantage enjoyed by the affluent starts long before adolescence. Children from poor families are much more likely to have cognitive deficits than their peers from better-off backgrounds. Young people who grow up in poor households consistently score lower on tests of intelligence and executive functioning. These socioeconomic differences are apparent very early in life—as early as two years of age. And being born into economic disadvantage has long-lasting effects on a wide range of outcomes—not only educational achievement, but mental and physical health, antisocial behavior, substance use and abuse, and, of course, earnings.

Many factors contribute to intellectual differences between children from different socioeconomic strata. One of the most notable factors is also one that's unpopular to acknowledge—genetics. This must be so, given the high heritability of intelligence, and of executive functions in particular; strong and well-documented genetic influences on brain anatomy; and what social scientists call "assortative mating"—the tendency for people who bear children together to have certain characteristics in common, including socioeconomic background and intelligence.

Genes clearly contribute to socioeconomic differences in intelligence, but environmental influences actually may be more important in explaining the relative intellectual deficiencies of children from poorer families. These environmental factors include both extreme trauma, such as violence inside and outside the home, and the chronic distress associated with poverty. Stress appears to have particularly toxic effects on brain regions like the prefrontal cortex that are crucial to advanced cognitive abilities and self-control. The good news is that, because the environment plays such a strong role in the development of this part of the brain, targeted interventions can help reduce inequality. We can narrow the divide between the haves and have-nots.

As we've seen, brain systems that govern functions like self-regulation remain very plastic for a long time and hence are very susceptible to environmental insult, particularly from persistent stresses like poverty. Not surprisingly, then, socioeconomic differences are especially pronounced in behaviors regulated by the prefrontal cortex, including things like self-control. Even when exposure to stressors that affect prefrontal brain systems occurs in early childhood, many of the more severe consequences of this experience may not become apparent until adolescence, when these brain systems become even more crucial for psychological health and scholastic success. It's easier to see the effects of poverty on poor self-regulation in adolescence, when we expect people to be able to exercise self-control, than in early childhood, when we know that it is normal for children to have occasional problems with self-regulation.

Brain imaging has shown how socioeconomic differences in executive functioning are reflected in brain anatomy. Recent studies have revealed structural differences in children's prefrontal regions that are linked to their parents' level of education. One aspect of brain development that is most disrupted by early stress involves the circuits that connect the prefrontal cortex with the limbic system. Early disruption of these circuits will tend to impair people's later ability to rein in sensation seeking and control their emotions. So it's hardly surprising that people from poor backgrounds are more likely to have all sorts of problems associated with impulse control, like substance abuse, crime, and aggression.

We've known for a long time that economic disadvantage hurts children's intellectual development, of course. In the United States, there's a fifty-year history of interventions like Head Start designed to stimulate the early cognitive development and enhance the school readiness of underprivileged children. These interventions have been largely disappointing in their effects. Certainly, they've done nothing to close the income gap between rich and poor, which is considerably wider now than it was when Head Start began in 1965. Income inequality in the United States, which was at an all-time low in the late 1960s, is at an all-time high today. Perhaps it was too much to expect a program like Head Start to significantly affect income inequality. But early-childhood interventions haven't closed the achievement gap, either. Despite billions of dollars invested in these programs, the gap in school performance between rich and poor children is wider now than it was fifty years ago.

In the last several years, advances in developmental neuroscience have begun to change the way we approach early intervention. The focus is beginning to shift away from academic achievement toward self-regulation. No one knows yet how well these new kinds of interventions will work. If successful, though, this focus on self-regulation will not only facilitate school readiness, but may also help reduce unemployment, increase college retention, lower rates of childhood obesity and teen pregnancy, and bring down the crime rate, since all of these problems are in some way related to deficits in self-control. We can argue about what the ultimate sources of these problems are — genes, poverty, discrimination, poor socialization, and so forth — but their immediate causes are problems in the ability to delay gratification.

Self-Regulation and Crime

Robert had terrible self-control.*

I got to know him over the course of several years because he took part in a study I helped lead, which tracked 1,350 adolescents who had been convicted of serious crimes as teenagers into their early and mid twenties. Many study participants had been convicted of very violent crimes, like armed robbery and aggravated assault. We carried out the study in Philadelphia and Phoenix, two cities we chose because they have enough crime to provide the number of participants we'd need to do a large-scale study, and because together they provided us with an ethnically diverse sample of offenders. Most of the serious juvenile offenders in Philadelphia are black, and most of the ones in Phoenix are either Latino or white. Although we went out of our way to enroll as many young women into the study as possible, the sample was overwhelmingly male — not unusual given the disproportionate amount of crime, and serious crime in particular, that is committed by young men.

Most teenage delinquents don't become persistent adult criminals. People tend to grow out of crime, just as with other sorts of risky and dangerous behavior, which decline as people mature through their twenties. As they lose some of their interest in sensation seeking and become better at self-regulation, most adolescents with a delinquent past start to turn their lives

---

* This individual's name and some of the minor details of his life have been changed.

around. Some delinquents re-offend while they are in their late teens, but few continue much beyond that.

We wanted to understand the differences between the adolescents who stopped committing crimes and those who didn't. What sets apart that small percentage of juvenile offenders who keep offending, long after their peers have ceased? Answering this question could help us design better programs to prevent crime and reduce recidivism.

One of the strengths of our study was that we interviewed the adolescents frequently enough to track their psychological development closely and obtain frequent reports on events in their lives. Each time we spoke with them, they completed a "life calendar" that took them through every month since the previous assessment and asked them to systematically recount what had been going on at home, in school, at work, and so forth. We could then use this information to construct a picture of their lives over time. At each interview, in addition to completing the life calendar, participants were given a series of standardized psychological tests, including measures of reward seeking and self-control.

When they were first enrolled in the study, the participants took part in a four-hour, one-on-one assessment with a trained interviewer. They completed a long battery of personality and intelligence tests, as well as dozens of questionnaires about various aspects of their lives. We asked about their families, friends, and neighborhoods, as well as their experiences in school and at work. During the first three years of the study, the adolescents were interviewed every six months, and after that, annually. We got to know these young people very well.

When the study began, most of the subjects were off the charts on tests measuring their attraction to immediate rewards and their inability to exercise self-restraint — not surprising, perhaps, in light of their criminal histories. This combination is unfortunate, and when taken to the extremes that we frequently saw in our sample, absolutely toxic. Fortunately, as they aged, most of the participants in our study became less shortsighted and better at regulating their impulses. And as they did, they stopped committing crimes. Only 10 percent of our subjects became chronic adult criminals. Other studies of juvenile delinquents have yielded similar numbers.

Robert, one of our Phoenix participants, was one of the small minority of offenders in our study who kept committing crimes. He was in and out of prison, in and out of therapeutic programs, on and off probation. Nothing the system did to or for Robert made a difference to his criminal behavior. Examining his psychological profile helps explain why.

Unlike most of the other adolescents in the sample, Robert's scores on measures of impulse control didn't improve as he got older. In fact, at the age of twenty-four, his scores were actually *lower* than they were when he was seventeen, which is remarkable, since almost no one becomes *more* impulsive during their twenties. Robert's life calendar and criminal history reflected his striking inability to exercise self-restraint. When we first met him, he'd been convicted of aggravated assault and was headed for prison, where he would spend the next eighteen months. After his release, Robert found a job at a fast-food restaurant, but lasted only a few months there, leaving work to re-enroll in high school, but remaining there for only four months. He took a job cleaning office buildings after dropping out, but was rearrested for drug dealing and was locked up again briefly. By nineteen, he had already fathered three children with two different girlfriends.

After his release, Robert was unemployed and out of school for a while, then took a new job, as a dishwasher, that he held for about three months, until he was arrested yet again — this time for robbery. In the first four years of the study, Robert held four different jobs and spent three different spells incarcerated.

This pattern continued for the next three years. During the seven years of the study, Robert was incarcerated five times.

The Four Rules

Social science teaches us that there are four basic rules to follow if you want to have a decent life. Stay in school — at least through high-school graduation, but longer if possible. Don't have children until you're married. Don't break the law. And, if you are not in school, do whatever you can to avoid being idle: if you have a job, don't quit it unless you have another one lined up, and if you're unemployed, take any job that you can get.

Breaking any of these rules will not guarantee disaster — there clearly are high-school dropouts, unmarried parents, lawbreakers, and idlers who escape poverty — but statistics show that if you play by these rules, you will almost certainly manage to make it. Research shows that people who follow these rules almost never end up in poverty.

Robert had broken all of them before he turned twenty-two. When our study ended, he was serving a long sentence in an Arizona state prison for robbery. As far as I know, he is still incarcerated.

The four rules share two important things in common. First, all of these choices have something to do with delaying gratification. Staying in school requires strong self-control and the ability to persevere through an often-tedious ordeal to attain a long-term goal, like a diploma. Avoiding unsafe sex requires setting aside the prospect of an immediate small reward (the enjoyable sensation of spontaneous, flesh-to-flesh intercourse) in favor of a longer-term benefit (not having to raise an infant without the necessary resources, or being able to continue one's schooling without the burden of parenthood). Breaking the law, especially during adolescence, is usually an impulsive act motivated by the prospect of an immediate reward, such as cash, stolen goods, or drugs. Turning down a job when one is unemployed, because the job isn't "good enough," or quitting one without having another one lined up, is likely caused by valuing the immediate reward (most likely, free time) over the possibility of a larger one in the future. The circumstances one grows up in surely affect these choices, but if you were to compare a sample of people who followed the four rules with a sample from the exact same background who did not, the rule breakers would score higher on measures of reward sensitivity and lower on measures of self-control, just like Robert. In fact, of all the factors that we looked at in our attempt to forecast which juvenile offenders would follow the usual pattern and become law-abiding adults, and which would continue in their criminal ways, the failure to develop mature self-control was one of the only consistent psychological predictors of persistent offending.

Because the participants in our study were already adolescents when we first met them, we do not have detailed information on their early years. I can't say with any certainty what contributed to Robert's chronic impulsivity. But other studies that have tracked people from birth have found that the antecedents of chronic offending are all associated with the failure to develop adequate self-regulation: birth complications, exposure to stress and trauma, poverty, harsh parenting, and early alcohol and drug use. Each of these has been shown to interfere with normal prefrontal development. My suspicion is that if we could see into Robert's past, we'd find several of these contributors.

The other quality shared by the four rules is that they all concern choices that are most often made during adolescence. Seldom is one faced with these decisions before this period. People in their late twenties and early thirties may also face these choices, but typically they've acquired the life experience and cognitive skills to approach them sensibly.

Imagine walking into the office of a counseling service that gave advice on these sorts of life decisions, the way financial planners help people manage their money. You sign in with the receptionist, who informs you that two counselors are available. One is seventeen and the other is thirty. Knowing what you now know about how adolescents think, if you were facing any of these decisions—whether to stay in school or drop out, whether to have a baby or not, and so forth—is there any doubt about which counselor you would be wiser to consult? Few of us would choose to be advised by a seventeen-year-old. Yet many seventeen-year-olds make these very sorts of decisions on their own. It is ironic that some of the most significant, life-changing, destiny-determining decisions we ever make arise at a time when our abilities to exercise good judgment are not fully developed.

The Coercive Cycle

As I explained in chapter 7, children are more likely to develop self-control when their parents are caring and affectionate but at the same time have explicitly expressed, patiently explained, developmentally appropriate, and consistently enforced expectations for their children's behavior. When parents are hostile or aloof, erratic, dictatorial, and either overly controlling or overly lenient, their children are less likely to develop mature self-regulation. How parents discipline their children matters, too. Parents who use physical force or express intense emotions when punishing are less likely to raise kids with good self-control than are parents who are calmer and gentler, while still maintaining their authority.

It takes a lot of time to raise a child with an eye toward her self-regulation. It's easier and faster to say, "Do it because I said so," or "Do whatever you want," than to say, "Here's what I'd like you to do, and here's why." Even the most patient parents often resort to these overly autocratic or overly permissive shortcuts when they're tired, preoccupied, or stressed out.

Unfortunately, poor parents often have less time to invest in their children's self-regulation than wealthier parents do, whether because their work schedules are more erratic or because one parent must handle a greater share of child-rearing duties because the other parent is absent. For these reasons, and a host of others we'll soon see, parents from lower-class backgrounds rear their children in ways that are less likely to lead to strong self-regulation. They're more likely to use harsh discipline and physical punishment. They tend to be more erratic and inconsistent, veering from excessive control to excessive permissiveness. They generally are less warm and less gentle. This is not the case for all lower-class parents, of course, nor is it true that all middle-class parents are models of temperance, kindness, and understanding. But these general differences between poor and affluent parents have been found in hundreds of studies.

Socioeconomic differences in parenting arise from many causes. The circumstances under which poorer parents raise their children are more stressful and taxing. The communities in which they live tend to be more chaotic, dangerous, and unpredictable, which tends to make parents more controlling and less patient. They're more likely to be parenting on their own, which often makes them more permissive. They have fewer resources that might allow them to take breaks from parenting when they're burnt out, which makes it harder to stand firm when their children are demanding. And because there is a good chance that they themselves were raised in similar circumstances, they're less likely to have good self-control, which is essential to good parenting.

Another reason that lower-SES parents are less likely to be calm and gentle is that, like all parents, their behavior is shaped by what their children do. Kids with weaker self-regulation are more impulsive and disobedient. Interacting with an impulsive and disobedient child makes parents themselves behave similarly—because their child flies off the handle easily, so do they. A "coercive cycle" is set in motion, in which harsh and inconsistent parenting produces problematic behavior in the child, which in turn evokes more harsh and inconsistent parenting. This cycle is more likely to occur in households where parents are stressed out.

In theory this familial liability could be offset by experiences outside the home that help build self-regulation—in school, for example—but these experiences are far less likely to be available in schools that serve poor communities. These schools are not only worse at teaching the basic intellectual skills needed for success in modern society, they're worse at providing opportunities to develop self-control. As a result, the kids who are most in need of this training because they haven't received it at home are the least likely to get it outside the family.

It is always politically dicey to describe the parenting of one segment of society as worse than another. Choosing how to parent ultimately is a matter of one's personal goals, tastes, and preferences. But in a society that rewards self-regulation, some parents' goals, tastes, and preferences are simply not in their children's best interests.

Poverty and Puberty

Most research on socioeconomic differences in executive function and self-regulation has focused on the implications of these inequities for the academic achievement of children from different socioeconomic backgrounds, which are substantial. There is another, perhaps more profound, disadvantage that lower-SES children bring to adolescence, however. They are less prepared than their more fortunate peers to respond to the neurobiological challenges of puberty.

The declining age of puberty means that, on average, children today are facing these challenges when they are younger and less able to regulate their emotions and behavior; remember, puberty hastens the arousal of the limbic system, but it doesn't speed the development of the prefrontal cortex. Going through puberty at an early age makes it more challenging, no matter what one's social background is. But because their self-control is weaker from an early age, poorer children are even more likely to be harmed by the fact that they're starting puberty earlier.

Moreover, as we saw in chapter 3, poor kids are entering puberty earlier than others. One would think that poverty would slow children's growth and development, if only because it is associated with poorer nutrition and health. This isn't true in modern society, though it was in the past, when poorer children went through puberty later, a pattern still seen in developing countries today. But once a society crosses the threshold from developing to developed, the relationship between socioeconomic status and pubertal timing flip-flops.

In developed countries, the causes of early puberty are more likely to manifest among disadvantaged children. Remember that the major contributors to the more recent decline in the age of puberty (as opposed to the drop that took place during the nineteenth and early twentieth centuries) are the increase in childhood obesity, the more likely survival of premature infants, the increased exposure of children to artificial light, higher rates of father absence, and greater exposure to endocrine-disrupting chemicals.

Although each of these factors by itself only contributes slightly to earlier puberty, their cumulative impact is much greater among children from poor families because *all* of these factors are more common in disadvantaged households. Within more affluent countries like the United States, for example, obesity is far more prevalent in lower socioeconomic strata; about 20 percent of poor kids are obese, but "only" 12 percent of better-off kids are. Premature births are about 50 percent more common among poor mothers than affluent ones. Kids' exposure to screen-based entertainment is widespread, but it is a lot more common in lower-class households; adolescents from poorer families not only spend more time watching television and playing video games, but are more likely to have these forms of entertainment in their bedrooms. This is especially a problem because children from poorer homes have later bedtimes and sleep less each night, which likely means that they have more exposure to light. Father absence is also primarily a problem of poor communities; 70 percent of children growing up in single-mother households are poor or low income. Exposure to bisphenol A (BPA), one of the commonly encountered endocrine disruptors that is hastening puberty, is significantly greater among the poor. In addition, the use of hair-care products that contain hormone-disrupting chemicals is especially common among poor black girls.

Although poor kids' diets and health care are inferior to that of middle-class kids, they're not bad enough to offset the combined puberty-accelerating effects of obesity, prematurity, light exposure, father absence, and endocrine disruptors.

Protection During a Tenuous Time

Because self-control matures gradually, adolescents go through a long period — now longer than ever, especially for poor people — in which that capacity can be easily disrupted. During this period, mature self-control is tenuous, present when conditions are optimal but absent when they are not.

During this fragile time, the best protection against lapses in self-control is external control of the sort that parents usually provide. Many studies confirm that adolescents who are closer to their parents and more consistently monitored by them are much less likely to engage in problem behavior than their peers. This is true of every problem associated with early puberty, including delinquency, substance use, and precocious sexual activity. Authoritative parenting lessens the risks associated with puberty at every age, even in cases of children who reach puberty unusually early.

How does good parenting mitigate the effects of early physical maturation? One thought is that it may take hanging around with older peers to actually turn the sensation seeking that is stimulated by early puberty into actual problem behaviors. A hormonally aroused adolescent may be motivated to experiment with sex, but she has to find a sex partner to make the fantasy a reality. If her parents closely monitor her whereabouts, this is less likely to happen. The same holds true for using alcohol and drugs, or for experimenting with minor delinquency. Early puberty is a risk factor for many types of behavioral problems, but early maturers who are closely supervised are at no greater risk than their peers who mature at an average age.

Simply put, adolescents who have trouble managing themselves benefit from having parents who can do it for them. The main tools in a parent's management toolbox are strictness, warmth, and supervision. Strict parents create and enforce rules and guidelines concerning how, where, and with whom their adolescents spend time. Warmth encourages adolescents to comply with these expectations because they want to make their parents happy. Supervision is added protection against rebellion. Lower-SES parents are less likely to use successful "management" strategies when their children are adolescents, however. Stress, poverty, and chaos all make it harder to be firm, warm, and vigilant. Plus, the common genetic liabilities that contribute to poor self-regulation in parents and their young children have the same impact on parents and their teenagers.

Adolescents from poor families, who need more help managing themselves, are less likely to get it from their parents. They're also less likely to get it from social institutions that provide supervision when parents can't. Studies have confirmed a fact that many might find obvious: adolescents who aren't supervised after school are more likely to get into various types of trouble. Teenagers from poor households are more likely to spend afterschool time in unstructured, unsupervised arrangements, and are more likely to do so in neighborhoods in which many families are socially isolated. When adults aren't around to watch over the neighborhood, antisocial peer groups are more likely to gather and lead teenagers into trouble.

In contrast, adolescents from middle-class households are more likely to participate in structured afterschool activities, like sports or theater, or to hold afterschool jobs, both of which provide structure and, at least in the case of school-sponsored extracurriculars, adult supervision. And if such opportunities are unavailable, affluent parents can pay for lessons, clubs, or other activities that offer the supervision and oversight that they themselves can't provide.

The bottom line is that children from wealthier families enter adolescence at a psychological advantage, and opportunities to further build the capacity for self-control are more plentiful for them. They enter secondary education with stronger self-regulation skills to begin with, having been raised in homes in which parents have stressed this trait. They're more likely to have parents and schools that can develop it further. Once they graduate high school, affluent adolescents are therefore more likely to have the psychological wherewithal and the financial resources to continue their education. And because higher education itself contributes to prefrontal development, self-regulation begets more self-regulation. Young people from poorer families are more likely to enter into environments where opportunities for novelty and stimulation are lacking. The fact that poor children are less likely to receive environmental stimulation when they are young, and when the brain is still malleable, has received a great deal of attention. The fact that this deprivation continues well into adolescence, when the brain is also very plastic, is something that warrants more attention than it receives.

The benefits of strong self-control don't end with college enrollment. Adolescents who enter college with a strong capacity for self-control are more likely to graduate on time. The ones who lack the capacity are less so, but adolescents who go to college are more likely than those who don't to have families who can bail them out when they falter — they can afford to take five years to finish college rather than four, six rather than five. They can take courses over the summer to make up for credits they've lost during the academic year. In college, as everywhere else in life, privilege provides protection.

Capital Formation

Adolescence has gotten longer for everyone. But *where* the period has been stretched differs between the classes. Puberty starts earlier among the poor, but the transition into adulthood takes place later among the affluent, who are far more likely to stay in school longer, delay getting married, and put off becoming parents. This is extremely important, because the impact of early puberty on the development of self-control is negative, whereas the impact of delayed adulthood on self-control is positive. As a result, the general trend toward a longer adolescence has been far more advantageous to the privileged than to the underprivileged.

In order to fully appreciate how the delayed transition into adulthood has disproportionately benefited the haves and hindered the have-nots, we must consider the different forms of "capital" and how they contribute to success in school, work, and life.

In addition to financial capital, adolescents growing up in more affluent families are more likely to accumulate human capital (the skills and abilities necessary for success at school and work), cultural capital (the cultural knowledge, manners of speech and dress, and ways of behaving that signal membership in the higher social classes), and social capital (connections with others who are able to provide assistance). In case you had any doubts, social science has confirmed that it's easier to succeed in life if you're wealthy, educated, sophisticated, and well connected.

Those who grow up in affluence have still another advantage that has become increasingly important: "psychological capital." This term refers to the noncognitive skills that are now recognized as just as crucial to success as the skills that are ordinarily included in the category of human capital—it includes things like social intelligence, vitality, enthusiasm, and, of course, self-regulation. We don't deliberately foster these things in school (although, as I pointed out in the previous chapter, we could), but being able to skillfully interact with others, light up a room, make people feel good about themselves, and exercise self-restraint are just as important, if not more so, than intelligence or talent.

Various aspects of psychological capital contribute to well-being in different ways, but self-regulation is probably the most critical to success in school and at work, especially in a world in which the ability to delay gratification has become so crucial. Plenty of people succeed without being cheery, extroverted, or vivacious, but few people do so without being determined, hardworking, and persevering.

I believe there is still another type of capital essential for success. For lack of a better label, let's call it "neurobiological capital." This is the advantage that accrues from having a protracted period of brain plasticity in an environment that is appropriately stimulating. The privileged have an advantage in neurobiological capital in early life, because they are likely to be exposed to environmental stimulation during infancy, the first period of heightened brain plasticity. But they also accumulate neurobiological capital by extending adolescence, because delaying the transition to adulthood keeps the window of plasticity open for a longer period of time while people can continue to expose themselves to the kinds of experience that improve the brain. The affluent also have the resources they need to buy access to stimulating environments during this time.

As we've seen, prefrontal systems become stronger through scaffolded stimulation — challenges that require us to use them in ways that are slightly more demanding than we're accustomed to. These are precisely the sort of challenges offered by the colleges and universities young people from privileged families attend. The advantage of staying in school longer is not just in the additional skills, credentials, connections, and capacities that are accumulated through this experience — although these advantages in human, cultural, social, and psychological capital are certainly considerable. It also comes from the opportunity to accumulate neurobiological capital.

The Privilege and Promise of a Delayed Adulthood

As mentioned in an earlier chapter, many people have expressed concern that delaying the transition into adulthood is bad for young people's psychological development. My colleagues and I have taken a look at whether delaying adulthood seems to be having a negative impact on the mental health of young people, using data from the Monitoring the Future study, described in chapter 3. To refresh your memory, each year since 1976, researchers at the University of Michigan have been conducting surveys of representative samples of Americans in their late teens and twenties. The different "cohorts" of young people — that is, people who were in high school during different eras — are followed over time, surveyed every two years from high-school graduation until they approach the age of thirty.

The surveys ask a range of questions about psychological functioning, attitudes, and values, but they also ask about peoples' life circumstances at the time of each survey, including whether they were enrolled in school or employed, with whom they were living, and how they were supporting themselves. It is therefore possible to determine how old people were at the time they passed a certain milestone, like finishing school, getting married, or having a child.

Monitoring the Future confirms that today's young people are taking longer to complete their formal education, take full-time jobs, establish economic independence from their parents, get married, and become parents. Despite the substantial differences among the different high-school cohorts in the timing of these transitions, however, respondents' answers to the questions about their quality of life indicate that the generations are remarkably similar in their reports of how things were going when they were in their twenties. Indeed, compared with their parents' generations, today's young adults are no more or less happy, no more or less satisfied with the way life is treating them, and no more or less likely to report that they are having fun.

Given all the fuss that has been made about the extent to which today's young people seem "stuck," these findings are surprising. The journalistic accounts that dominate the narratives of popular magazines simply do not match the data. Nor do the portraits of carefree, self-indulgent millennials.* Today's young adults aren't any more self-satisfied or self-absorbed than their parents were at this age. In short, the psychological similarities between young people today and their parents at the same age are far more striking than the differences. Other researchers who have examined data sets similar in scope to Monitoring the Future have drawn the same conclu-

---

* The widely reported assertion that today's young adults are more narcissistic than their elders is misleading. The study that led to this conclusion found that young adults scored higher on a measure of narcissistic personality disorder than people sixty-five and older. But so did adults in their thirties, forties, fifties, and early sixties. Young adults did not differ from these groups, however.

sion. Unfortunately, reporting that today's young people are pretty much the same as their parents is boring, whereas bashing "kids today" gets headlines (just as it did in their parents' day).

In our analysis, we found that levels of happiness and satisfaction are largely uncorrelated with the age at which people complete the various milestones. People who entered the labor force, got married, or finished school at an older age were, on average, no less happy than those who made these transitions when they were younger — if anything, the respondents who delayed these transitions were *more* satisfied with life. This was especially the case with respect to having kids, where doing so at a later age correlated with higher reports of happiness and life satisfaction. I should stress, though, that the strength of the association between happiness and life satisfaction, on the one hand, and the age at which one entered various adult roles, on the other, was extremely small.

Given the growing evidence that the early twenties is a time of continued brain plasticity, and the likely possibility that this potential asset begins to fade as we stop putting ourselves in intellectually challenging situations, delaying the movement into the routinized life that adulthood generally entails actually may be a good decision, at least for people who are able to use the flexibility of their young-adult years wisely. By remaining in school longer, putting off marriage, and waiting before settling into careers and parenthood, those who can afford to delay the transition into adulthood not only gain the benefits of additional schooling, but also have more time to take advantage of the brain plasticity that is more likely to be maintained by experiences in novel and stimulating environments. A longer adolescence not only builds their human capital, but it also builds their psychological and neurobiological capital as well.

Rather than lamenting how long it takes young people to become adults and encouraging them to speed things up, we should focus our attention on how to help all young people in their twenties — not just the economically advantaged — benefit from the delayed transition into adulthood, and to think more about encouraging young adults to use these years in ways that will stimulate further brain development, not only by making college more accessible, but by expanding opportunities for apprenticeships and for voluntary community service through programs like AmeriCorps. This will go a long way toward closing the gap between the haves and have-nots. Encouraging more adolescents to go to college, while laudable in principle, is not enough, however. In order to reduce inequality, we will need to focus on promoting the development of self-regulation, through early interventions, by teaching parents how to facilitate their children's self-control through authoritative parenting, and by using schools to help do what many families can't or don't do on their own.

We also need to take a closer look at how society treats adolescents. In many respects, those who most need our protection are the least likely to receive it. As the next chapter reveals, much of our treatment of young people is completely misaligned with what science is teaching us about adolescence. And nowhere is this more evident than in how we respond to young people who break the law.

10   *Brains on Trial*

The return address on the envelope didn't specify an individual, only an identification number and the name of a state prison in Michigan. The handwritten letter, on neatly folded yellow legal paper, recounted a thirty-five-year story of violence, regret, remorse, and redemption.

Joseph Mahoney had contacted me to ask my assistance in his quest to be released from prison, where he had been since the age of fifteen.* He was about to turn fifty. Without any opportunity for parole, he would spend the rest of his life inside the Harrison Correctional Facility.

I've received several letters like Joseph's every month for the past eight years. His story was similar to most of the other ones. He'd been one of four boys who had robbed a convenience store. As the youngest member of the group, Joseph didn't have much say in the crime's planning — although "planning" would be a generous way to describe their actions on that February night in 1977.

The boys had been sitting around one of their homes, drinking beer and getting high. One of them, Hakeem, who was seventeen, was going on about a corner grocery in a nearby neighborhood whose owner was an old man named Jerome Williams. Hakeem had been by the place at least a doz

---

* I've changed the names of some of the people and altered some of the details in the cases discussed in this chapter.

times on his way to and from his girlfriend's apartment. He knew the store's routines well, and was confident that the old man would be an easy target.

Hakeem described his plan. In an hour or so, the shopkeeper would be alone behind the counter. It would all happen so quickly, he said, no one's face would be remembered. It was cold and raining—they'd have their sweatshirt hoods pulled up. They'd hang outside the store until there were no customers inside, enter as a group, and demand that the clerk turn over the cash in the register. He'd have no choice but to comply—a sixty-year-old man would see that he was outnumbered and easily overpowered. Once they took the cash, they'd run out the back door, into the alley. It would take the police at least ten minutes to respond—convenience stores in Detroit were held up all the time. By the time the police arrived, the kids would be long gone. Divvied up among them, the amount of money each would get wasn't much—maybe a hundred dollars apiece. But it was too easy to pass up the opportunity. Hakeem assured them that his older brother, Isaiah, had pulled off similar robberies in other neighborhoods, and he'd never been caught. Better still, no one had ever been hurt.

Only Hakeem and two others would enter the store. Joseph, as the youngest, would be the lookout. If another customer approached the store while the rest of them were inside, it was his job to stop the person from coming in, by engaging him in a conversation and keeping him occupied. "How am I doing that?" Joseph asked, simultaneously insulted and relieved that he had been given this assignment.

Hakeem, who was a head taller than Joseph, put his hand on Joseph's shoulder. He squeezed it—not hard enough to hurt him, but firmly enough to remind the younger boy that he was older and stronger. "Little man, you just tell him your mother sent you out to get some milk and bread, and you were in such a rush that you forgot to take the money she left you. Explain the situation. You can't go back home without anything. Your brother and sister are hungry. Maybe he can have a little sympathy. Stand between him and the door. You only need to keep him out for a minute or so." Hakeem knew that Joseph would do as he said—not only was Joseph the youngest of the four, he was, by nature, a follower.

Things didn't unfold as planned, though. The shopkeeper refused to open the register as Hakeem had assumed he would. Rattled, Hakeem panicked. He hadn't told any of his friends that he had a .32-caliber handgun inside his waistband. Hakeem pulled the gun out, the clerk grabbed for it, and the gun went off. It fell to the floor and skidded away. The boys didn't wait to see if anyone had been shot. They turned and ran out the front of the store as quickly as they could.

Joseph heard the gunshot but was too scared to move. Once he saw his friends tearing out of the store, though, he took off after them. No one knew that the shopkeeper's wife had been in the back room and had seen everything through a small crack in the wall. Between Lenora Williams's account and the reports of several people who had seen the boys running down the street, it wasn't hard for the police to track them down and make an arrest. Hakeem's fingerprints were all over the gun.

Jerome Williams died in the hospital a few days later.

In Michigan, if someone is killed during the commission of a felony, the homicide is treated as first-degree murder. And under the state's "felony murder" law, any co-offenders fourteen and older are equally responsible for the victim's death, regardless of who did the actual killing. Joseph, who hadn't been in the store when Jerome Williams was shot — who hadn't even known that Hakeem had been carrying a weapon — was convicted and sentenced to life in prison without the possibility of parole.

No one liked the felony murder law. The state's attorney knew that Joseph hadn't shot anybody. He knew Joseph was only fifteen. He knew that this was Joseph's first offense. He didn't think Joseph should spend the rest of his life in prison. But his hands had been tied by the state legislature. Once it was evident that Joseph had been involved in the shooting, no matter how minimal his involvement, his life sentence was a foregone conclusion.

Joseph's letter arrived at my office a few months after the U.S. Supreme Court's decision in *Miller v. Alabama,* a 2012 case in which the Court ruled, by a 5–4 margin, that mandatory life sentences for juveniles were unconstitutional. Joseph was seeking a new sentence, on the grounds that the *Miller* decision applied retroactively. His lawyers contended that anyone who had been sentenced to life as a juvenile had the right to a resentencing hearing, in which the now-unconstitutional sentence could be replaced with one that was shorter. Joseph had written to ask if I would help his lawyers argue that the thirty-five years he had spent in prison constituted more than enough punishment for a crime he had committed when he was fifteen — at an age when his judgment, and his brain, were still immature. Joseph had read

job training. More than a few have undergone some sort of religious conversion. Many, like Joseph, have participated in programs designed to help younger inmates and reduce recidivism.

Their letters by and large are intelligent, thoughtful, and remarkably well informed by both science and legal precedent. They all ask my help in their quest for a second chance. They thank me and my colleagues for doing research that demonstrates what their own experiences have taught them — that people change, and that it is wrong to judge them forever on the basis of what they did as teenagers. They ask for copies of articles on adolescent brain development that they can read and give to their public defenders. I answer all of them, and send information and materials I think might be useful.

As far as I know, none of these inmates has been released from prison.

As Any Parent Knows

Joseph Mahoney is one of more than twenty-five hundred inmates currently serving a life sentence in an American prison for crimes they had committed when they were younger than eighteen. The *Miller* Supreme Court decision didn't ban life sentences for juvenile murderers outright, but the Court ruled that the imposition of this sentence could no longer be automatic — it had to be determined on a case-by-case basis.

Under the new law, some juveniles convicted of homicide could still be given life without the possibility of parole, but not all of them would. Most would undoubtedly receive long sentences, but they might be eligible for parole after serving a period of time. At sentencing, judges and juries would be expected to take into account factors like the offender's prior criminal record and psychological maturity, as well as the circumstances of the crime. After *Miller,* a fifteen-year-old like Joseph, who was obviously taking orders from a more powerful peer, would presumably be treated less harshly and given the second chance that a shorter sentence or the possibility of parole would allow. He would receive much more than a slap on the wrist, but neither would he be locked up forever.

Miller was the third in a series of Supreme Court cases that drew on scientists' new understanding of adolescent development. The *Miller* decision had been preceded by *Graham v. Florida,* a 2010 case in which the Supreme

Court banned life sentences for juveniles who had been convicted of crimes other than homicide. *Graham,* in turn, had grown out of a landmark ruling in 2005, *Roper v. Simmons,* which abolished the juvenile death penalty. It is considered one of the most important cases involving juveniles in the history of the Court.

In all three cases I was one of several experts who helped amass the scientific evidence and incorporate it into the argument presented to the Court — that adolescents are inherently less mature than adults in ways that make them less responsible for their crimes, which renders them less deserving of sentences like life without parole. We argued that the immaturity of the adolescent brain — the combination of an easily aroused engine but a still-developing braking system — makes minors more impulsive than adults and more easily influenced by peers. If this is true, we pointed out, it makes them less responsible for their behavior.

Under American criminal law, individuals found guilty of the same crime may differ in their degree of responsibility for their acts. Criminal culpability can be mitigated by the circumstances of the crime and by the perceived character of the criminal. Someone with no prior record of violence who acts in a way he has never acted before and kills another person impulsively or after being coerced may be guilty of homicide, but he would likely be punished less harshly than someone with a long arrest record who painstakingly plans and carries out a murder on his own.

The fact that adolescents' immaturity is something over which they have no control — the incomplete maturation of their brain — was a key part of our reasoning. There are plenty of irresponsible adults in the world, but when they commit crimes, the fact that they are irresponsible doesn't matter. The law recognizes that some conditions lessen people's criminal responsibility, but unless a criminal's act is the obvious product of mental retardation or mental illness, poor judgment isn't a mitigating factor. We expect that by the time people reach a certain age, they've learned how to behave as members of society. We have little patience for adults whose behavior indicates that they won't — or can't — play by the rules.

Adolescents are immature in a way that is different from the typical immature adult, though. An impulsive adolescent will almost certainly develop into an adult who is able to exercise self-restraint. Someone who is still behaving like an impetuous teenager, even though he is thirty, is probably going to be that way forever. He's a bad horse to bet on.

Our laws recognize that adolescents are different from adults, and there are many things we don't let minors do because we believe them to be too immature. This is precisely why we don't let people under twenty-one buy alcohol — because we don't think they're responsible enough to handle it. This is the logic behind having a minimum age for driving, or dropping out of school, or even getting married without parental permission. Somehow, though, we lose sight of this logic when a young person commits a serious crime. But committing a crime, no matter how serious, doesn't turn an adolescent brain into an adult brain.

It's not only adolescents' immature judgment that demands that we treat them differently when they break the law. If the plasticity of the adolescent brain makes juveniles more amenable to rehabilitation, this argues against mandatory life sentences that don't allow courts to consider whether an impulsive or impressionable teenager might grow into a law-abiding adult who can control his impulses and stand up to peer pressure. Of course a teenager who kills another person deliberately should be punished — no one is arguing otherwise. But should he be incarcerated for the rest of his life, with no chance to prove that he has matured? Suppose he turned out to be like Joseph Mahoney — a concerned and responsible adult who might make a significant contribution to his community?

For some people, treating juveniles who commit serious crimes differently than we treat adults for the same offenses makes no sense. As they are quick to point out, adolescents clearly know right from wrong. Why should we let them off the hook? Moreover, they usually ask, how can a particular sentence be overly harsh when applied to a juvenile but not when applied to an adult who has committed the same crime?

The answer to these questions is that in order to make the punishment fit the crime, we need to look not just at the crime, but at the criminal. Adolescents' immaturity doesn't mean that they are *not* guilty, but it does mean that they are *less* guilty.

To take an extreme example, imagine that someone drops a stone from an overpass, and that the stone shatters the windshield of a car, causing the driver to lose control, crash, and suffer a severe injury. Now consider the person's age in deciding how he or she ought to be punished. Few of us would conclude that an eight-year-old and a twenty-eight-year-old should be held equally responsible for this act, and few would think it fair to punish an eight-year-old child to the same degree that we might punish an adult, despite the fact that the crime and the resulting harm are the same in each case. A severe punishment for a young adult who committed such an act might be entirely appropriate, but that same sanction would be excessive when applied to a young child. Even those who insist that adolescents who break the law be treated like adults have trouble with the prospect of adult time for adult crime if the criminal is still in the second grade.*

Most people agree that there is some age below which we shouldn't hold people to adult standards of criminal responsibility. It's harder to find consensus on *where* that line should be drawn. The difference between an eight-year-old and a twenty-eight-year-old is obvious. The difference between a fifteen-year-old and a twenty-eight-year-old is not. But science confirms that there is still a good deal of development that takes place between these two ages.

The Supreme Court reached this conclusion in the cases concerning the juvenile death penalty and life without parole. "As any parent knows," Justice Anthony Kennedy famously wrote in the Court's majority opinion in *Roper*, the juvenile-death-penalty case, adolescents are less mature than adults. He noted that they are impulsive and shortsighted and highly susceptible to peer pressure, and that their character is still developing. In his view, they shouldn't be candidates for the sentences we reserve for the worst of the worst — those who are fully responsible for their crimes and who are probably irredeemable. The Court ruled that the juvenile death penalty was unfairly harsh in light of adolescents' immaturity, and that it therefore violated the Eighth Amendment of the Constitution, which prohibits "cruel and unusual" punishment.

Justice Kennedy had the advantage of not having to rely just on what "any parent knows." By the time these cases came to the Court, evidence had been accumulating that adolescents were not only more impulsive, vulnerable to peer pressure, and unformed than adults, but that scientists could point to some of the neurobiological underpinnings that accounted for these differences. Using neuroscience to buttress commonsense observations about teenagers — what "any parent knows" — as well as the psychological research that was consistent with these beliefs didn't change the basic

---

* Not all of them do, though. When a reporter once asked my opinion of a California prosecutor's initial decision in 1996 to charge a six-year-old with attempted murder, I said that perhaps he was trying to send a message to first-graders all over the country.

argument that adolescents were inherently less responsible than adults, but it gave it more force. The brain science allows us to describe adolescent immaturity in physical, not just psychological, terms. People are persuaded much more by concrete than by abstract evidence, and by neuroscience in particular. In this instance, a brain scan was worth a thousand words.

The United States versus Omar Khadr

The oddest question I have ever been asked during the forty years that I have been studying adolescent development is whether I thought that someone would need to be capable of formal operational thinking in order to build an improvised explosive device (IED).

According to Jean Piaget's influential theory of child development, "formal operational thinking" is the highest level of cognitive development, a stage not attained until the beginning of adolescence, at the earliest. It requires a level of abstract reasoning that depends on brain systems that develop throughout childhood and early adolescence, but don't fully mature until age fifteen or sixteen.

This unusual question was posed to me during a pretrial investigation held at Guantánamo Bay, where I was serving as an expert witness in a case involving a detainee who had been accused of building and setting IEDs in eastern Afghanistan, as an assistant to al-Qaeda operatives, and throwing a hand grenade that killed an American soldier. Omar Khadr, the detainee, was fifteen at the time he was captured by American soldiers. Khadr's defense team, which had retained me, was planning to argue in court that a fifteen-year-old, by virtue of his developmental immaturity, warranted special consideration under the law, consideration he had not been given by the interrogators who questioned him after his capture, and that he would not likely be given by those prosecuting him for his alleged actions.

The person questioning me at Guantánamo Bay about formal operations and IEDs was Marine Major Jeff Groharing, the attorney prosecuting the case against Khadr for the U.S. government. I was interviewed by him and an army psychologist in a small room down the hall from the lawyers' offices, across from the courthouse where the tribunals were to take place. Groharing was looking for evidence that Khadr, by virtue of his bomb-building ability, demonstrated adult-like cognitive maturity, which argued in favor of treating him as an adult and viewing his responses during the interrogation as no different than those an adult would have provided.

He was hoping I'd say that in order to do what he did, Khadr would have had to be functioning at an adult level of logical ability and, more important, would have to have had a fully developed prefrontal cortex. By January of 2009, when I was being deposed, a mature prefrontal cortex had become a defining feature of adulthood. By then, the adolescent brain had appeared in *New Yorker* cartoons and on the covers of both *Newsweek* and *Time*. I was questioned repeatedly about what the recent research on the adolescent brain implied for understanding Khadr's behavior.

Because Piaget never created any tasks designed to study whether abstract reasoning was required for bomb making, I explained that my answer to the prosecutor's questions would have to extrapolate from the broader literature on cognitive development in childhood and adolescence. I replied that I thought it likely that a typical elementary-school student had the intellectual abilities required for building an IED. After all, it doesn't require abstract reasoning to follow instructions to connect one colored wire to another, or to connect a series of parts together in a predetermined sequence that can be copied from a picture or a model. Even young children can do this, I pointed out, as evidenced by their ability to assemble Legos or Tinkertoys according to the instructions included in the box.

Omar Khadr's case had received worldwide attention for a number of reasons. He had been interrogated repeatedly between August and October of 2002 at the U.S. detention center housed at Bagram Air Base, in Afghanistan, where he was taken after his capture, and for several years after his transfer to Guantánamo. He is the youngest person to have been detained at Guantánamo and is the first child soldier ever tried by the United States for war crimes. He was detained for so long because it was believed that he could be an important source of intelligence. His father, who had been killed a few years before Khadr's capture, had been a close associate of Osama bin Laden's. Omar himself had met the al-Qaeda leader often.

I was asked to weigh in on two issues in the Khadr case. The first concerned his degree of criminal culpability. Even if it were proven that he had participated in the manufacture and planting of IEDs, a fifteen-year-old working under the supervision and authority of adults is not fully responsible for criminal behavior in which he might have been encouraged to take part. For the same reasons that the Supreme Court had abolished the juvenile death penalty and placed strict limits on the use of life without parole for juveniles convicted of serious crimes, it seemed to me that a reasonable case for mitigation, and lesser punishment, could be made on Khadr's behalf, should he be found guilty.

It may seem odd to extend this logic to the case of a terrorist, but an adolescent is an adolescent, whether he is making fun of his teachers, committing armed robbery, or building a bomb. No matter how "adult-like" the crime is, it doesn't change the fact that brain systems that govern abilities like thinking ahead and impulse control are still developing. It's easy to lose sight of this when an adolescent is accused of something as serious as homicide. It is almost guaranteed that this will be ignored when the adolescent is working for a terrorist organization that is an avowed enemy of the United States.

I had seen videotapes of Khadr assembling and planting bombs and had little doubt that he was guilty of these terrorist acts. In evaluating his conduct, though, and in determining an appropriate sentence, it is important to focus not only on whether he was guilty, but whether he was fully responsible for his behavior. Khadr had spent his entire life among people who had repeatedly told him that the United States was an evil enemy intent on killing him, his family, and anyone who was like them. Think about the messages American children hear about the Taliban, and just reverse the situation.

Khadr had been sent by his father to live with a group of operatives who closely oversaw his behavior. It was inconceivable for a fifteen-year-old under these circumstances to have done anything other than follow the orders he was given — and just as unimaginable for him to have developed a worldview that was different from that held by those around him. In my opinion, adolescent immaturity mitigated Omar Khadr's responsibility, just as it had Joseph Mahoney's on the night that the grocery store robbery had spiraled out of control, or Justin Swidler's, when he created and circulated Teacher Sux, the derogatory website discussed in chapter 4.

The second issue I was prepared to discuss concerned the reliability of statements Omar Khadr had made during the many hours of his interrogations, as his confessions provided the basis for much of the government's case against him. Khadr had later said that he had confessed to throwing the grenade that killed the American soldier only because he wanted his interrogators to stop hurting him. He insisted that he hadn't thrown it. Given his age and the circumstances of his interrogations, I thought that there was reason to be concerned about the dependability of Khadr's statements. I had no idea what the truth was, but I worried that the interrogations might have produced untrustworthy information. There is considerable evidence that, because of their developmental immaturity, juveniles are more prone to giving false confessions.

I spent most of my time at Guantánamo reading interrogation reports. I met Khadr a couple of times. By then he was in his early twenties. I didn't need to meet him to serve as an expert. My testimony was going to focus on how fifteen-year-olds think and behave. He requested both meetings — he wanted to personally meet all the experts who were working with his attorneys.

I was struck by how normal Khadr seemed for someone who had spent the last seven years in a stark prison cell, much of it in solitary confinement, and who had been subjected to some unbelievably harsh treatment on a daily basis for much of that time (and that's just the treatment that was documented in the files I was given to review). Khadr was an exceptionally friendly, gentle, and articulate young man, fluent in multiple languages, including English (he had spent part of his childhood in Canada). He was not at all forbidding. He was hardly what one expects an al-Qaeda terrorist to be like.

On the ride out from our office to Camp Delta, where I met Khadr, my escorts, a psychiatrist and clinical psychologist who had gotten to know him on previous visits, stopped at the commissary to buy him some of the foods he liked. They met with him first while I waited nearby. When I entered his cell, a small, blindingly white room, he insisted that I help myself to the hummus, pita chips, and cherry tomatoes my colleagues had brought him — remarking that I was *his* guest. I sat across from him at a table. His ankle was shackled to a ring cemented into the floor of the cell. The overhead fluorescents, which glowed twenty-four hours a day, buzzed. It was one of the most surreal experiences I've ever had.

Khadr asked many questions about my work and my family. He had been told that I was a professor, and he asked what courses I taught. I learned that he was hoping to attend college and then medical school, if he ever was released. He said he was interested in reading papers about our research on adolescent decision making. When he learned that I had a son who was close to his age, he wanted to know about him as well. We even discussed the Philadelphia Eagles, who had made it into the NFL playoffs that season, and who were in the midst of losing to the Arizona Cardinals just as I was being deposed. Khadr knew little about American football, but he was amused by the fact that my son and I would watch Eagles games "together," in different cities but connected by telephone and text messaging.

Whether Khadr's confessions to having thrown the grenade were obtained under duress needed to be resolved before the military tribunal went any further. Because they were an essential part of the government's case against him, the tribunal needed to determine if the statements were admissible. If they weren't, it would be difficult to prove that he had thrown the grenade, because there had been no witnesses who had survived the firefight.

The preliminary hearing on this question began with testimony from the government's witnesses, who testified that Khadr had confessed willingly and without being coerced. His interrogators all denied having tortured him. As far as I was concerned, whether his treatment rose to the level of torture wasn't the issue. I was prepared to testify that even in the absence of torture, a fifteen-year-old who was being held captive under the conditions that prevailed in the detention camps was highly susceptible to false confessions. There have been dozens of cases in which adolescents have falsely confessed under far more benign circumstances. Of course, no one other than Khadr and his interrogators really knew what went on during the questioning, but it seemed plausible, to say the least, that a frightened and badly wounded fifteen-year-old in Khadr's position might have told his interrogators what he thought they wanted to hear.

As it turned out, I never had to take the stand. The hearing didn't even last long enough for the government to fully present its case, much less the defense team. The day after it began was Barack Obama's inauguration, and soon after he was sworn in as president, he suspended all Guantánamo tribunals. Khadr's case was ultimately settled in an agreement the following year, in which he pleaded guilty to war crimes, conspiracy, spying, and providing material support for terrorism. In 2012, as part of the arrangement, he was released from the detention camp and transferred to a Canadian prison, where he is serving an additional seven years.

False Confessions

Adolescents' relatively greater propensity to give false confessions has arisen as an important issue in a number of prominent cases, including the 1989 Central Park jogger case, in which five adolescents were falsely convicted of assaulting and raping a twenty-eight-year-old woman who had been running in the park. The key evidence that led to the boys' conviction were the confessions made by four of the five suspects — admissions that were later discovered to be untrue and, according to the boys' attorneys, coerced. The identity of the person who had actually committed the crime came out twelve years later, and was corroborated by DNA evidence. The convictions were vacated in 2002, but by then, the five had all served prison terms. A lawsuit brought by them against New York City still has not been settled.

Many people can't fathom why anyone would confess to a crime he did not commit, but this happens more often than one would imagine. In the United States, interrogators are permitted to use deception when questioning suspects, and many use tactics that have been shown to increase the likelihood of people admitting to things they didn't do. Adolescents are especially susceptible to these techniques, not only because they are less savvy than adults, but because the methods exploit adolescents' cognitive immaturity.

One of the most common tricks is "minimization," in which the alleged act is played down by the interrogator ("After all, you were only doing what your buddies told you to do"), and the suspect is led to believe that confessing to the more understated version of the crime will lead to kinder treatment and facilitate a speedier release from custody ("If you cooperate with me, I'm going to see if we can get you out of here as soon as possible, so that you can go home and see your parents"). Because adolescents, younger ones in particular, are especially drawn to immediate rewards and less likely to think about the consequences of their actions, they are more likely than adults to respond positively to these sorts of ruses.

Even when adolescents' confessions aren't false, they are often problematic because they are obtained without the adolescent's full knowledge that what he says can be used against him in court. In theory, the requirement that adolescents be read their Miranda rights ("You have the right to remain silent," and so forth) is supposed to prevent adolescents from making false or ill-advised confessions, but studies have found that adolescents under the age of fifteen don't really understand what the Miranda warning actually means. I once asked a very intelligent twelve-year-old if he understood what it meant when a police officer told someone that he had the right to remain silent. (He had told me that he had seen people being read their rights on plenty of episodes of *Law and Order*.) The child thought about it for a moment and replied, "It means that you don't have to say anything until the police officer asks you a question."

Drawing the Line

Studies of adolescents' susceptibility to false confessions, as well as their criminal responsibility, are part of a larger discussion of where we should define the age of legal majority. All societies have to grapple with deciding who is old enough to take on the responsibilities and be granted the privileges of adulthood, and who is still too young for this. There was a time when societies drew distinctions between adolescents and adults on the basis of things like whether they had matured physically or entered into some specific role of adulthood, like owning property, but those days disappeared long ago in most parts of the world. In modern society, such distinctions are normally based on chronological age. Most countries pick an age — usually eighteen — and use this for all legal purposes. People of the same age are all treated the same way, regardless of how mature they are in comparison to their peers.

The "one age fits all" definition of adulthood is both efficient and not subject to discriminatory bias. A system in which psychological maturity is judged on a case-by-case basis is not only cumbersome, but open to prejudice. This was the reason to disagree with the more conservative members of the Supreme Court who dissented from the majority opinions in the cases that banned the juvenile death penalty and mandatory life without parole for juveniles. The dissenting justices acknowledged that most adolescents were less mature than adults, but pointed out that surely some of them were just as capable. Instead of banning the death penalty or life without parole for *all* people younger than eighteen, they asked, why not let judges and juries make these decisions on an individual basis? That would permit them to punish the juveniles who thought and behaved just like adults as if they were adults under the law.

In theory this makes sense. In practice, though, it is loaded with potential problems. Judgments of adolescents' maturity are fraught with error and tainted by bias — for instance, studies find that black adolescents are judged as more adult-like than white adolescents who've committed the same crimes, even when black people are doing the judging. Additionally, an adolescent can be made to appear more mature (by dressing in an adult outfit) or less so (by dressing like a child). Aspects of the adolescents' appearance or behavior that are not genuinely indicative of his maturity — facial expressions or posture, for example — can affect people unconsciously.

It is true that using chronological age alone to make decisions about who is an adult and who isn't doesn't allow reasonable exceptions to the rule — for example, permitting especially mature sixteen-year-olds to vote, or prohibiting exceptionally irresponsible twenty-two-year-olds from buying alcohol. But the alternative isn't practical. Even if it were possible to fairly and accurately assess a person's psychological maturity, doing so would be enormously burdensome. Imagine what it would be like if passing a maturity "test" (if one even existed) were required to purchase liquor or be admitted to an R-rated movie.

There is a different problem with using a single chronological age to define legal adulthood, though. The same age may not be appropriate for different kinds of decisions. In the United States, as opposed to most of the rest of the world, we address this concern by deciding what age is "mature enough" on an issue-by-issue basis. Although the presumptive age of majority in America is eighteen, as it is in most other countries, we deviate from this guideline more often than we adhere to it. Consider, for instance, the different ages we use to determine when people can make independent medical decisions, drive, hold various types of employment, drop out of school, marry without their parents' permission, view R-rated movies without an adult chaperone, vote, serve in the military, enter into contracts, buy cigarettes, and purchase alcohol. The ages generally range from fifteen to twenty-one, although there are some outliers, such as when someone can be tried as an adult (in most states, this is fourteen, but in some, a child accused of murder can be tried as an adult at any age), or the age at which someone can rent a car without paying an "underage premium," which can be as old as twenty-five, depending on the rental company.

Although this issue-by-issue approach is also reasonable in principle, it's problematic in how we apply it. Because we don't rely on science to link specific ages to specific rights or responsibilities, we end up with laws that are bafflingly inconsistent, at least when viewed through the lens of science. Here's an example: A friend of mine who directs a national organization that advocates on behalf of juveniles in trouble with the law once received a phone call from the director of an adult prison, asking for advice on how to handle the request of an adolescent inmate who wanted to smoke cigarettes, but who was below the minimum legal age to purchase tobacco. In other words, it was fine to prosecute and punish this person as an adult, but illegal to let him enjoy the privileges of adulthood while he was serving his adult sentence in an adult prison! How can we rationalize sentencing juveniles to adult prisons before they are old enough to buy cigarettes, or sending young people into combat before they can buy beer? The answer is that policies that distinguish between adolescents and adults are made for all sorts of reasons, and science is only one of many considerations.

The reason we use sixteen as the minimum driving age in the United States is a case in point. There are very few activities more dangerous than driving a car. Of all the things we let adolescents do before they have developed mature judgment, driving makes the least sense.

When automobiles were first introduced, there were no age restrictions — indeed, there were no driver's licenses of any sort. As it became clear that traffic safety was an issue, states began licensing drivers and setting a minimum driving age, most commonly eighteen, which is where it stands today in most of the developed world.

In the 1920s and 1930s, many states lowered the driving age from eighteen to sixteen, but not because people suddenly discovered that sixteen-year-olds were more mature than they had thought. In urban areas, lowering the driving age allowed sixteen- and seventeen-year-olds to take jobs that required operating a car or truck. In rural areas, it permitted teens to drive motorized vehicles on public roads in order to transport farm equipment. (Operating motorized equipment within a family farm was already permitted, even for much younger children, but this permission did not extend to driving these vehicles on roads.) As concerns about the high rate of teen driving fatalities have grown in recent years, many states have adopted a policy called "graduated driver-licensing," which lets sixteen-year-olds drive, but only under certain circumstances (e.g., no other passengers in the car, not driving after a certain hour).

The regulation of drinking is similarly disconnected from the science of adolescent development. After Prohibition ended, the minimum drinking age was established at twenty-one in the majority of states. During the early 1970s, several of these states lowered this age to eighteen, nineteen, or twenty. The voting age recently had been lowered to eighteen, which was done because many politicians argued — most vociferously, Edward Kennedy — that it hadn't been fair to send eighteen-year-olds to Vietnam but prohibit them from voting. Some states extended this logic by bringing their drinking age closer in line with the military draft and the new voting age. Some politicians felt it also was unfair to make people serve in the military but deny them the right to drink.

After it emerged that lowering the drinking age led to an increase in highway fatalities, advocacy groups launched an effort to persuade these states to return the age to twenty-one. Because some states agreed but others did not, minors began driving across state lines to purchase alcohol — or, worse yet, to drink — and then drive back home. In 1984, the federal government passed legislation that mandated a reduction in highway funding for any states that did not set the minimum drinking age at twenty-one. Every state complied.

Today, the United States is one of only three developed countries that doesn't permit people to drink when they reach eighteen (the others are Iceland and Japan, which set the minimum drinking age at twenty). The important point, though, is that no new discoveries about adolescent development have ever prompted changes in the minimum drinking age. It is unlikely that adolescents are either less or more mature today than they were when they were allowed to buy alcohol at the age of eighteen.

Adolescents' Right to Make Decisions About Abortion

Whether one age of majority should apply to multiple legal issues became a point of controversy after the Supreme Court abolished the juvenile death penalty. The court's decision in that case drew extensively on an amicus curiae (friend of the court) brief submitted by the American Psychological Association. Citing evidence from both the brain and behavioral sciences, psychologists had taken the position that adolescents are inherently less blameworthy than adults because of their developmental immaturity.

Although this argument stood on solid scientific footing, it appeared to contradict a stance the same organization had taken in an earlier case, which concerned whether a minor should be allowed to obtain an abortion without notifying her parents. In its brief to the Court in that case, psychologists had argued that adolescents had comparable decision-making skills to those of adults, and that there was no reason to require young women to notify their parents before terminating a pregnancy.

It looked like the American Psychological Association was trying to have it both ways. In opposing the juvenile death penalty, the organization said that science showed that adolescents were not as mature as adults, but in arguing for adolescents' right to make abortion decisions without telling their parents, the APA contended that the science showed that they were plenty mature. To some observers, it looked like the whole developmental-immaturity argument was just a convenient fabrication concocted by liberal child psychologists to suit their political goals.

Within two years of abolishing the juvenile death penalty, the Supreme Court heard a new case about parental involvement in adolescents' abortion decisions. Those who opposed allowing adolescents to make these decisions on their own seized on the Court's characterization of adolescent immaturity in the juvenile death-penalty case and used it to argue in favor of parental-involvement requirements. They pointed out that if adolescents were too immature for the death penalty, they were too immature to make abortion decisions.

This debate highlights the problem with using one age for every legal line we draw between adolescents and adults. Simply put, there isn't a single age when people become psychologically mature.

Different regions of the brain develop along different timetables, and as a result, different abilities reach adult levels of maturity at different ages. It's not until age eighteen or older that we can reliably control our impulses, stand up to peer pressure, and resist the temptation to take risks because of the prospect of an attractive reward. But under good conditions — when they are not overly aroused emotionally or pressured by time or by other people — fifteen- and sixteen-year-olds can reason just as well as adults.

This is why it is not hypocritical or disingenuous to suggest one age for death-penalty eligibility and another for the right to get an abortion without parental permission. The circumstances surrounding each situation are different. Adolescents' decisions to commit crimes — if one can even call them "decisions" — are usually rash and often made in the presence of peers, like the convenience store robbery that led to Joseph Mahoney's life imprisonment. But their decisions about terminating a pregnancy can be made in an unhurried fashion and in consultation with adults. Indeed, to help ensure that abortion decisions are not made rashly, more than two-thirds of all states require any woman seeking an abortion — regardless of her age — to receive some type of counseling before the procedure is performed, usually including information about the specific procedure as well as the health risks of abortion and pregnancy. Twenty-five states mandate a waiting period of at least twenty-four hours between the counseling and the medical procedure. Very few pregnant teenagers decide to terminate a pregnancy hastily or without adult advice. It's pretty much impossible.

That's not the case where crime is concerned. Adolescents' crimes more often than not are impulsive and unplanned and typically committed with peers. Emotions often get in the way of good judgment. As a consequence, the circumstances that define "mature" behavior in each situation are clearly different. Resisting peer influence and checking one's impulses are far more important in criminal decision making than abortion decision making, in part because society structures the latter to encourage consultation with adults and avoid hasty choices.

Thus far, research on adolescent brain development has had its most far-reaching impact on criminal law. In addition to the Supreme Court cases that banned the juvenile death penalty and placed limits on life without parole, several states have changed, or are reconsidering, their laws governing whether juveniles can be tried as adults. Drawing on research indicating that brain systems governing impulse control are slow to mature, some states have raised the age at which juveniles can be prosecuted in adult court, and others have mandated that younger adolescents' competence to stand trial be evaluated before they can be transferred to the adult system. In other states, added protections have been mandated for adolescents undergoing interrogations, such as requiring the presence of a parent or attorney, or videotaping the questioning so that it can be reviewed later to evaluate whether unduly coercive techniques were used.

about our research in the prison library, and he was confident he had science on his side. In his letter, he explained how he had grown up a lot since
he was a fifteen-year-old. Surely a parole board would see that. Surely they
would conclude that he was no longer dangerous—if in fact he ever had
been. They would see that he had no disciplinary blemishes on his prison
record.

It certainly looked to me like Joseph would be an asset to the community. He had been a model prisoner during his time in Harrison, not only
getting his GED, but completing a two-year associate's degree in criminal
justice through a program for inmates run by the local community college.
Once he had turned twenty, Joseph had decided that he was going to focus
his time on self-improvement; he didn't care whether he'd ever be able to
use these skills on the outside. His accomplishments were remarkable: During his thirty-five years of incarceration, he had received certifications in
auto repair, plumbing, landscape management, carpentry, electrical main-
tenance, refrigeration repair, and both basic and advanced computer operations. He took part in several poetry-writing workshops that had been
led by students from a nearby university. Joseph was so well respected by
the prison administrators and his fellow inmates that he had been selected
to serve two terms as the inmates' official representative to the Harrison
administration. When he was thirty, he had started a program within the
prison for young inmates who were eligible for parole. He wanted to help
them adjust to life behind bars and make themselves better candidates for
early release. Joseph might never be free, but he hoped to enjoy their freedom vicariously.

Over the years, I've received about a hundred letters like Joseph's. They
usually come from men in their thirties or forties who had committed a serious, violent crime sometime in their midteens. Rarely do the writers deny
culpability for what they did or try to pass themselves off as victims of circumstances, although in most cases, the childhood and early-adolescent
years they describe in gruesome detail had been horrifyingly traumatic,
filled not only with poverty and violence, but with constant exposure to explosive, abusive, drug-addicted parents and siblings, many of whom themselves rotated in and out of prison. The inmates write, with considerable
remorse, about the foolish and reckless things they did as teenagers, and
they acknowledge the harm they have caused. Almost all of them have been
well-behaved prisoners, taking advantage of counseling, education, and

Rethinking the Boundary Between Adolescence and Adulthood

We don't yet know whether findings from the study of adolescent brain development will influence changes in arenas other than criminal law. As is usually the case when science appears in court, research on adolescent brain development is usually used to justify a change in the law that already had support for other reasons. After all, there is no good scientific reason to maintain the minimum legal driving age at sixteen, and plenty of evidence that this age is too low, but attempts to raise the driving age to eighteen have been unpopular. Often, the most vehement opponents have been parents, who are annoyed at the prospect of having to chauffeur their teenagers.

Research on adolescent brain development does not point to an obvious chronological age at which a sharp legal distinction between adolescents and adults should be drawn for all purposes. Generally speaking, science indicates that people reach various kinds of maturity between the ages of roughly fifteen and twenty-two. Adolescents' judgment in situations that permit unhurried decision making and consultation with others — what psychologists call "cold cognition" — is likely to be as mature as that of adults by age sixteen. In contrast, adolescents' judgment in situations characterized by emotional arousal, time pressure, or the potential for social coercion — what psychologists call "hot cognition" — is unlikely to be as mature as adults until they are older, certainly no earlier than age eighteen and perhaps as late as twenty-one.

If developmental science were an important consideration in establishing the age of legal adulthood — as I believe it should be — a reasonable starting point would be to distinguish between two sets of regulations: those that involve cold cognition and those that involve hot cognition. Cold cognition is relevant to matters such as voting, granting informed consent for medical procedures (including abortion) or being the subject in a scientific study, and competence to stand trial in court. In all of these instances, adolescents can gather evidence, consult with advisors (such as their parents, physicians, or attorneys), and take time before making a decision. Time pressure and peer pressure aren't usually factors. Given an adequate waiting period and the opportunity to discuss the decision with an adult, I see no reason why a pregnant sixteen-year-old shouldn't be able to get an abortion or contraception without her parents' involvement, or why we shouldn't let sixteen-year-olds vote. (People this young can vote in Austria, Argentina, Brazil, Ecuador, and Nicaragua.)

I certainly wouldn't recommend changing the age of legal adulthood to sixteen for all purposes, though. A later age is more sensible for matters that involve hot cognition, like driving, drinking, and criminal responsibility. Here the circumstances are usually those that bring out the worst in adolescents' judgment — they frequently pit the temptation of immediate rewards against the prudent consideration of long-term costs, occur against a backdrop of high emotional arousal, and include other adolescents. These are the very conditions under which adolescents' decision making is more impulsive, more risky, and more myopic than that of adults. Given this, I believe we ought to raise the minimum driving age to eighteen, set the minimum age of adult criminal responsibility at eighteen, and continue to restrict minors' access to alcohol, tobacco, and, where it is legal, marijuana.

Whether the drinking age should be lowered from twenty-one to eighteen is a difficult and contentious issue. I must admit that I have a philosophical problem with prohibiting adolescents from purchasing alcohol until they are twenty-one but allowing them to serve in the military and face the dangers of combat when they are as young as eighteen (seventeen, actually, with their parents' permission). Evidently, although drinking is considered too risky to leave to teenagers, the suggestion that combat may be too dangerous for people this age is seldom entertained.

It's no mystery why this is. The military would have trouble meeting its staffing requirements without enlisting older teenagers. Males between the ages of seventeen and nineteen make up about 3 percent of the male civilian population, but account for more than 6 percent of all males in the military. The same is true for females. Females between seventeen and nineteen make up less than 4 percent of the civilian population, but nearly 8 percent of all females in the military. Male teenagers account for 13 percent of all males in the Marines. Female teenagers account for 16 percent of the Marines' females.

Apart from the fairness issue, there is empirical evidence on both sides of the minimum-legal-drinking-age debate. On the one hand, setting the minimum legal drinking age at twenty-one has diminished automobile deaths among younger drivers, although the evidence is not as clear-cut as one might think. One problem in interpreting the drop in fatal crashes that occurred when the drinking age was raised to twenty-one in 1984 is that a decline in auto fatalities was already taking place before the age was changed, as a result of improvements in auto safety and increased awareness of the hazards of drinking and driving. It isn't clear how much raising the drinking age further accelerated this trend. Given the fact that alcohol accounts for a large proportion of automobile fatalities at *all* ages (and especially between twenty-one and thirty), raising the drinking age to any degree will result in fewer highway deaths. There is nothing magical about picking twenty-one as the minimum age to purchase alcohol, though, and as I noted earlier, the United States has the highest minimum drinking age in the developed world.

Nor does it seem that the drinking age is the main problem, at least as far as highway safety is concerned. Virtually all European countries that set both the driving age and the drinking age at eighteen have significantly lower automobile-fatality rates than the United States. If we were genuinely concerned about improving adolescents' health, raising the driving age would be the single most important policy change we could make. A scientifically informed discussion might lead to setting eighteen as the minimum age for both driving and drinking. That's how most countries do it — and most countries have far fewer auto fatalities than the United States.

I don't harbor any delusions about the use of scientific evidence to inform policymaking, though. Policymakers and advocacy groups use science the way that drunks use lampposts — for support, not illumination. If the political will is absent, no amount of science, no matter how persuasive it is, is going to change the law.

Conclusion

The discovery that adolescence is a time of heightened brain plasticity — comparable in many respects to the first few years of life — should radically transform our vision of the period. Traditionally, we have thought of adolescence as a period so inevitably fraught with difficulty — a perilous time for young people, a worrisome one for their families, and an exasperating one for their teachers — that most of our advice to adolescents, parents, and educators has been aimed at helping them avoid the pitfalls and hazards we presumed to be unavoidable. This has led to a view of adolescence as a struggle young people must suffer through and a battle the adults who care for them must endure.

Not surprisingly, most of our efforts to influence adolescent development are aimed at preventing or treating problems, rather than optimizing healthy development. Unlike zero to three, where our focus has been largely on encouraging positive growth and development through early intervention and education, our emphasis during adolescence has been almost entirely on preventing problems. We spend our time telling adolescents what they shouldn't do, rather than guiding them toward what they should — and can — do.

As I described in chapter 1, it's obvious that our current approach to adolescence has not been working. American high-school students' achievement has not improved in three decades and lands at or near the bottom of global rankings despite relentless efforts at school reform; surveys reveal high rates of mental health problems and unhappiness among our teenagers and young adults; and we face continuing epidemics of adolescent obesity, binge drinking, violence, and unsafe sex, despite substantial investments in efforts to educate young people about risky and unhealthy behavior.

Our current approach has been calibrated to help young people *survive,* when we should be helping them *thrive.* And thriving during adolescence depends above all on developing strong self-control. Countless studies indicate that people with a superior ability to regulate their feelings, thoughts, and behaviors are more successful in school and at work; less vulnerable to a wide range of psychological difficulties, such as depression, anxiety, and eating disorders; and less likely to engage in risky behavior, such as drug use, delinquency, reckless driving, and unprotected sex. If we can help children and adolescents develop better self-regulation, we will significantly improve the health and well-being of the nation as a whole.

The fact that adolescence lasts longer than ever gives this goal added import and urgency. The elongation of adolescence, a product of the declining age of puberty and the increasingly older age at which young people enter the conventional roles of adulthood, has three profound implications.

First, a longer adolescence has made self-control more important than ever before, because people must be able to delay the gratification that comes with the independence of adulthood that much longer. I've used the example of waiting until one is married before having sex to illustrate just how hard (if not impossible) it is to endure such a long period between the beginning and end of adolescence, but this example is also a reasonable metaphor for what adolescence has become: an incredibly lengthy time between the first taste of adulthood and the opportunity to satisfy the urges it stimulates. As I've pointed out, puberty sparks all sorts of arousal, not just the sex drive. The fact that it takes place so much earlier today than in the past means a much longer period between when the "engines" are ignited and when the "brakes" have matured. This has made adolescence a much riskier period.

Second, the fact that adolescence starts earlier and lasts longer has increased the advantage that the affluent enjoy over the underprivileged, because the former are more likely to have the neurobiological, psychological, familial, and institutional resources necessary for successful self-regulation. Adolescents who grow up in middle-class families enter the world with stronger self-control to begin with, and they are more likely to be raised in ways that foster its maturation, have easier access to educational and extracurricular experiences that further its growth, and have people in their lives who can protect them from the dire consequences of occasional lapses in self-control that are inevitable at this age. Adolescents without these advantages are not only less likely to acquire the additional years of schooling needed for success in the world of work, they are also more likely to cut adolescence short by taking on the roles of adulthood at an earlier age. This not only hurts them financially, but neurobiologically and psychologically too. Rather than criticize those young people who are lucky enough to be able to take more time before becoming adults, we might instead think about how we might share this opportunity with those who are less psychologically and socioeconomically fortunate.

Finally, a longer time between the beginning and end of adolescence means that the window of risk and opportunity created by the brain's exceptional sensitivity to the environment is open that much longer. The increased brain plasticity that marks adolescence is especially good news because the brain systems that govern self-control are particularly malleable. The challenge we face as parents, educators, and adults concerned with the well-being of young people is figuring out how to take advantage of this opportunity, by providing adolescents with new experiences and responsibilities that stimulate brain development, while limiting their exposure to situations and substances that threaten their health while their self-control is still immature.

Some Recommendations

Our new understanding of adolescence should inspire significant changes in how we raise, educate, and treat young people. Based on this new knowledge, I offer the following recommendations for parents, educators and employers, and policymakers.

FOR PARENTS:

Lessen the chance that your child will go through puberty early. The early onset of puberty increases adolescent boys' and girls' risk taking, substance abuse, and delinquency, and elevates girls' risk for depression and eating disorders. Early puberty also increases a woman's chances of developing cancer (the jury is still out on whether it has a similar impact on men). A century ago, the decline in the age of puberty was due mainly to improvements in health and nutrition. Today, however, it is due to more worrisome causes, including obesity, the proliferation of endocrine-disrupting chemicals, and increased exposure to artificial light.

In order to reduce the chances of obesity, parents should see that their kids eat less sugar and fat and more fresh fruit and vegetables, and get at least an hour of aerobic exercise each day. In order to reduce children's exposure to light, parents must establish and enforce reasonable bedtimes (preschoolers need between eleven and twelve hours of sleep each day; elementary-school children need at least ten) and limit their children's screen-based entertainment, which not only contributes to overall light exposure but disrupts their sleep as well.

There is growing awareness of the harmful effects of endocrine disruptors, and perhaps their presence in the environment will decline if sufficient pressure is placed on regulatory agencies to prohibit their use. In the meantime, parents should minimize their children's exposure to pesticides and plastics that contain chemicals known to interfere with normal hormonal development. These chemicals are, unfortunately, ubiquitous in modern society, but special care should be taken to read product labels and avoid exposure to soft vinyl products with a strong smell, certain plastics (especially those labeled with the numbers 3 and 7, or known to contain BPA), and substances that contain phthalates (which are found in many soft plastics as well as many cosmetics) or parabens (a type of preservative contained in many cosmetics, shampoos, and sunscreens).

Taking steps to reduce childhood obesity, screen time, and exposure to harmful chemicals will have added benefits beyond postponing puberty. Obesity is a risk factor for numerous maladies, including cardiovascular disease and diabetes. The increased time children spend in front of TV and computer screens contributes to sleep deprivation, which is associated with lower school achievement, higher rates of psychological disorder, and accidental injuries. Exposure to manmade chemicals that alter our biological functioning is linked to many types of illness, most notably cancer.

Practice authoritative parenting. The earlier onset of puberty makes it more crucial than ever that parents help their kids develop stronger self-regulation. By practicing authoritative parenting during childhood and adolescence, parents will enhance their children's school achievement and lower the chances that their adolescents will engage in risky and reckless behavior; use or abuse alcohol, tobacco, and illicit drugs; get in trouble with the law; have precocious or unprotected sex; and develop mental health problems like depression, anxiety, and eating disorders.

Authoritative parenting requires that parents do three things as often and as consistently as possible: be warm, be firm, and be supportive. Parents can increase the level of warmth in their relationship with their children by making a concerted effort to be more physically affectionate, more forthcoming with compliments when they are deserved, more actively involved in their children's lives, and more attentive and responsive to their children's emotional needs. Because children's emotional needs change as they get older, it is helpful to read up on different stages of development to know what to expect as your child matures. It's also important to just spend time together having fun. Every interaction doesn't need to culminate in a life lesson.

Parents can make sure that they are firm by clearly expressing and explaining their expectations for their children's behavior, by enforcing rules in a consistent but flexible manner, and by imposing consequences for misbehavior. Parents should not use physical punishment or be verbally hostile, though. A parent who has difficulty regulating his or her own behavior, and finds it hard to avoid lashing out physically or verbally, should seek help from a professional. If you're not careful you'll pass on your own poor self-regulation to your child.

Parents can support their children's developing ability to exercise self-control in several ways. Use the technique of scaffolding (explained in chapter 7) to create learning situations in which your child is challenged but has a good chance of success. Don't micromanage your child's life in a way that deprives him of the opportunity to make any decisions or practice self-control. When you praise your child's accomplishments, focus on the effort she invested, not on the outcome or her native ability. By focusing on her effort, you are sending the important message that determination and hard work are the keys to success.

Encourage activities that are likely to contribute to self-regulation. Children's self-regulation can be strengthened through deliberate practice. Remember that self-control begets more self-control. Some specific exercises that may help your child are mindfulness meditation, yoga, and disciplined physical activity like tae kwon do or tai chi. Many helpful resources for meditation are available in books and apps. These apps typically have a narrator who explains the technique and guides you through the process. Meditation is also taught through workshops and classroom-based instruction, as are yoga, tai chi, and tae kwon do. Video instruction is also available for yoga and tai chi.

Organized sports, when overseen by coaches who understand and genuinely care about their players' mental as well as physical health, can also contribute to the development of self-control, grit, and the ability to function as a member of a team. Even for young people who are not inclined toward organized athletics, getting sufficient aerobic exercise and rest — including adequate sleep — are crucial. All of these factors contribute to psychological and physical health in adults as well as children and teenagers, so it makes sense for you to do them, too.

Be aware of the emotional and social circumstances that can undermine your child's judgment. Many adolescents who display excellent judgment and good self-regulation under optimal conditions don't when they're stressed, fatigued, or in groups with other teenagers. Watch out for these situations, and try to provide additional support and supervision when they arise. Remember that unsupervised, unstructured time with peers is often a recipe for risky and reckless behavior. The more you limit your adolescent's time in these sorts of settings, the safer he will be. If your state has graduated driver-licensing that prohibits new drivers from driving with teen passengers, make sure that your child is in compliance, or retract his driving privileges. If your state has no such law, you would be wise to enforce this as a family rule. Multiple teen passengers in a car driven by an adolescent is as dangerous as drinking and driving.

Reduce your child's exposure to stress. Just as the disciplined practice of self-control through things like meditation or yoga help strengthen the capacity, so can stress undermine it, by causing what psychologists call "dysregulation."

Making your home feel as gentle and calm as possible will help minimize your child's dysregulation. This means keeping arguments to a minimum (both with your children and between you and your partner). Children benefit from being raised in a loving and happy family where people are kind, physically affectionate, and relaxed. Conversely, they are harmed by living in a home that is conflict-ridden, tense, unpredictable, or frenetic.

Strive to keep outside sources of stress, like work, from impinging on your home environment. I realize that this has become so much more difficult because the boundaries between home and work have been eroded by nonstop electronic communication. But filling your home with the pressures of the workplace adversely affects the mental health of everyone in your family—not just yourself. You may not feel as if you need a sanctuary from the office (you're just kidding yourself if you really believe this), but that doesn't mean that your child needs to live inside your pressure cooker, too. A healthy home environment is a calm and pleasant place where people can relax and have fun, not an extension of a stress-filled, deadline-driven workplace.

The same principle applies to pressures that can arise from kids' own activities. Children benefit from extracurricular activities, but they also need time after school and on weekends when they can just unwind and do nothing in particular. Adolescents who attend demanding schools especially need time to decompress from very full days.

Don't worry about whether your twenty-something child is taking too long to grow up. Prolonging adolescence isn't necessarily bad; it may even be beneficial, at least under the right circumstances. The longer one can stay immersed in a world characterized by new and stimulating experiences, the longer one can benefit from the positive effects such experiences have on the brain.

It's important for you and your adolescent to remember that this period is an opportunity for growth, but not a guarantee—growth depends entirely on how well the new activities are tailored to one's needs and talents. For many, college will be the main source of stimulation. But not all adolescents are ready for the psychological demands of higher education immediately after high school. They might benefit from some time in the military or pursuing challenging service opportunities, like AmeriCorps. These activities are preferable to employment in an unstimulating entry-level job, like working behind the counter of a fast-food restaurant.

Reimagine what secondary schools can accomplish. Growing interest in developing noncognitive skills, including self-regulation, is welcome. Schools must now incorporate activities into their curricula that build noncognitive skills. These activities include computer-based training to develop executive functions, meditation, aerobic exercise, structured physical activity that demands concentration, and programs explicitly designed to teach self-regulation. At a time of shrinking school budgets, I realize that any call to add more programs to the curriculum won't be warmly embraced and may be ridiculed as extravagances. To this resistance I can only say that our persistently mediocre record of secondary-school achievement, despite the relatively long school days we force our adolescents to endure, suggests there's plenty of room to rethink how that time might be more profitably spent. Given what we know about the importance of exercise for the development of self-regulation, one hour of each school day should be devoted to physical education. This will likely raise students' test scores more than additional instruction.

Incorporate social and emotional learning into the middle-school curriculum. I noted in chapter 8 that there is good evidence that social and emotional learning (SEL) programs contribute to the development of self-regulation, especially when implemented in elementary or middle school, so long as they follow the "SAFE" principles: they are sequenced, active, focused, and explicit. Anyone who's interested in bringing SAFE SEL programs to their school should consult the website of the Collaborative for Academic, Social, and Emotional Learning (CASEL), a nonprofit organization that conducts systematic evaluations of SEL program effectiveness, as well as the U.S. Department of Education's What Works Clearinghouse, which maintains lists of school-based social and emotional learning programs with proven track records of success.

Make high school more demanding. It is laudable to incorporate more activities that promote noncognitive skills into our schools. But we cannot continue to ignore the fact that American students graduate with far less proficiency in academic skills than they should. A recent report on adults' literacy and proficiency in math and technology indicates that Americans' relative standing internationally is actually getting worse—a sorry comment indeed on the results of three decades of intensive school reform. Among those between fifty-five and sixty-five—that is, people who graduated high school around 1970—U.S. adults were above average in comparison to the rest of the world. Among those between forty-five and fifty-four, who graduated around 1980, Americans placed in the middle of the field. But among adults younger than forty-five—who graduated around 1990 or later—Americans' performance was well below the international average.

Many factors have likely contributed to this disappointing trend. But one major contributor is the fact that American high schools are considerably less demanding than in the rest of the industrialized world. American teenagers describe school as boring and unchallenging, a view shared by students from other countries who spend part of their adolescence in the United States. Too much instruction is aimed at the rote memorization of facts. With the exception of students who are bound for the nation's most prestigious colleges and universities, and those who are enrolled in AP and other advanced classes, young people are rarely pushed beyond their current capabilities. They don't get the sort of stimulation necessary to develop brain regions that support higher-order cognitive skills and self-regulation. This is especially unfortunate in light of what neuroscience is teaching us about the importance of novelty and challenge during periods of brain plasticity. A false dichotomy has been drawn between the need to test students and monitor school performance, on the one hand, and the need for schools to help develop critical thinking, on the other. We can, and should, do all of these.

Spend less money and time on classroom-based health education. Everyone agrees that we must deter adolescents from risky activities like reckless driving and unprotected sex, but our efforts continue to yield meager results. That's because adolescent risk-taking is not substantially reduced by classroom-based instruction, the customary preventive measure. Our schools and communities spend hundreds of millions of dollars every year on health-education programs that either have proven ineffective or have never been rigorously evaluated. Some instruction is necessary in order to communicate information and facts to students, of course, but much of what schools do is wasteful of time and resources. Concerted efforts to promote self-regulation will probably do more to reduce substance use, unprotected sex, and reckless driving than will conventional drug, sex, and driver's education.

Promote authoritative parenting. Schools and communities can teach parents how to be more effective at home. This can be accomplished through community-based parent-education programs, counseling from health care practitioners about effective parenting, school-sponsored "clinics" for parents, and public service programming. Children whose parents do not practice authoritative parenting will be at a distinct disadvantage in school and in the workplace.

Prepare adolescents for the psychological demands of college, not just the academic ones. Promoting cognitive development beyond high school is essential to closing the gap between the haves and the have-nots. This can't be accomplished simply by expanding college opportunities, however. Indeed, encouraging all students to enroll in college will have disastrous consequences unless our high-school graduates have the self-discipline, as well as the academic skills and financial resources, necessary to complete the requirements for a college degree. The high college-dropout rate reflects how poorly we prepare our high-school students for the demands that college places on self-regulation. We need to rethink college-preparatory education so that it includes activities that help foster self-regulation in addition to building academic skills. Having a few years of college no longer provides any occupational or financial advantage over merely graduating from high school. Increasing the number of people who attend college, but not the number who earn a degree (which is the current trend), only creates a larger pool of people who carry debt they can't repay.

Employers of teenagers and young adults should learn about the latest findings on adolescent brain and behavioral development. For employers, the most important new news is that adolescents are sharply biased toward immediate rewards, less attentive to the potential downside of bad decisions, more shortsighted, less able to control their impulses, and more likely to make reckless decisions when they're in groups of their peers. More careful, scientifically informed management of adolescent employees can enhance young people's work experiences and improve employers' bottom lines.

FOR POLICYMAKERS:

Rethink our approach to public health policies aimed at young people. A lot of adolescents' risky behavior results from neurobiological immaturity rather than ignorance or misinformation. An approach to public health that attempts to change the context in which teenagers and young adults live is more likely to reduce reckless and dangerous behavior than will one that tries to change their basic natures. There are many examples of effective "contextual" approaches to deterring risky behavior. Graduated driver-licensing significantly reduces teen auto crashes. Smoking can be deterred by raising the minimum purchase age for tobacco to twenty-one, which will help keep cigarettes out of high-school peer groups. Stronger enforcement of laws prohibiting the sale of alcohol to minors, as well as laws that punish adults who make "proxy purchases" for adolescents, will lower rates of teen drinking. Making condoms available through school-based clinics has been shown to lower rates of unprotected sex without increasing rates of sexual activity. Providing more extensive afterschool activities for adolescents will limit opportunities for unstructured and unsupervised time, a well-known contributor to delinquency.

Treat juveniles who commit crimes as juveniles, not as adults. In practice this means maintaining a separate juvenile justice system for adolescents under the age of eighteen, an approach to juvenile sentencing that emphasizes rehabilitation rather than punishment, and strict limits on trying juveniles as adults. This latter option should be used very rarely and prohibited in the case of first-time offenders, nonviolent offenders, and offenders under age fifteen. Transferring adolescents to the adult system increases, rather than decreases, their risk for recidivism.

Rethink age boundaries between adolescents and adults to bring them more in line with the findings from scientific studies. Many of our legal boundaries simply don't make sense in light of what we've learned about how adolescents think. By the time people are sixteen, their competence to make informed decisions when they are given opportunities to think them through is comparable to that of adults. People as young as sixteen therefore should be permitted to vote, grant informed consent to receive health care (including abortions and contraceptive services), participate as subjects in research without needing parental permission, and view and purchase the same mass media as adults. On the other hand, adolescents are worse than adults at regulating impulses and exercising sound judgment when they are emotionally aroused and with friends. For this reason, we should raise the driving age to eighteen and maintain and enforce minimum purchase ages for substances such as alcohol and, where it's legal, marijuana.

Some Final Thoughts

I am not the first person to raise concerns about the well-being of America's youth, by any means. But the conversation I believe we need to have is a different one than those we have had over the past three decades, in several respects.

First, the conversation cannot be limited to just one group of involved parties. Parents, educators, politicians, businesspeople, health care professionals, and other adults who assist in the rearing of our adolescents all need to be involved, because no single group on this list is the sole cause of the problems adolescents have, and no single group can possibly provide the solution. Nor is it useful to pin the blame for these problems on any one sector of society. The usual finger-pointing has gotten us nowhere, because the problems our adolescents exhibit are multiply determined, typically with small, but nevertheless significant, contributions from numerous forces. This makes it virtually impossible to make headway by addressing any one contributing cause in isolation from the others, because each cause by itself only contributes a small amount to the problem.

Second, the conversation needs to be about the whole range of issues we need to address, treating them not as separate problems but as interrelated ones. Seemingly different problems that are common during adolescence, like obesity, reckless driving, dropping out of college, substance abuse, unintended pregnancy, bullying, and suicidal thinking, share many of the same underlying causes, and our failure to recognize their commonalities has impeded our progress in ameliorating them. Many of the same factors that lead some adolescents to binge drink encourage others to have unprotected sex, others to commit crimes, and still others to fail in school. Unfortunately, funding for research on these problems and programs to address them provides inadequate support for studying or addressing their interrelatedness or shared causes. A good deal of lip service is paid to the need for cross-disciplinary collaboration, but this is by far the exception rather than the rule.

Third, the discussion must focus not only on how to prevent problematic development, but on how to promote positive development. Preventing problems is crucial, of course, but most of us want more for our young people than for them to merely survive adolescence. We want our teenagers and young adults to be healthy and vibrant, not simply free of disease; optimistic and exuberant, not simply "nondepressed"; ethical and compassionate, not simply law-abiding; intellectually curious and eager to succeed in academic and occupational pursuits, not simply content to do just what it takes to avoid failing; and goal-oriented and hopeful, not simply satisfied with maintaining the status quo. Most of what is written for parents and practitioners is aimed at preventing or treating problems, rather than on optimizing healthy development. This needs to change.

Finally, the conversation needs to be grounded in a new concept of adolescence, which recognizes that it is now a longer and more important stage of development. This conversation must also apply the insights into adolescent brain development that have emerged over the past two decades. We need a national focus on this age period that is similar in magnitude to that which has focused on zero to three.

Periods of heightened brain plasticity are times when our experiences are likely to have enduring effects. We have known for some time that the first few years of life constitute one such period. We now know that adolescence is another.

The brain will never again be as plastic as it is during adolescence. We cannot afford to squander this second opportunity to help young people be happier, healthier, and more successful. Adolescence is our last best chance to make a difference.

Acknowledgments

I have been steeped in the study of adolescence for nearly forty years. This book weaves together many different topics of research in which I've been involved over this time, among them adolescent brain development, the growth of psychological maturity, adolescent decision making and risk-taking, the impact of puberty on psychological functioning, the importance of authoritative parenting, student achievement and school engagement, adolescents' susceptibility to peer pressure, juvenile crime and delinquency, and the influence of psychological science on social and legal policy. Accordingly, I have many people and organizations to acknowledge and thank, and I am delighted to do so.

I was extraordinarily fortunate to be a member of three separate interdisciplinary projects funded by the John D. and Catherine T. MacArthur Foundation during the past twenty years, and my thinking has been greatly influenced by my involvement in these enterprises. Some of my ideas about the ways in which brain development in adolescence influences risky decision making grew out of many years of collaboration with members of the foundation's Research Network on Psychopathology and Development. Much of my thinking about adolescent development and legal policy was shaped by my colleagues on the foundation's Research Network on Adolescent Development and Juvenile Justice. And my understanding of adolescent brain development continues to deepen as a result of my participation in the foundation's Research Network on Law and Neuroscience.

Several of the specific programs of work in which I was directly involved are described in this book. Many thanks to Marie Banich, Beth Cauffman, Sandra Graham, and Jen Woolard for collaborating on the original study of adolescent decision making; to Ken Dodge, Jen Lansford, and our international collaborators for their assistance in collecting the data for the cross-national follow-up to this project; to Ed Mulvey and the rest of the Pathways team for their work on our study of juvenile offenders; and to Jason Chein and the members of Temple's Neurocognition Lab for their many contributions to our studies of peer-influence processes. I wish I had room to acknowledge by name all of the undergraduates, graduate students, postdoctoral fellows, and colleagues who worked on these projects over the years, but the list is simply too long to include here. One person I do want to single out is my longtime administrative assistant, Marnia Davis, whose organizational talents are exceeded only by her relentlessly sunny disposition.

Although a large part of this book draws on studies of adolescent brain development, I am not a neuroscientist by training, and I have had to depend on many generous colleagues for the incredible tutoring I have received over the past fifteen years. I am especially grateful to B. J. Casey, Jason Chein, Ron Dahl, Chuck Nelson, Danny Pine, and Linda Spear. In addition, many scientists whose research I relied on in this book took the time to patiently answer questions about their work. Thanks to Cliff Abraham, Daphne Bavelier, Fulton Crews, Alev Erisir, Ron Haskins, Marcia Herman-Giddens, Tony Koleske, Marina Kvaskoff, Angeline Lillard, Bruce McEwen, Jane Mendle, Lynn Selemon, Cheryl Sisk, and Kali Trzesniewski. Of course, I assume full responsibility for the accuracy with which I represented their science.

Several friends, students, and colleagues read portions of the manuscript and discussed various parts of the book with me as I was struggling to make sense of things. I am particularly grateful to Angela Duckworth, Ellen Greenberger, Jens Ludwig, Kate Monahan, Ingrid Olson, Bob Schwartz, Elizabeth Scott, Liz Shulman, Karol Silva, Ashley Smith, and Marsha Weinraub for their helpful insights and suggestions. I had the opportunity to discuss the ideas that form the basis for the book during visits to Duke University, Emory University, the University of Pennsylvania, and the University of Virginia, and I thank my colleagues at these institutions for their critiques and comments. I am also grateful to the graduate students who participated in my seminar on adolescent development during the fall of 2013, where early drafts of several chapters were discussed.

Research of the sort described in this book is expensive, and if it weren't for the generosity of numerous funding agencies and foundations, the science could not have been conducted. I'm especially grateful to Laurie Garduque and her colleagues at the MacArthur Foundation for their long-standing and generous support of my work; to the Jacobs Foundation, whose funding enabled me to carry out the cross-national study of decision making; to the Office of Juvenile Justice and Delinquency Prevention, National Institute of Justice, National Institute on Drug Abuse, Centers for Disease Control and Prevention, MacArthur Foundation, William T. Grant Foundation, Robert Wood Johnson Foundation, William Penn Foundation, and the states of Arizona and Pennsylvania, which funded our study of juvenile offenders; and to the National Institute on Drug Abuse, National Institute on Alcohol Abuse and Alcoholism, and U.S. Army Medical Research and Materiel Command, which have supported our work on peer influences on adolescents' risky behavior. My home institution, Temple University, has been exceptionally supportive during the past twenty-five years, and many of the ideas that eventually developed into this book were first hatched during a study leave that was granted by the university.

The final form of this book was greatly shaped, and substantially improved, by my agent, Jim Levine, and my editor, Eamon Dolan. I cannot fully convey just how involved each of them was in this project, from beginning to end. If there is a harder-working literary agent in the business than Jim, I'd sure like to meet that person. And if there is a more meticulous or demanding editor than Eamon — well, I think I'd rather not. I am also grateful to the entire team at Houghton Mifflin Harcourt, especially Ben Hyman and Taryn Roeder, and to Melissa Dobson, for her careful copyediting.

It is customary for authors to end their acknowledgments with an expression of gratitude to their families for their love and support during the writing process. I, too, am incredibly fortunate to have a loving and supportive family, but I'm luckier than most, because in addition to their unconditional affection and encouragement, I also was able to count on my family's technical expertise. My wife, Wendy, who is a writer, has discussed this book with me on a near-daily basis for the past two years (not to mention the past three decades during which she patiently endured endless conversations about adolescence). She also read the entire manuscript and vastly improved the writing in many places, especially in sections that attempted to describe brain science to nonscientists. At the time I was first developing the idea for the book, our son, Ben, was an editor of nonfiction at a major publishing house. He read countless drafts of the book proposal, provided wise counsel while I was shopping the idea around, and propped me up during periods of discouragement. So when I say I could not have done this without the two of them, I mean it literally.

Notes

INTRODUCTION

page

1   *adults are far more bewildered:* Laurence Steinberg, "We Know Some Things: Parent-Adolescent Relationships in Retrospect and Prospect," *Journal of Research on Adolescence* 11, no. 1 (2001), 1–20.

4   *neuroscience has come under attack:* Sally Satel and Scott O. Lilienfield, *Brainwashed: The Seductive Appeal of Mindless Neuroscience* (New York: Basic Books, 2013).

      how important the environment is: Robert Plomin, "Genetics and Experience," *Current Opinion in Psychiatry* 7, no. 4 (1994), 297–99.

5   *prejudice against young people cloaked in pseudoscience:* Michael Males, "Does the Adolescent Brain Make Risk-Taking Inevitable?" *Journal of Adolescent Research* 24, no. 1 (2009), 3–20.

      substantial and systematic changes in the brain's anatomy and functioning: "The Teenage Brain," special issue, *Current Directions in Psychological Science* 22, no. 2 (2013).

6   *the brain doesn't completely mature until sometime during the early twenties:* Ibid.

7   *Fewer of today's teens drink alcohol or smoke:* Data on adolescent drug use are from the Monitoring the Future survey, www.monitoringthefuture.org. *Youth crime is lower today:* Data on youth crime are from FBI arrest statistics, www.fbi.gov. *Teen pregnancy has decreased:* Data on teen pregnancy are from the National Campaign to Prevent Teen and Unplanned Pregnancy, www.thenationalcampaign.org.

1. SEIZING THE MOMENT

9   *earlier puberty places people at significantly greater risk:* Sonya Negriff and Elizabeth J. Susman, "Pubertal Timing, Depression, and Externalizing Problems: A Framework, Review, and Examination of Gender Differences," *Journal of Research on Adolescence* 21, no. 3 (2011), 717–46; Emily C. Walvoord, "The Timing of Puberty: Is It Changing? Does It Matter?" *Journal of Adolescent Health* 47, no. 5 (2010), 433–39.

people in their midtwenties are being unfairly criticized: Kali H. Trzesniewski and M. Brent Donnellan, "'Young People These Days . . .': Evidence for Negative Perceptions of Emerging Adults," *Emerging Adulthood,* February 18, 2014, doi:10.1177/2167696814522620; Jeffrey J. Arnett, Kali H. Trzesniewski, and M. Brent Donnellan, "The Dangers of Generational Myth-Making: Rejoinder to Twenge," *Emerging Adulthood* 1, no. 1 (2013), 17–20.

10   *only within the past twenty-five years:* The first published study of the adolescent brain was Terry L. Jernigan et al., "Maturation of Human Cerebrum Observed *In Vivo* During Adolescence," *Brain* 114, no. 5 (1991), 2037–49.

the brain's last *period of especially heightened malleability:* Anthony J. Koleske, "Molecular Mechanisms of Dendrite Stability," *Nature Reviews Neuroscience* 14 (2013), 536–50; Angeline S. Lillard and Alev Erisir, "Old Dogs Learning New Tricks: Neuroplasticity Beyond the Juvenile Period," *Developmental Review* 31, no. 4 (2011), 207–39.

11   *Adolescents' drug use is on the rise:* Monitoring the Future, www.monitoringthefuture.org.

attempted suicide: Centers for Disease Control and Prevention, Youth Risk Behavior Surveillance System, www.cdc.gov.

bullying: Kenneth C. Land, *The 2011 FCD-CWI Special Focus Report on Trends in Violent Bullying Victimization in School Contexts for 8th, 10th, and 12th Graders, 1991–2009* (Durham, NC: Foundation for Child Development and Child and Youth Well-Being Index [FCD-CWI] Project, Duke University, 2011).

remedial education among college freshmen: Dinah Sparks and Nat Malkus, *First-Year Undergraduate Remedial Coursetaking* (Washington, DC: National Center for Education Statistics, 2013).

The United States spends more per student on secondary and postsecondary education: OECD, *Education at a Glance 2013: OECD Indicators* (Paris: OECD, 2013).

a collection of unproven, ineffective, and only marginally successful programs: Laurence Steinberg, "A Social Neuroscience Perspective on Adolescent Risk-Taking," *Developmental Review* 28, no. 1 (2008), 78–106.

we spend nearly $6 billion each year incarcerating adolescents: Amanda Petteruti, Tracy Velázquez, and Nastassia Walsh, *The Costs of Confinement: Why Good Juvenile Justice Policies Make Sense* (Washington, DC: Justice Policy Institute, 2009).

There have been no gains: Data from the National Assessment of Educational Progress, U.S. Department of Education.

12   *performance of our high-school students is undeniably lackluster:* Daniel Koretz, "How Do American Students Measure Up? Making Sense of International Comparisons," *Future of Children* 19, no. 1 (2009), 37–51.

underachievement is costly: Complete College America, *Remediation: Higher Education's Bridge to Nowhere* (Washington, DC: Complete College America, 2012).

doesn't even make the top ten: OECD, *Education at a Glance 2013.*

obtain their degrees from for-profit universities of questionable quality: Catherine Rampell, "Data Reveal a Rise in College Degrees Among Americans," *New York Times,* June 12, 2013.

economic returns on college completion: OECD, *Education at a Glance 2013.*

proportion of students who smoke marijuana: Data on drinking and drug use from Monitoring the Future, www.monitoringthefuture.org.

American adolescents are among the most frequent binge drinkers and users of illegal drugs in the world: George C. Patton et al., "Health of the World's Adolescents: A Synthesis of Internationally Comparable Data," *Lancet* 379, no. 9826 (2012), 1665–75.

Nearly a third of young women in the United States will get pregnant: National Campaign to Prevent Teen and Unplanned Pregnancy.

United States continues to lead the industrialized world: Data on teen pregnancy and STDs from the National Campaign to Prevent Teen and Unplanned Pregnancy. Data on abortion from Gilda Sedgh et al., "Legal Abortion Levels and Trends by Woman's Age at Termination," *Perspectives on Sexual and Reproductive Health* 45, no. 1 (2013), 13–22.

13   *Aggression continues to be a widespread problem:* Centers for Disease Control and Prevention, Youth Risk Behavior Surveillance System, www.cdc.gov.

highest rates of youth violence in the developed world: Dirk Enzmann et al., "Self-Reported Youth Delinquency in Europe and Beyond: First Results of the Second International Self-Report Delinquency Study in the Context of Police and Victimization Data," *European Journal of Criminology* 7, no. 2 (2010), 159–83; National Research Council, *U.S. Health in International Perspective: Shorter Lives, Poorer Health* (Washington, DC: National Academies Press, 2013).

physically threatened by students: National Center for Education Statistics, School Staffing Survey; Dorothy Espelage et al., "Understanding and Preventing Violence Directed Against Teachers," *American Psychologist* 68, no. 2 (2013), 75–87.

Nearly two-thirds of our high schools have security guards: U.S. Department of Education, National Center for Education Statistics, 2005–06, 2007–08, and 2009–10 School Survey on Crime and Safety (SSOCS).

Twenty percent of all high-school-aged boys in America take prescription medication for ADHD: Allan Schwarz and Sarah Cohen, "ADHD Seen in 11% of U.S. Children as Diagnoses Rise," *New York Times,* March 31, 2013.

the United States consumes more than 75 percent of the world's ADHD medication: Richard Scheffler et al., "The Global Market for ADHD Medications," *Health Affairs* 26, no. 2 (2007), 450–57.

Adolescent obesity: Data on obesity from Harvard School of Public Health, Obesity Prevention Source, www.hsph.harvard.edu/obesity-prevention-source. International comparisons from National Research Council and Institute of Medicine, 2013.

14   *near the top in soft drink and french fry consumption:* U.S. Department of Health and Human Services, Health Resources and Services Administration, *U.S. Teens in Our World* (Rockville, MD: U.S. Department of Health and Human Services, 2003).

high-school students who try to kill themselves each year: Centers for Disease Control and Prevention.

suicide attempts and suicidal ideation among American high-school students are both on the rise: World Health Organization, WHO Mortality Database, 2011.

American teenagers are among the world's most miserable: U.S. Department of Health and Human Services, Health Resources and Services Administration, 2003.

one recent national study of more than forty thousand people: Carlos Blanco et al., "Mental Health of College Students and Their Non-College-Attending Peers," *Archives of General Psychiatry* 65, no. 12 (2008), 1429–37.

Adolescents' psychological problems have gotten worse over time: Jean M. Twenge et al., "Birth Cohort Increases in Psychopathology Among Young Americans, 1938–2007: A Cross-Temporal Meta-Analysis of the MMPI," *Clinical Psychology Review* 30 (2010), 145–54.

16   *those who score high on measures of self-regulation invariably fare best:* Terrie Moffitt, Richie Poulton, and Avshalom Caspi, "Lifelong Impact of Early Self-Control: Childhood Self-Discipline Predicts Adult Quality of Life," *American Scientist* 101, no. 5 (2013), 352–59.

2. THE PLASTIC BRAIN

19   *"reminiscence bump":* David C. Rubin et al., "Autobiographical Memory Across the Adult Life Span," in *Autobiographical Memory,* edited by David C. Rubin (Cambridge, UK: Cambridge University Press, 1986), 202–21.

our ability to remember things remains excellent until the midforties: Lars-Göran Nilsson, "Memory Function in Normal Aging," *Acta Neurologica Scandinavia* 107, sup. 179, 7–13. But see Timothy A. Salthouse, "When Does Age-Related Cognitive Decline Begin?" *Neurobiology of Aging* 30, no. 4 (2009), 507–14, and Lars-Göran Nilsson et al., "Challenging the Notion of an Early-Onset of Cognitive Decline," *Neurobiology of Aging* 30, no. 4 (2009), 521–24.

20   *We recall emotionally intense events with special clarity:* Alafair Burke, Friderike Heuer, and Daniel Reisberg, "Remembering Emotional Events," *Memory & Cognition* 20, no. 3 (1992), 277–90.

incorporate these occurrences into our developing autobiographies: Martin A. Conway, Jefferson A. Singer, and Angela Tagini, "The Self and Autobiographical Memory: Correspondence and Coherence," *Social Cognition* 22, no. 5 (2004), 491–529.

Researchers have studied this: Herbert F. Crovitz and Harold Schiffman, "Frequency of Episodic Memories as a Function of Their Age," *Bulletin of the Psychonomic Society* 4, no. 5 (1974), 517–18.

21   *more likely to remember music, books, and films:* Steve M. J. Janssen, Antonio G. Chessa, and Jaap M. J. Murre, "Temporal Distribution of Favourite Books, Movies, and Records: Differential Encoding and Re-sampling," *Memory* 15, no. 7 (2007), 755–67.

chemically primed to encode memories more deeply: Brian Knutson and R. Alison Adcock, "Remembrance of Rewards Past," *Neuron* 45, no. 3 (2005), 331–32.

22   *studies of institutionally reared infants:* Charles A. Nelson III and Margaret A. Sheridan, "Lessons from Neuroscience Research for Understanding Causal Links Between Family and Neighborhood Characteristics and Educational Outcomes," in *Whither Opportunity?: Rising Inequality, Schools, and Children's Life Chances,* edited by Greg J. Duncan and Richard J. Murnane (New York: Russell Sage Foundation, 2011), 27–46.

25   *two types of brain plasticity:* Ibid.

26   *our brains don't produce many new neurons:* Richard S. Nowakowski, "Stable Neuron Numbers from Cradle to Grave," *Proceedings of the National Academy of Sciences* 103, no. 33 (2006), 12219–20.

one hundred thousand new connections between neurons are formed every second: Jane W. Couperus and Charles A. Nelson, "Early Brain Development and Plasticity," in *Blackwell Handbook of Early Childhood Development,* edited by Kathleen McCartney and Deborah Phillips (Malden, MA: Blackwell, 2008), 85–105.

an area about the size of Manhattan: Jamie Ward, *The Student's Guide to Cognitive Neuroscience,* 2nd ed. (New York: Psychology Press, 2010).

the focus of pruning during adolescence: Zdravko Petanjek et al., "Extraordinary Neoteny of Synaptic Spines in the Human Prefrontal Cortex," *Pro-*

ceedings of the National Academy of Sciences 108, no. 32 (2011), 13281–86; Fulton Crews, Jun He, and Clyde Hodge, "Adolescent Cortical Development: A Critical Period of Vulnerability for Addiction," *Pharmacology, Biochemistry, and Behavior* 86, no. 2 (2007), 189–99.

27   *the two kinds of plasticity differ:* Angeline S. Lillard and Alev Erisir, "Old Dogs Learning New Tricks: Neuroplasticity Beyond the Juvenile Period," *Developmental Review* 31, no. 4 (2011), 207–39.

    the developing brain is chemically predisposed to be modified by experiences: Linda Patia Spear, "Adolescent Neurodevelopment," *Journal of Adolescent Health* 52, no. 2, sup. 2 (2013), S7–S13.

    sculpted both by passive exposure and by active experience: Lillard and Erisir, "Old Dogs Learning New Tricks."

28   *one type of plasticity . . . disrupts the effects of another:* Sheena A. Josselyn and Paul W. Frankland, "Infantile Amnesia: A Neurogenic Hypothesis," *Learning and Memory* 19, no. 9 (2012), 423–33.

    "sensitive periods": Sharon E. Fox, Pat Levitt, and Charles A. Nelson III, "How the Timing and Quality of Early Experiences Influence the Development of Brain Architecture," *Child Development* 81, no. 1 (2010), 28–40.

    don't fully mature until the early or even mid twenties: Spear, "Adolescent Neurodevelopment."

29   *"experience expectant":* William T. Greenough, James E. Black, and Christopher S. Wallace, "Experience and Brain Development," *Child Development* 58, no. 3 (1987), 539–59.

30   *debates about when the brain is most plastic are pointless:* P. A. Howard-Jones, E. V. Washbrook, and S. Meadows, "The Timing of Educational Investment: A Neuroscientific Perspective," *Developmental Cognitive Neuroscience* 2, sup. 1 (2012), S18–S29.

    the region adversely affected by the abuse differed: Susan L. Andersen, "Preliminary Evidence for Sensitive Periods in the Effect of Childhood Sexual Abuse on Regional Brain Development," *Journal of Neuropsychiatry and Clinical Neuroscience* 20, no. 3 (2008), 292–301.

33   *myelination stabilizes the circuits that have already been formed:* R. Douglas Fields, "Myelination: An Overlooked Mechanism of Synaptic Plasticity?" *Neuroscientist* 11, no. 6 (2005), 528–31; Julie A. Markham and William T. Greenough, "Experience-Driven Brain Plasticity: Beyond the Synapse," *Neuron Glia Biology* 1, no. 4 (2004), 351–63; Robert J. Zattore, R. Douglas Fields, and Heidi Johansen-Berg, "Plasticity in Gray and White: Neuroimaging Changes in Brain Structure During Learning," *Nature Neuroscience* 15, no. 4 (2012), 528–36.

    increase during adolescence in certain brain proteins: L. A. Glantz et al., "Synaptophysin and Postsynaptic Density Protein 95 in the Human Prefrontal Cortex from Mid-Gestation into Early Adulthood," *Neuroscience* 149, no. 3 (2007), 582–91; Anthony J. Koleske, "Molecular Mechanisms of

Dendrite Stability," *Nature Reviews Neuroscience* 14 (2013), 536–50; Zattore et al., "Plasticity in Gray and White."

a study of London taxi drivers: Eleanor A. Maguire, "London Taxi Drivers and Bus Drivers: A Structural MRI and Neuropsychological Analysis," *Hippocampus* 16, no. 12 (2006), 1091–1101.

strengthened each time we do it: Lillard and Erisir, "Old Dogs Learning New Tricks."

34   *repetition stimulates myelination:* Ibid.

35   *the demands we place on our brain must exceed the brain's capacity:* Martin Lovden et al., "A Theoretical Framework for the Study of Adult Cognitive Plasticity," *Psychological Bulletin* 136, no. 4 (2010), 659–76.

"zone of proximal development": L. S. Vygotsky, *Mind in Society: The Development of Higher Psychological Processes* (Cambridge, MA: Harvard University Press, 1978).

ten thousand hours need to be devoted to deliberate practice: K. Anders Ericsson, Ralf Th. Krampe, and Clemens Tesch-Romer, "The Role of Deliberate Practice in the Acquisition of Expert Performance," *Psychological Review* 100, no. 3 (1993), 363–406.

36   *"metaplasticity":* Wickliffe C. Abraham and Mark F. Bear, "Metaplasticity: The Plasticity of Synaptic Plasticity," *Trends in Neurosciences* 19, no. 4 (1996), 126–30; Wickliffe C. Abraham, "Metaplasticity: Tuning Synapses and Networks for Plasticity," *Nature Reviews Neuroscience* 9 (2008), 387–99; Sarah R. Hulme, Owen D. Jones, and Wickliffe C. Abraham, "Emerging Roles of Metaplasticity in Behaviour and Disease," *Trends in Neurosciences* 36, no. 6 (2013), 353–62.

learning primes the brain: Hulme, Jones, and Abraham, "Emerging Roles of Metaplasticity in Behaviour and Disease."

intelligent people enjoy longer sensitive periods: Angela M. Brant et al., "The Nature and Nurture of High IQ: An Extended Sensitive Period for Intellectual Development," *Psychological Science* 24, no. 8 (2013), 1487–95.

Hundreds of studies of age differences in brain activity: "The Teenage Brain," special issue, *Current Directions in Psychological Science* 22, no. 2 (2013).

37   *falls somewhere in the period between ages ten and twenty-five:* R. C. Kessler et al., "Lifetime Prevalence and Age-of-Onset Distributions of DSM-IV Disorders in the National Comorbidity Survey Replication," *Archives of General Psychiatry* 62, no. 6 (2005), 593–602.

38   necessary *in order to experience normal amounts of pleasure:* Michael G. Hardin and Monique Ernst, "Functional Brain Imaging of Development-Related Risk and Vulnerability for Substance Use in Adolescents," *Journal of Addiction Medicine* 3, no. 2 (2009), 47–54; Nora Volkow and Ting-Kai Li, "The Neuroscience of Addiction," *Nature Neuroscience* 8 (2005), 1429–30.

exposure to drugs during adolescence is more closely associated with addiction than is exposure during adulthood: Ralph W. Hingson, Timothy

Heeren, and Michael R. Winter, "Age at Drinking Onset and Alcohol Dependence: Age at Onset, Duration, and Severity," *Archives of Pediatric and Adolescent Medicine* 160, no. 7 (2006), 739–46; Maria Orlando et al., "Developmental Trajectories of Cigarette Smoking and Their Correlates from Early Adolescence to Young Adulthood," *Journal of Consulting and Clinical Psychology* 72, no. 3 (2004), 400–410.

39   *High-school football players who suffer concussions:* C. C. Reddy, M. Collins, and G. A. Gioia, "Adolescent Sports Concussions," *Physical Medicine Rehabilitation Clinics of North America* 19, no. 2 (2008), 247–69; E. Toledo et al., "The Young Brain and Concussion: Imaging as a Biomarker for Diagnosis and Prognosis," *Neuroscience and Biobehavioral Reviews* 36, no. 6 (2012), 1510–31.
      old brains are changed when they learn new tricks, but not as much as young brains: Zattore, Fields, and Johansen-Berg, "Plasticity in Gray and White."
      actively studying whether people in their teens are more responsive: Dietsje D. Jolles and Eveline A. Crone, "Training the Developing Brain: A Neurocognitive Perspective," *Frontiers in Human Neuroscience* 6 (April 9, 2012), doi:10.3389/fnhum.2012.00076.

40   *"transcranial magnetic stimulation":* Catarina Freitas, Faranak Farzan, and Alvaro Pascual-Leone, "Assessing Brain Plasticity Across the Lifespan with Transcranial Magnetic Stimulation: Why, How, and What Is the Ultimate Goal?" *Neuroscience* 7 (April 2, 2013), doi:10.3389/fnins.2013.00042.
      the adolescent brain is more responsive to TMS: Julia B. Pitcher et al., "Physiological Evidence Consistent with Reduced Neuroplasticity in Human Adolescents Born Preterm," *Journal of Neuroscience* 32, no. 46 (2012), 16410–16.

41   *several neuroscientists have come to a similar, albeit speculative, conclusion:* Susan L. Andersen, "Trajectories of Brain Development: Point of Vulnerability or Window of Opportunity?" *Neuroscience and Biobehavioral Reviews* 27, nos. 1–2 (2003), 3–18; Ezekiel P. Carpenter-Hyland and L. Judson Chandler, "Adaptive Plasticity of NMDA Receptors and Dendritic Spines: Implications for Enhanced Vulnerability of the Adolescent Brain to Alcohol Addiction," *Pharmacology, Biochemistry, and Behavior* 86, no. 2 (2007), 200–208; Crews, He, and Hodge, "Adolescent Cortical Development"; K. Cohen Kadosh, D. E. Linden, and J. Y. Lau, "Plasticity During Childhood and Adolescence: Innovative Approaches to Investigating Neurocognitive Development," *Developmental Science* 16, no. 4 (2013), 574–83; Russell D. Romeo and Bruce S. McEwen, "Stress and the Adolescent Brain," *Annals of the New York Academy of Sciences* 1094 (2006), 202–14; L. D. Selemon, "A Role for Synaptic Plasticity in the Adolescent Development of Executive Function," *Translational Psychiatry* 3, no. 3 (2013), e238; Cheryl L. Sisk and Julia L. Zehr, "Pubertal Hormones Organize the Adolescent Brain and Behavior," *Frontiers in Neuroendocrinology* 26, nos. 3–4 (2005), 163–74.

hard to document in an animal with such a short lifespan: I am grateful to Elizabeth Shirtcliff for pointing this out.

we are born twice: Jean-Jacques Rousseau, *Emile: or, On Education* (New York: Basic Books, 1979).

42   *the adolescent brain is more responsive to stress and arousal:* Lisa Eiland and Russell D. Romeo, "Stress and the Developing Adolescent Brain," *Neuroscience* 249 (2013), 162–71; Laura R. Stroud et al., "Stress Response and the Adolescent Transition: Performance Versus Peer Rejection Stressors," *Development and Psychopathology* 21, no. 1 (2009), 47–68.

the brain's response to rewarding images: Leah H. Somerville et al., "The Medial Prefrontal Cortex and the Emergence of Self-Conscious Emotion in Adolescence," *Psychological Science* 24, no. 8 (2013), 1554–62.

chemically altering the actual structure of its circuits: Jiska S. Peper et al., "Sex Steroids and Connectivity in the Human Brain: A Review of Neuroimaging Studies," *Psychoneuroendocrinology* 36, no. 8 (2011), 1101–13; Bruce S. McEwen et al., "Estrogen Effects on the Brain: Actions Beyond the Hypothalamus via Novel Mechanisms," *Behavioral Neuroscience* 126, no. 1 (2012), 4–16.

43   *Sex hormones promote myelination, stimulate the development of new neurons, and facilitate synaptic pruning:* I. G. Campbell et al., "Sex, Puberty, and the Timing of Sleep EEG Measured Adolescent Brain Maturation," *Proceedings of the National Academy of Sciences* 109, no. 15 (2012), 5740–43; R. A. Hill, "Interaction of Sex Steroid Hormones and Brain-Derived Neurotrophic Factor-Tyrosine Kinase B Signalling: Relevance to Schizophrenia and Depression," *Journal of Neuroendocrinology* 24, no. 12 (2012), 1553–61; Cecile D. Ladouceur et al., "White Matter Development in Adolescence: The Influence of Puberty and Implications for Affective Disorders," *Developmental Cognitive Neuroscience* 2, no. 1 (2012), 36–54; M. A. Mohr and C. L. Sisk, "Pubertally Born Neurons and Glia Are Functionally Integrated into Limbic and Hypothalamic Circuits of the Male Syrian Hamster," *Proceedings of the National Academy of Sciences* 110, no. 12 (2013), 4792–97; Tomas Paus, "How Environment and Genes Shape the Adolescent Brain," *Hormones and Behavior* 64, no. 2 (2013), 195–202; Jennifer S. Perrin et al., "Growth of White Matter in the Adolescent Brain: Role of Testosterone and Androgen Receptor," *Journal of Neuroscience* 28, no. 38 (2008), 9519–24.

fears we acquire during adolescence: Siobhan S. Pattwell et al., "Altered Fear Learning Across Development in Both Mouse and Human," *Proceedings of the National Academy of Sciences* 109 no. 40 (2012), 16318–23.

the brain's chemistry shifts: Spear, "Adolescent Neurodevelopment."

these processes taper off considerably as the brain matures into adulthood: Jun He and Fulton T. Crews, "Neurogenesis Decreases During Brain Maturation from Adolescence to Adulthood," *Pharmacology, Biochemistry, and Behavior* 86, no. 2 (2007), 327–33; Koleske, "Molecular Mechanisms of Dendrite Stability"; Yi Zuo et al., "Development of Long-Term Dendritic Spine Stability in Diverse Regions of Cerebral Cortex," *Neuron* 46, no. 2 (2005), 181–89.

Even after this genetic switch has been flipped, its effects can be reversed: Feras V. Akbik et al., "Anatomical Plasticity of Adult Brain Is Titrated by Nogo Receptor 1," *Neuron* 77, no. 5 (2013), 859–66.

a pattern seen in other animals: Spear, "Adolescent Neurodevelopment."

44   *many of the fears we may have developed during childhood are temporarily squelched:* Siobhan S. Pattwell et al., "Selective Early-Acquired Fear Memories Undergo Temporary Suppression During Adolescence," *Proceedings of the National Academy of Sciences* 108, no. 3 (2011), 1182–87.

brain plasticity in adulthood is facilitated by a mismatch: Lovden et al., "A Theoretical Framework for the Study of Adult Cognitive Plasticity."

45   *college contributes to brain development:* Kimberly G. Noble et al., "Higher Education Is an Age-Independent Predictor of White Matter Integrity and Cognitive Control in Late Adolescence," *Developmental Science* 16, no. 5 (2013), 653–64.

3. THE LONGEST DECADE

48   *the average age at which boys' voices broke:* S. F. Daw, "Age of Boys' Puberty in Leipzig, 1727–49, as Indicated by Voice Breaking in J. S. Bach's Choir Members," *Human Biology* 42, no. 1 (1970), 87–89; Jane Mendle and Joseph Ferrero, "Detrimental Psychological Outcomes Associated with Pubertal Timing in Adolescent Boys," *Developmental Review* 32, no. 1 (2012), 49–66.

49   *"accident hump":* Joshua R. Goldstein, "A Secular Trend Toward Earlier Male Sexual Maturity: Evidence from Shifting Ages of Male Young Adult Mortality," *PLoS ONE* 6, no. 8 (2011), e14826.

A 2012 report based on information provided by pediatricians: Marcia E. Herman-Giddens et al., "Secondary Sexual Characteristics in Boys: Data from the Pediatric Research in Office Settings Network," *Pediatrics* 130, no. 5 (2012), e1058–68.

average age at which men marry: U.S. Bureau of the Census.

51   *The most recent U.S. study:* Frank M. Biro et al., "Pubertal Assessment Method and Baseline Characteristics in a Mixed Longitudinal Study of Girls," *Pediatrics* 126, no. 3 (2010), e583.

a mix of genetic and environmental influences: Alejandro Lomniczi et al., "Epigenetic Control of Female Puberty," *Nature Neuroscience* 16, no. 3 (2013), 281–89.

52   *stimulated by an increase in a brain chemical called kisspeptin:* A. K. Roseweir and R. P. Millar, "The Role of Kisspeptin in the Control of Gonadotrophin Secretion," *Human Reproduction Update* 15, no. 2 (2009), 203–12.

production of kisspeptin in the brain is affected by other chemicals: Valérie Simonneaux et al., "Kisspeptins and RFRP-3 Act in Concert to Synchronize Rodent Reproduction with Seasons," *Frontiers in Neuroscience* 7, no. 22 (2013), doi:10.3389/fnins.2013.00022; Sandra Steingraber, *The Falling Age of Puberty in U.S. Girls: What We Know, What We Need to Know* (San Francisco: Breast Cancer Fund, 2007).

54   *hastened by increases in our children's exposure to "endocrine disruptors":* Steingraber, *The Falling Age of Puberty in U.S. Girls*; Emily C. Walvoord, "The Timing of Puberty: Is It Changing? Does It Matter?" *Journal of Adolescent Health* 47, no. 5 (2010), 433–39.

55   *the proportion of very-low-birthweight children who survive:* Ibid.

puberty begins earlier among adolescents: Jay Belsky et al., "Family Rearing Antecedents of Pubertal Timing," *Child Development* 78, no. 4 (2007), 1302–21.

56   *a decline in obesity among very young children:* Sabrina Tavernise, "Obesity Studies Tell Two Stories, Both Right," *New York Times,* April 14, 2014.

more likely to wish they were older: Nancy L. Galambos, Erin T. Barker, and Lauree C. Tilton-Weaver, "Who Gets Caught at Maturity Gap? A Study of Pseudomature, Immature, and Mature Adolescents," *International Journal of Behavioral Development* 27, no. 3 (2003), 253–63.

draws early maturers into behaviors: Sonya Negriff and Elizabeth J. Susman, "Pubertal Timing, Depression, and Externalizing Problems: A Framework, Review, and Examination of Gender Differences," *Journal of Research on Adolescence* 21, no. 3 (2011), 717–46.

early maturation is a boost to their egos: Laurence D. Steinberg, *Adolescence,* 10th ed. (New York: McGraw-Hill, 2014).

57   *early-maturing girls are at elevated risk for sexual abuse:* M. Celio, N. S. Karnik, and H. Steiner, "Early Maturation as a Risk Factor for Aggression and Delinquency in Adolescent Girls: A Review," *International Journal of Clinical Practice* 60, no. 10 (2006), 1254–62; Penelope K. Trickett et al., "Child Maltreatment and Adolescent Development," *Journal of Research on Adolescence* 21, no. 1 (2011), 3–20.

Early-maturing girls are vulnerable to emotional distress in general: Dale A. Blyth, Roberta G. Simmons, and David F. Zakin, "Satisfaction with Body Image for Early Adolescent Females: The Impact of Pubertal Timing Within Different School Environments," *Journal of Youth and Adolescence* 14, no. 3 (1985), 207–26; Xiaojia Ge et al., "Parenting Behaviors and the Occurrence and Co-Occurrence of Adolescent Depressive Symptoms and Conduct Problems," *Developmental Psychology* 32, no. 4 (1996), 717–31.

58   *their school achievement never fully recovers:* David Magnusson, Hakan Stattin, and Vernon L. Allen, "Differential Maturation Among Girls and Its Relation to Social Adjustment in a Longitudinal Perspective," in *Life-Span Development and Behavior,* vol. 7, edited by David L. Featherman and Richard M. Lerner (Hillsdale, NJ: Erlbaum, 1986).
Some aspects of brain development in adolescence are driven by puberty: Ashley R. Smith, Jason Chein, and Laurence Steinberg, "Impact of Socio-Emotional Context, Brain Development, and Pubertal Maturation on Adolescent Decision-Making," *Hormones and Behavior* 64, no. 2 (2013), 323–32.
Menarche at twelve or earlier elevates a woman's risk of breast cancer: Steingraber, *The Falling Age of Puberty in U.S. Girls.*

59   *risk factor for testicular cancer:* Ibid.
surveys that have been conducted for nearly four decades: The Monitoring the Future study of high-school students, carried out by researchers at the University of Michigan, conducted biennial follow-ups when the participants were in their twenties.

61   *economic returns on a college degree are still huge:* OECD, *Education at a Glance 2013: OECD Indicators* (Paris: OECD, 2013).
"What Is It About 20-Somethings?": Robin Marantz Henig, "What Is It About 20-Somethings?" *New York Times Magazine,* August 18, 2010.

62   *an experience that has been shown to stimulate brain development:* Kimberly G. Noble et al., "Higher Education Is an Age-Independent Predictor of White Matter Integrity and Cognitive Control in Late Adolescence," *Developmental Science* 16, no. 5 (2013), 653–64.
a sharp drop in marital satisfaction: Stephen A. Anderson, Candyce S. Russell, and Walter R. Schumm, "Perceived Marital Quality and Family Life-Cycle Categories: A Further Analysis," *Journal of Marriage and the Family* 45, no. 1 (1983), 105–14.
whose self-control is still developing: Laurence Steinberg, "A Social Neuroscience Perspective on Adolescent Risk-Taking," *Developmental Review* 28, no. 1 (2008), 78–106.
there are frequent lapses: Dustin Albert and Laurence Steinberg, "Judgment and Decision Making in Adolescence," *Journal of Research on Adolescence* 21, no. 1 (2011), 211–24.

63   *nearly doubled since 1980:* Susan Aud, Angelina KewalRamani, and Lauren Frohlich, *America's Youth: Transitions to Adulthood,* NCES 2012–026 (Washington, DC: U.S. Department of Education, National Center for Education Statistics, 2011).
Compared with people in their early twenties: Carlos Blanco et al., "Mental Health of College Students and Their Non-College-Attending Peers,"

Archives of General Psychiatry 65, no. 12 (2008), 1429–37; Kim Fromme, William R. Corbin, and Marc I. Kruse, "Behavioral Risks During the Transition from High School to College," *Developmental Psychology* 44, no. 5 (2008), 1497–1504; Wendy S. Slutske et al., "Do College Students Drink More Than Their Non-College-Attending Peers? Evidence from a Population-Based Longitudinal Female Twin Study," *Journal of Abnormal Psychology* 113, no. 4 (2004), 530–40.

4. HOW ADOLESCENTS THINK

69   *risky behavior usually peaks somewhere during the late teens:* Data on self-inflicted injuries and drownings from the Centers for Disease Control and Prevention; on crime, from FBI arrest statistics; on crashes, from the Insurance Institute for Highway Safety; on unintended pregnancies, from Lawrence Finer and Mia Zolna, "Unintended Pregnancy in the United States: Incidence and Disparities," *Contraception* 84, no. 5 (2011), 478–85; and on drugs, from Wilson M. Compton et al., "Prevalence, Correlates, Disability, and Comorbidity of DSM-IV Drug Abuse and Dependence in the United States," *Archives of General Psychiatry* 64, no. 5 (2007), 566–76.

they're just as smart as adults: Laurence Steinberg, "A Social Neuroscience Perspective on Adolescent Risk-Taking," *Developmental Review* 28, no. 1 (2008), 78–106.

73   *it actually gets bigger as we grow from childhood into adolescence:* Snezana Urošević et al., "Longitudinal Changes in Behavioral Approach System Sensitivity and Brain Structures Involved in Reward Processing During Adolescence," *Developmental Psychology* 48, no. 5 (2012), 1488–1500.

stronger preference for sweet things: J. A. Desor and G. K. Beauchamp, "Longitudinal Changes in Sweet Preferences in Humans," *Physiology and Behavior* 39, no. 5 (1987), 639–41.

the teen's reward centers are also more sensitive: Monica Luciana et al., "Dopaminergic Modulation of Incentive Motivation in Adolescence: Age-Related Changes in Signaling, Individual Differences, and Implications for the Development of Self-Regulation," *Developmental Psychology* 48, no. 3 (2012), 844–61.

74   *peaking around age sixteen:* Laurence Steinberg et al., "Age Differences in Sensation Seeking and Impulsivity as Indexed by Behavior and Self-Report: Evidence for a Dual Systems Model," *Developmental Psychology* 44, no. 6 (2008), 1764–78.

adolescents are relatively more attentive and responsive to rewards: Adriana Galvan et al., "Earlier Development of the Accumbens Relative to Orbitofrontal Cortex Might Underlie Risk-Taking Behavior in Adolescents," *Jour-*

nal of Neuroscience 26, no. 25 (2006), 6885–92; Janna Marie Hoogendam et al., "Different Developmental Trajectories for Anticipation and Receipt of Reward During Adolescence," *Developmental Cognitive Neuroscience* 6 (October 2013), 113–24; Leah H. Somerville, "The Teenage Brain: Sensitivity to Social Evaluation," *Current Directions in Psychological Science* 22, no. 2 (2013), 129–35.

they're actually less sensitive to losses: Anastasia Christakou et al., "Neural and Psychological Maturation of Decision-Making in Adolescence and Young Adulthood," *Journal of Cognitive Neuroscience* 25, no. 11 (2013), 1807–23; Monique Ernst, Daniel S. Pine, and Michael Hardin, "Triadic Model of the Neurobiology of Motivated Behavior in Adolescence," *Psychological Medicine* 36, no. 3 (2006), 299–312.

75   *maximum fertility in the late teen years:* Richard G. Bribiescas and Peter T. Ellison, "How Hormones Mediate Trade-offs in Human Health and Disease," in *Evolution in Health and Disease,* edited by Stephen C. Stearns and Jacob C. Koella, 2nd ed. (New York: Oxford University Press, 2008), pp. 77–93.

a well-timed act of intercourse: David B. Dunson, Bernardo Colombo, and Donna D. Baird, "Changes with Age in the Level and Duration of Fertility in the Menstrual Cycle," *Human Reproduction* 17, no. 5 (2002), 1399–1403.

hormones make us more sensitive to rewards: Jean-Claude Dreher et al., "Menstrual Cycle Phase Modulates Reward-Related Neural Function in Women," *Proceedings of the National Academy of Sciences* 104, no. 7 (2007), 2465–70; Adriana Galván, "The Teenage Brain: Sensitivity to Rewards," *Current Directions in Psychological Science* 22, no. 2 (2013), 88–93.

76   *Connections between neurons in the prefrontal cortex proliferate from birth until around age ten, and are then gradually pruned:* "The Teenage Brain," special issue, *Current Directions in Psychological Science* 22, no. 2 (2013); Monica Luciana, ed., "Adolescent Brain Development: Current Themes and Future Directions," special issue, *Brain and Cognition* 72, no. 1 (2010).

77   *adolescents can exercise self-control:* C. F. Geier et al., "Immaturities in Reward Processing and Its Influence on Inhibitory Control in Adolescence," *Cerebral Cortex* 20, no. 7 (2010), 1613–29; Theresa Teslovich et al., "Adolescents Let Sufficient Evidence Accumulate Before Making a Decision When Large Incentives Are at Stake," *Developmental Science* 17, no. 1 (2014), 59–70.

The brain continues to grow more interconnected: Nico U. F. Dosenbach et al., "Prediction of Individual Brain Maturity Using fMRI," *Science* 329, no. 5997 (2010), 1358–61.

78   *Justin Swidler was an excellent student:* The facts of the case are reported in J.S., a Minor By and Through His Parents and Natural Guardians, H.S. and

I.S., Appellants v. Bethlehem Area School District, Commonwealth Court of Pennsylvania, No. 2259 C.D. 1999.

80   *She urged listeners to send the school district money:* Christian D. Berg, "'Dr. Laura' Rips 'Scummy' Web-Threat Teen," *Allentown (PA) Morning Call,* May 21, 1999, A1.

The district prevailed: "Pennsylvania High Court Upholds Student's Expulsion over Web Site," Associated Press, September 27, 2002.

a civil suit brought by Kathleen Fulmer against Justin: Lauri Rice-Maue, "Swidler Says He Created Site to Vent," *Allentown (PA) Morning Call,* Northampton County edition, October 28, 2000.

81   *I testified that Justin's behavior struck me as wrong, but nonetheless pretty typical:* Lauri Rice-Maue, "Professor Testifies on Swidler's Behalf," *Allentown (PA) Morning Call,* Northampton County edition, November 1, 2000.

83   *The picture of adolescence:* Steinberg, "A Social Neuroscience Perspective on Adolescent Risk-Taking."

demonstrated in numerous studies: Luciana et al., "Dopaminergic Modulation of Incentive Motivation in Adolescence."

85   *when mice go through puberty:* Ibid.

5. PROTECTING ADOLESCENTS FROM THEMSELVES

88   *"age-crime curve":* Alex R. Piquero, David P. Farrington, and Alfred Blumstein, "The Criminal Career Paradigm," in *Crime and Justice: A Review of Research,* edited by Michael Tonry, vol. 30 (Chicago: University of Chicago Press, 2003), 359–506.

89   *Adolescents are also more likely than other age groups:* Statistics on many forms of risky behavior are tabulated by the Centers for Disease Control and Prevention.

Risky driving is especially common during adolescence: National Highway Traffic Safety Administration, *National Survey of Speeding and Other Unsafe Driving Actions* (Washington, DC: NHTSA, 1998).

90   *higher crash rates among teenagers:* Anne T. McCartt, "Rounding the Next Curve on the Road Toward Reducing Teen Drivers' Crash Risk," *Journal of Adolescent Health* 53, no. 1 (2013), 3–5; Divera A. M. Twisk and Colin Stacey, "Trends in Young Driver Risk and Countermeasures in European Countries," *Journal of Safety Research* 38, no. 2 (2007), 245–57.

people in their teens and early twenties have quicker reaction times: Rachael D. Seidler et al., "Motor Control and Aging: Links to Age-Related Brain Structural, Functional, and Biochemical Effects," *Neuroscience and Biobehavioral Reviews* 34, no. 5 (2010), 721–33.

morbidity and mortality both increase: R. E. Dahl, "Adolescent Brain Development: A Period of Vulnerabilities and Opportunities," *Annals of the New York Academy of Sciences* 1021 (June 2004), 1–22.

half of all deaths during adolescence are due to accidents: Centers for Disease Control and Prevention.

major causes of morbidity in adolescence: Robert W. Blum and Kristin Nelson-Mmari, "The Health of Young People in a Global Context," *Journal of Adolescent Health* 35, no. 5 (2004), 402–18; Elizabeth M. Ozer and Charles E. Irwin Jr., "Adolescent and Young Adult Health: From Basic Health Status to Clinical Interventions," in *Handbook of Adolescent Psychology,* edited by Richard M. Lerner and Laurence Steinberg, vol. 1, 3rd ed. (Hoboken, NJ: Wiley, 2009), 618–41.

School-based health education is nearly universal in the United States: Steinberg, "A Social Neuroscience Perspective on Adolescent Risk-Taking."

92 *they place a lot more emphasis on the potential rewards:* Susan G. Millstein and Bonnie L. Halpern-Felsher, "Perceptions of Risk and Vulnerability," *Journal of Adolescent Health* 31, no. 1, parts I–II, sup. 1 (2002), 10–27.

One of my favorite illustrations: Abigail A. Baird, Jonathan A. Fugelsang, and Craig M. Bennett, "'What Were You Thinking?': An fMRI Study of Adolescent Decision Making" (poster presented at the 12th Annual Cognitive Neuroscience Society [CNS] Meeting, New York, April 2005).

93 *more than quadruples the chance of a crash:* Bruce Simons-Morton, Neil Lerner, and Jeremiah Singer, "The Observed Effects of Teenage Passengers on the Risky Driving Behavior of Teenage Drivers," *Accident Analysis and Prevention* 37, no. 6 (2005), 973–82.

they're far more likely to offend in groups: Data from the National Crime Victimization survey.

experimentation with alcohol and illicit drugs: Laurie Chassin, Andrea Hussong, and Iris Beltran, "Adolescent Substance Use," in *Handbook of Adolescent Psychology,* edited by Richard M. Lerner and Laurence Steinberg, vol. 1, 3rd ed. (Hoboken, NJ: Wiley, 2009), 723–63.

Even in Italy: Silvia Bonino, Elena Cattelino, and Silvia Ciairano, *Adolescents and Risk: Behaviors, Functions, and Protective Factors* (New York: Springer, 2005).

a study of risky driving: Margo Gardner and Laurence Steinberg, "Peer Influence on Risk Taking, Risk Preference, and Risky Decision Making in Adolescence and Adulthood: An Experimental Study," *Developmental Psychology* 41, no. 4 (2005), 625–35.

94 *When adolescents drive with their parents in the car:* Bruce G. Simons-Morton et al., "The Effect of Passengers and Risk-Taking Friends on Risky Driving and Crashes/Near Crashes Among Novice Teenagers," *Journal of Adolescent Health* 49, no. 6 (2011), 587–93.

95 *"the social brain":* Stephanie Burnett et al., "The Social Brain in Adoles-

cence: Evidence from Functional Magnetic Resonance Imaging and Behavioural Studies," *Neuroscience and Biobehavioral Reviews* 35 (2011), 1654–64.

Many autism researchers: Carrie L. Masten et al., "An fMRI Investigation of Responses to Peer Rejection in Adolescents with Autism Spectrum Disorders," *Developmental Cognitive Neuroscience* 1, no. 3 (2011), 260–70.

The social brain is still changing in adolescence: K. L. Mills et al., "Developmental Changes in the Structure of the Social Brain in Late Childhood and Adolescence," *Social Cognitive and Affective Neuroscience* 9, no. 1 (2014), 123–31.

the pain of social rejection: C. Nathan DeWall et al., "Acetaminophen Reduces Social Pain: Behavioral and Neural Evidence," *Psychological Science* 21, no. 7 (2010), 931–37.

96   *adolescents' fixation on others' emotions:* Lihong Wang, Scott Huettel, and Michael D. De Bellis, "Neural Substrates for Processing Task-Irrelevant Sad Images in Adolescents," *Developmental Science* 11, no. 1 (2008), 23–32.

"wisdom of crowds": James Surowiecki, *The Wisdom of Crowds: Why the Many Are Smarter Than the Few and How Collective Wisdom Shapes Business, Economies, Societies, and Nations* (New York: Doubleday, 2004).

97   *stimulate a desire for others:* Piotr Winkielman et al., "Affective Influence on Judgments and Decisions: Moving Towards Core Mechanisms," *Review of General Psychology* 11, no. 2 (2007), 179–92.

Obese adolescents: Eric Stice et al., "Youth at Risk for Obesity Show Greater Activation of Striatal and Somatosensory Regions to Food," *Journal of Neuroscience* 31, no. 12 (2011), 4360–66.

Feeling good makes us want to feel even better: Piotr Winkielman, Kent C. Berridge, and Julia L. Wilbarger, "Unconscious Affective Reactions to Masked Happy Versus Angry Faces Influence Consumption Behavior and Judgments of Value," *Personality and Social Psychology Bulletin* 31, no. 1 (2005), 121–35.

98   *peers light up the same reward centers:* Amanda E. Guyer et al., "Probing the Neural Correlates of Anticipated Peer Evaluation in Adolescence," *Child Development* 80, no. 4 (2009), 1000–1015.

socializing with peers provokes chemical changes: Elena I. Varlinskaya et al., "Social Context Induces Two Unique Patterns of c-Fos Expression in Adolescent and Adult Rats," *Developmental Psychobiology* 55, no. 7 (2013), 684–97.

adolescents' heightened sensitivity to social rewards: Dustin Albert, Jason Chein, and Laurence Steinberg, "The Teenage Brain: Peer Influences on Adolescent Decision-Making," *Current Directions in Psychological Science* 22, no. 2 (2013), 114–20.

activates adolescents' reward centers: Jason Chein et al., "Peers Increase

Adolescent Risk Taking by Enhancing Activity in the Brain's Reward Circuitry," *Developmental Science* 14, no. 2 (2011), F1–F10.

make immediate rewards especially compelling: Lia O'Brien et al., "Adolescents Prefer More Immediate Rewards When in the Presence of Their Peers," *Journal of Research on Adolescence* 21, no. 4 (2011), 747–53; Alexander Weigard et al., "Effects of Anonymous Peer Observation on Adolescents' Preference for Immediate Rewards," *Developmental Science* 17, no. 1 (2014), 71–78.

99   *a high probability of something bad happening:* Ashley Smith, Jason Chein, and Laurence Steinberg, "Peers Increase Adolescent Risk-Taking Even When the Probabilities of Negative Outcomes Are Known," *Developmental Psychology* 17 (2014), 79–85.

this doesn't happen for adult mice: Viviana Trezza, Patrizia Campolongo, and Louk J.M.J. Vanderschuren, "Evaluating the Rewarding Nature of Social Interactions in Laboratory Animals," *Developmental Cognitive Neuroscience* 1, no. 4 (2011), 444–58.

human adolescents also learn more from group projects: Cary J. Roseth, David W. Johnson, and Roger T. Johnson, "Promoting Early Adolescents' Achievement and Peer Relationships: The Effects of Cooperative, Competitive, and Individualistic Goal Structures," *Psychological Bulletin* 134, no. 2 (2008), 223–46.

adolescent mice drank more alcohol: Sheree Logue et al., "Adolescent Mice, Unlike Adults, Consume More Alcohol in the Presence of Peers Than Alone," *Developmental Science* 17, no. 1 (2014), 79–85.

100   *more effective than driver education:* Susan P. Baker, Li-Hui Chen, and Guohua Li, *National Evaluation of Graduated Driver Licensing Programs,* report no. DOT HS 810 614 (Washington, DC: National Highway Traffic Safety Organization, 2006), www.nhtsa.gov.

prime time for adolescents' initial experimentation with alcohol, drugs, sex, and delinquent behavior: D. Wayne Osgood, Amy L. Anderson, and Jennifer N. Shaffer, "Unstructured Leisure in the After-School Hours," in *Organized Activities as Contexts of Development: Extracurricular Activities, After-School, and Community Programs,* edited by Joseph L. Mahoney, Reed W. Larson, and Jacquelynne S. Eccles (Mahway, NJ: Erlbaum, 2005), 45–64.

101   *posters on the city's subways:* Kate Taylor, "Posters on Teenage Pregnancy Draw Fire," *New York Times,* March 6, 2013.

"a powerful weapon to reduce teen pregnancy": Richard V. Reeves, "Shame Is Not a Four-Letter Word," *New York Times,* March 15, 2013.

102   *these efforts are based on faulty premises:* Steinberg, "A Social Neuroscience Perspective on Adolescent Risk-Taking."

We've made considerable progress: Karen Hein, *Issues in Adolescent Health: An Overview* (Washington, DC: Carnegie Council on Adolescent Development, 1988).

no decline in adolescents' risky behavior in several years: Data come from the annual Youth Risk Behavior Survey, conducted by the Centers for Disease Control and Prevention.

good reason to be skeptical about the effectiveness of these programs: Data on various forms of risk taking are from the CDC's annual Youth Risk Behavior Survey.

103 *one-third of American high-school students are overweight or obese:* Cynthia L. Ogden et al., "Prevalence of Obesity and Trends in Body Mass Index Among U.S. Children and Adolescents, 1999–2010," *Journal of the American Medical Association* 307, no. 5 (2012), 483–90.

more eighth graders use illicit drugs today: Data from Monitoring the Future, www.monitoringthefuture.org.

because the price of cigarettes has increased: Jonathan Gruber, "Youth Smoking in the 1990s: Why Did It Rise, and What Are the Long-Run Implications?" *American Economic Review* 91, no. 2 (2001), 85–91.

104 *DARE:* S. T. Ennett et al., "How Effective Is Drug Abuse Resistance Education? A Meta-Analysis of Project DARE Outcome Evaluations," *American Journal of Public Health* 84, no. 9 (1994), 1394–1401.

abstinence education: Christopher Trenholm et al., *Impacts of Four Title V, Section 510 Abstinence Education Programs* (Princeton, NJ: Mathematica Policy Research, 2007).

driver training: National Research Council, *Preventing Teen Motor Crashes: Contributions from the Behavioral and Social Sciences* (Washington, DC: National Academies Press, 2007).

enhancing adolescents' general capacity for self-regulation: Daniel Romer et al., "Can Adolescents Learn Self-Control?: Delay of Gratification in the Development of Control over Risk Taking," *Prevention Science* 11 (2010), 319–30.

105 *enable adolescents to exercise self-control:* Gilbert J. Botvin, "Advancing Prevention Science and Practice: Challenges, Critical Issues, and Future Directions," *Prevention Science* 5, no. 1 (2004), 69–72.

we should try to change the context: Committee on the Science of Adolescence, Institute of Medicine and the National Research Council, *The Science of Adolescent Risk-Taking* (Washington, DC: National Academies Press, 2011).

6. THE IMPORTANCE OF SELF-REGULATION

107 *the "marshmallow test":* Walter Mischel et al., "'Willpower' over the Life Span: Decomposing Self-Regulation," *Social Cognitive Affective Neuroscience* 6, no. 2 (2011), 252–56.

108 *higher SAT scores and better coping abilities:* Yuichi Shoda, Walter Mischel,

and Philip K. Peake, "Predicting Adolescent Cognitive and Self-Regulatory Competencies from Preschool Delay of Gratification: Identifying Diagnostic Conditions," *Developmental Psychology* 26, no. 6 (1990), 978–86.

adults who had problems delaying gratification when they were preschoolers: Mischel et al., "'Willpower' over the Life Span."

Even in middle age: B. J. Casey et al., "Behavioral and Neural Correlates of Delay of Gratification 40 Years Later," *Proceedings of the National Academy of Sciences* 108, no. 36 (2011), 14998–15003.

109   *an especially sharp drop in preference for immediate rewards:* Laurence Steinberg et al., "Age Differences in Future Orientation and Delay Discounting," *Child Development* 80, no. 1 (2009), 28–44.

110   *people who show a stronger preference for immediate rewards:* Amy L. Odum, "Delay Discounting: I'm a K, You're a K," *Journal of the Experimental Analysis of Behavior* 96, no. 3 (2011), 427–39; Rosalyn E. Weller et al., "Obese Women Show Greater Delay Discounting Than Healthy-Weight Women," *Appetite* 51, no. 3 (2008), 563–69.

report enjoying school less: Tom Loveless, *Brown Center Report on American Education 2006* (Washington, DC: Brookings Institution, 2006).

sitting in class every day is about as much fun as doing homework: Laurence Steinberg, with B. Bradford Brown and Sanford M. Dornbusch, *Beyond the Classroom: Why School Reform Has Failed and What Parents Need to Do* (New York: Simon & Schuster, 1996).

111   *the gap had been about that size for some time:* U.S. Census Bureau, *Current Population Survey,* 2012, Table A-3.

112   *front-page story in the* New York Times: Jason DeParle, "For Poor, Leap to College Often Ends in a Hard Fall," *New York Times,* December 22, 2012, A1.

113   *recent assessment of federal programs:* Ron Haskins and Cecilia Elena Rouse, "Time for Change: A New Federal Strategy to Prepare Disadvantaged Students for College," policy brief, *Future of Children* 23, no. 1 (2013), 1–6.

studies of financial-aid and student-loan programs: Ron Haskins, Harry Holzer, and Robert Lerman, *Promoting Economic Mobility by Increasing Postsecondary Education* (Philadelphia: Pew Charitable Trusts, 2009).

114   *tied for last in the rate of college* completion: OECD, *Education at a Glance 2013: OECD Indicators* (Paris: OECD, 2013).

117   *The remaining 75 percent is due to something else:* Ulric Neisser et al., "Intelligence: Knowns and Unknowns," *American Psychologist* 51, no. 2 (1996), 77–101.

"grit": Angela Duckworth et al., "Grit: Perseverance and Passion for Long-Term Goals," *Journal of Personality and Social Psychology* 92, no. 6 (2007), 1087–1101.

118   *"noncognitive skills":* James J. Heckman, Jora Stixrud, and Sergio Urzua,

"The Effects of Cognitive and Noncognitive Abilities on Labor Market Outcomes and Social Behavior," *Journal of Labor Economics* 24 (2006), 411–82.

distinguish children who succeed from those who don't: Paul Tough, *How Children Succeed: Grit, Curiosity, and the Hidden Power of Character* (New York: Houghton Mifflin Harcourt, 2012).

120   *Adolescents who score high on measures of perseverance:* Angela L. Duckworth and Martin E. P. Seligman, "Self-Discipline Outdoes IQ in Predicting Academic Performance of Adolescents," *Psychological Science* 16, no. 12 (2005), 939–44; Angela L. Duckworth, Patrick D. Quinn, and Eli Tsukayama, "What *No Child Left Behind* Leaves Behind: The Roles of IQ and Self-Control in Predicting Standardized Achievement Test Scores and Report Card Grades," *Journal of Educational Psychology* 104, no. 2 (2012), 439–51.

121   *predictors of many different types of success:* Adele Diamond, "Executive Functions," *Annual Review of Psychology* 64 (2013), 135–68; Terrie Moffitt, Richie Poulton, and Avshalom Caspi, "Lifelong Impact of Early Self-Control," *American Scientist* 101, no. 5 (2013), 352–59.

122   *many basic intellectual capacities are not plastic:* Flavio Cunha, James J. Heckman, and Susanne M. Schennach, "Estimating the Technology of Cognitive and Noncognitive Skill Formation," *Econometrica* 78, no. 3 (2010), 883–931.

highly determined by genes: Gail Davies et al., "Genome-Wide Association Studies Establish That Human Intelligence Is Highly Heritable and Polygenic," *Molecular Psychiatry* 16, no. 10 (2011), 996–1005; MacIej Trzaskowski et al., "DNA Evidence for Strong Genetic Stability and Increasing Heritability of Intelligence from Age 7 to 12," *Molecular Psychiatry* 19, no. 3 (2014), 380–84.

patterns of neural architecture: Arthur W. Toga and Paul M. Thompson, "Genetics of Brain Structure and Intelligence," *Annual Review of Neuroscience* 28 (2005), 1–23.

123   *influence of genes on self-control:* Sharon Niv et al., "Heritability and Longitudinal Stability of Impulsivity in Adolescence," *Behavior Genetics* 42, no. 3 (2012), 378–92.

regions of the brain responsible for self-control: Caroline Brun et al., "Mapping the Regional Influence of Genetics on Brain Structure Variability—a Tensor-Based Morphometry Study," *NeuroImage* 48, no. 1 (2009), 37–49.

correlation between early and later impulsivity: Moffitt, Poulton, and Caspi, "Lifelong Impact of Early Self-Control."

even the most impulsive, aggressive juvenile delinquents can be helped: Mark W. Lipsey et al., *Improving the Effectiveness of Juvenile Justice Programs: A New Perspective on Evidence-Based Practice* (Washington, DC: Center for Juvenile Justice Reform, Georgetown University, 2010).

one of the most important tendencies we inherit is plasticity: Jay Belsky and Michael Pluess, "Beyond Diathesis Stress: Differential Susceptibility to Environmental Influence," *Psychological Bulletin* 135, no. 6 (2009), 885–908; Bruce J. Ellis and W. Thomas Boyce, "Biological Sensitivity to Context," *Current Directions in Psychological Science* 17, no. 2 (2005), 183–87.

124   *influence of environmental forces that affect self-regulation:* Jay Belsky and Michael Pluess, "Beyond Risk, Resilience, and Dysregulation: Phenotypic Plasticity and Human Development," *Development and Psychopathology* 25, no. 4, pt. 2 (2013), 1243–61; Jay Belsky and Michael Pleuss, "Cumulative-Genetic Plasticity, Parenting, and Adolescent Self-Regulation," *Journal of Child Psychology and Psychiatry* 52, no. 5 (2011), 619–26.

the most important environmental contributor to self-regulation is the family: Nancy Eisenberg et al., "Conscientiousness: Origins in Childhood?" *Developmental Psychology*, December 17, 2012, doi:10.1037/a0030977.

7. HOW PARENTS CAN MAKE A DIFFERENCE

126   *scientifically proven prescription:* Laurence Steinberg, *The Ten Basic Principles of Good Parenting* (New York: Simon & Schuster, 2004).

136   *three parenting styles predominate:* Nancy Darling and Laurence Steinberg, "Parenting Style as Context: An Integrative Model," *Psychological Bulletin* 113, no. 3 (1993), 487–96.

"Tiger mothering": Amy Chua, *Battle Hymn of the Tiger Mother* (New York: Penguin, 2011).

roundly criticized: Charles Q. Choi, "Does Science Support the Punitive Parenting of 'Tiger Mothering'?" *Scientific American*, January 8, 2011.

137   *better mental health* and *fare better in school when their parents are warm and supportive:* Su Yeong Kim et al., "Does 'Tiger Parenting' Exist? Parenting Profiles of Chinese Americans and Adolescent Developmental Outcomes," *Asian American Journal of Psychology* 4, no. 1 (2013), 7–18.

138   *benefits of authoritative parenting accrue:* Steinberg, *The Ten Basic Principles of Good Parenting.*

8. REIMAGINING HIGH SCHOOL

141   *blue-ribbon commission report:* National Commission on Excellence in Education, *A Nation at Risk: The Imperative for Educational Reform* (Washington: U.S. Department of Education, 1983).

142   *the numbers aren't skewed by this diversity:* Daniel Koretz, "How Do American Students Measure Up? Making Sense of International Comparisons," *Future of Children* 19, no. 1 (2009), 37–51.

a little-known study that compared the world's fifteen-year-olds: Jon Douglas Willms, *Student Engagement at School: A Sense of Belonging and Participation; Results from Pisa 2000* (Paris: OECD, 2003).

143   *the teen-suicide rate is higher in the United States:* Danuta Wasserman, Qi Cheng, and Guo-Xin Jiang, "Global Suicide Rates Among Young People Aged 15–19," *World Psychiatry* 4, no. 2 (2005), 114–20.

American children's moods: Reed Larson and Maryse Richards, "Waiting for the Weekend: Friday and Saturday Night as the Emotional Climax of the Week," *New Directions for Child and Adolescent Development* 82 (Winter 1998), 37–52.

calibrating their level of effort: Jean Johnson et al., *Getting By: What American Teenagers Really Think About Their Schools* (New York: Public Agenda, 1997).

they have little interest in school: Laurence Steinberg, with B. Bradford Brown and Sanford M. Dornbusch, *Beyond the Classroom: Why School Reform Has Failed and What Parents Need to Do* (New York: Simon & Schuster, 1996).

20 percent or so of students who have dropped out: U.S. Department of Education, "States Report New High School Graduation Rates Using More Accurate, Common Measure," press release, November 26, 2012.

American high-school students spend far less time on schoolwork: Tom Loveless, *Brown Center Report on American Education* (Washington, DC: Brookings Institution, 2002), Amanda Ripley, *The Smartest Kids in the World* (New York: Simon & Schuster, 2013).

144   *small but statistically significant increases:* Data from the National Assessment of Educational Progress, U.S. Department of Education.

The list of unsuccessful experiments is long: Jal Mehta, "Teachers: Will We Ever Learn?" *New York Times,* April 12, 2013.

no advantage to going to private school: Loveless, *Brown Center Report on American Education.*

145   *Elementary schools in America are more than twice as likely:* Data from the National Center on Education Statistics, U.S. Department of Education.

secondary-school and elementary-school teachers have comparable years of education: Ibid.

the amounts of time that students spend in the classroom: OECD, *Education at a Glance 2012.*

spend a little more per capita on high-school students: Ibid.

146   *more training programs for secondary-school teachers received high marks:* National Council on Teacher Quality, *Teacher Prep Review* (Washington, DC: National Council on Teacher Quality, 2013).

no school-reform effort would have any impact: Steinberg, *Beyond the Classroom.*

147   *the "immigrant paradox":* Carola Suarez-Orozco, Jean Rhodes, and Michael

Milburn, "Unraveling the Immigrant Paradox: Academic Engagement and Disengagement Among Recently Arrived Immigrant Youth," *Youth & Society* 41, no. 2 (2009), 151–85.

become more important as students get older: Arthur E. Poropat, "A Meta-Analysis of the Five-Factor Model of Personality and Academic Performance," *Psychological Bulletin* 135, no. 2 (2009), 322–38.

148   *basic premise behind this movement:* Richard J. Davidson et al., "Contemplative Practices and Mental Training: Prospects for American Education," *Child Development Perspectives* 6, no. 2 (2012), 146–53.

149   *people from different socioeconomic backgrounds:* Melvin Kohn, *Class and Conformity: A Study in Values,* 2nd ed. (Chicago: University of Chicago Press, 1977).

151   *seven character strengths:* Information from KIPP website, www.kipp.org.
       a best-selling book: Paul Tough, *How Children Succeed: Grit, Curiosity, and the Hidden Power of Character* (New York: Houghton Mifflin Harcourt, 2012).

152   *two factors that have been shown time and again to contribute to scholastic success:* Steinberg, *Beyond the Classroom.*
       a recent evaluation of KIPP middle schools: Christina Clark Tuttle et al., *KIPP Middle Schools: Impacts on Achievement and Other Outcomes* (Washington, DC: Mathematica Policy Research, 2013).

153   *rates of college graduation among KIPP graduates:* KIPP Foundation, *The Promise of College Completion: KIPP's Early Successes and Challenges* (San Francisco: KIPP, 2011).

155   *in the degree of interconnection between different brain regions:* Sarah-Jayne Blakemore and Silvia A. Bunge, "At the Nexus of Neuroscience and Education," *Developmental Cognitive Neuroscience* 2S (2012), S1–S5; Lisa A. Kilpatrick et al., "Impact of Mindfulness-Based Stress Reduction Training on Intrinsic Brain Connectivity," *NeuroImage* 56, no. 1 (2011), 290–98; Allyson P. Mackey, Alison T. Miller Singley, and Silvia A. Bunge, "Intensive Reasoning Training Alters Patterns of Brain Connectivity at Rest," *Journal of Neuroscience* 33, no. 11 (2013), 4796–4803; Yi-Yuan Tang, Rongxiang Tang, and Michael I. Posner, "Brief Meditation Training Induces Smoking Reduction," *Proceedings of the National Academy of Sciences* 110, no. 34 (2013), 13971–75.

156   *how we retain information in our minds and use it:* Diamond, "Executive Functions."
       Practicing the n-back task: Alexandra B. Morrison and Jason M. Chein, "Does Working Memory Training Work? The Promise and Challenges of Enhancing Cognition by Training Working Memory," *Psychonomic Bulletin and Review* 18 (2011), 46–60.

157   *bolster performance on tests:* Ibid.
       Exercises that practice mindfulness: Davidson et al., "Contemplative Prac-

tices and Mental Training"; Alexandra B. Morrison et al., "Taming a Wandering Attention: Short-Form Mindfulness Training in Student Cohorts," *Frontiers in Human Neuroscience* 7 (January 6, 2014), doi:10.3389/fnhum.2013.00897.

focusing one's attention on the present moment: Scott R. Bishop et al., "Mindfulness: A Proposed Operational Definition," *Clinical Psychology Science and Practice* 11, no. 3 (2004), 230–41; Britta K. Hölzel et al., "How Does Mindfulness Meditation Work? Proposing Mechanisms of Action from a Conceptual and Neural Perspective," *Perspectives on Psychological Science* 6, no. 6 (2011), 537–59.

mindfulness meditation: Jon Kabat-Zinn, *Full Catastrophe Living: Using the Wisdom of Your Body and Mind to Face Stress, Pain, and Illness* (New York: Delta, 2005).

158   *improves sleep, cardiovascular health, and immune function:* Paul Grossman et al., "Mindfulness-Based Stress Reduction and Health Benefits: A Meta-Analysis," *Journal of Psychosomatic Research* 57, no. 1 (2004), 35–43; Richard J. Davidson et al., "Alterations in Brain and Immune Function Produced by Mindfulness Meditation," *Psychosomatic Medicine* 65, no. 4 (2003), 564–70; Robert H. Schneider et al., "Stress Reduction in the Secondary Prevention of Cardiovascular Disease: Randomized, Controlled Trial of Transcendental Meditation and Education in Blacks," *Circulation: Cardiovascular Quality and Outcomes* 5 (November 2012), 750–58.

aerobic exercise: John R. Best, "Effects of Physical Activity on Children's Executive Function: Contributions of Experimental Research on Aerobic Exercise," *Developmental Review* 30, no. 4 (2010), 321–51; Lot Verburgh et al., "Physical Exercise and Executive Functions in Preadolescent Children, Adolescents and Young Adults: A Meta-Analysis," *British Journal of Sports Medicine,* March 6, 2013, doi:10.1136/bjsports-2012-091441.

159   *team sports that combine aerobic activity with strategy:* Diamond, "Executive Functions."

organized athletics appears to help promote the development of self-regulation: Joseph L. Mahoney et al., "Adolescent Out-of-School Activities," in *Handbook of Adolescent Psychology,* edited by Richard M. Lerner and Laurence Steinberg, vol. 2, 3rd ed. (New York: Wiley, 2009), 228–69.

combine a challenging physical activity with mindfulness: Mark T. Greenberg and Alexis R. Harris, "Nurturing Mindfulness in Children and Youth: Current State of Research," *Child Development Perspectives* 6, no. 2 (2012), 161–66.

training in specific self-regulation strategies: J. A. Durlak et al., "The Impact of Enhancing Students' Social and Emotional Learning: A Meta-Analysis of School-Based Universal Interventions," *Child Development* 82, no. 1 (2011), 405–32.

review of effective, school-based SEL programs: Ibid.

160   *envision and plan long-term goals:* Angela Lee Duckworth et al., "Self-Regulation Strategies Improve Self-Discipline in Adolescents: Benefits of Mental Contrasting and Implementation Intentions," *Educational Psychology*
31, no. 1 (2011), 17–26.

imagine these potential impediments beforehand: Peter M. Gollwitzer and
Gabriele Oettingen, "Planning Promotes Goal Striving," in *Handbook of
Self-Regulation: Research, Theory, and Applications,* edited by Kathleen D.
Vohs and Roy F. Baumeister, 2nd ed. (New York: Guilford, 2011).

students who were taught and encouraged to use MCII: Angela Lee Duckworth et al., "From Fantasy to Action: Mental Contrasting with Implementation Intentions (MCII) Improves Academic Performance in Children,"
Social Psychological and Personality Science 4, no. 6 (2013), 745–53.

161   *requires three common principles:* Diamond, "Executive Functions."
the training must be stimulating: Ibid.

162   *deliberate practice:* K. Anders Ericsson, Ralf Th. Krampe, and Clemens
Tesch-Romer, "The Role of Deliberate Practice in the Acquisition of Expert
Performance," *Psychological Review* 100, no. 3 (1993), 363–406; K. Anders
Ericsson, Kiruthiga Nandagopal, and Roy W. Roring, "Toward a Science of
Exceptional Achievement: Attaining Superior Performance Through De-
liberate Practice," *Annals of the New York Academy of Sciences* 1172 (August
2009), 199–217.

9. WINNERS AND LOSERS

164   *gap between the haves and the have-nots:* World Bank, *World Development
Indicators,* http://data.worldbank.org.

165   *people who grow up in poor households:* Kimberly G. Noble et al., "Neural
Correlates of Socioeconomic Status in the Developing Human Brain," *Developmental Science* 15, no. 4 (2012), 516–27.

long-lasting effects on a wide range of outcomes: Elliot M. Tucker-Drob,
"How Many Pathways Underlie Socioeconomic Differences in the Development of Cognition and Achievement?" *Learning and Individual Differences* 25 (June 2013), 12–20.

executive functions in particular: Naomi P. Friedman et al., "Individual Differences in Executive Functions Are Almost Entirely Genetic in Origin,"
Journal of Experimental Psychology: General 137, no. 2 (2008), 201–25.

genetic influences on brain anatomy: Arthur W. Toga and Paul M. Thompson, "Genetics of Brain Structure and Intelligence," *Annual Review of Neuroscience* 28 (2005), 1–23.

"assortative mating": Christine R. Schwartz, "Trends and Variation in As-

sortative Mating: Causes and Consequences," *Annual Review of Sociology* 39 (2013), 451–70; Anna A. E. Vinkhuyzen et al., "Reconsidering the Heritability of Intelligence in Adulthood: Taking Assortative Mating and Cultural Transmission into Account," *Behavior Genetics* 42, no. 2 (2012), 187–98.

Stress appears to have particularly toxic effects: J. L. Hanson et al., "Early Neglect Is Associated with Alterations in White Matter Integrity and Cognitive Functioning," *Child Development* 84, no. 5 (2013), 1566–78; Eamon McCrory, Stephane A. De Brito, and Essi Viding, "The Impact of Childhood Maltreatment: A Review of Neurobiological and Genetic Factors," *Frontiers in Psychiatry* 2 (July 28, 2011), doi:10.3389/fpsyt.2011.00048; Pia Pechtel and Diego A. Pizzagalli, "Effects of Early Life Stress on Cognitive and Affective Function: An Integrated Review of Human Literature," *Psychopharmacology* 214, no. 1 (2011), 55–70.

166   *socioeconomic differences are especially pronounced:* Martha J. Farah, "Mind, Brain, and Education in Socioeconomic Context," in *The Developmental Relations Between Mind, Brain, and Education: Essays in Honor of Robbie Case,* edited by Michel Ferrari and Ljiljana Vuletic (Dordrecht: Springer, 2010).

linked to their parents' level of education: Jamie L. Hanson et al., "Family Poverty Affects the Rate of Human Infant Brain Growth," *PLoS One* 8, no. 12 (2013), e80954; Gwendolyn M. Lawson et al., "Associations Between Children's Socioeconomic Status and Prefrontal Cortical Thickness," *Developmental Science* 16, no. 5 (2013), 641–52.

most disrupted by early stress: Pechtel and Pizzagalli, "Effects of Early Life Stress on Cognitive and Affective Function."

interventions have been largely disappointing: Amy L. Wax, *Race, Wrongs, and Remedies: Group Justice in the 21st Century* (Lanham, MD: Rowman and Littlefield, 2009).

at an all-time high today: Data from the U.S. Census Bureau, Current Population Reports.

gap in school performance between rich and poor: Sean F. Reardon, "The Widening Academic Achievement Gap Between the Rich and the Poor: New Evidence and Possible Explanations," in *Whither Opportunity? Rising Inequality and the Uncertain Life Chances of Low-Income Children,* edited by Greg J. Duncan and Richard J. Murnane (New York: Russell Sage Foundation Press, 2011).

167   *adolescents who had been convicted of serious crimes:* Edward P. Mulvey, *Highlights from Pathways to Desistance: A Longitudinal Study of Serious Adolescent Offenders* (Washington, DC: Office of Juvenile Justice and Delinquency Prevention, U.S. Department of Justice, 2011).

delinquents don't become persistent adult criminals: Terrie E. Moffitt, "Adolescence-Limited and Life-Course-Persistent Antisocial Behavior: A Developmental Taxonomy," *Psychological Review* 100, no. 4 (1993), 674–701.

become better at self-regulation: Kathryn C. Monahan et al., "Trajectories of Antisocial Behavior and Psychosocial Maturity from Adolescence to Young Adulthood," *Developmental Psychology* 45, no. 6 (2009), 1654–68.

168   *few continue much beyond that:* Alex R. Piquero, David P. Farrington, and Alfred Blumstein, "The Criminal Career Paradigm," in *Crime and Justice: A Review of Research,* edited by Michael Tonry, vol. 30 (Chicago: University of Chicago Press, 2003), 359–506.

169   *four basic rules to follow:* There are various versions of this model, originally suggested by Isabel Sawhill and Christopher Jencks, and popularized most recently in Juan Williams, *Enough: The Phony Leaders, Dead-End Movements, and Culture of Failure That Are Undermining Black America — and What We Can Do About It* (New York: Broadway Books, 2007).

people who follow these rules almost never end up in poverty: Wax, *Race, Wrongs, and Remedies.*

170   *failure to develop mature self-control:* Kathryn Monahan et al., "Psychosocial (Im)maturity from Adolescence to Early Adulthood: Distinguishing Between Adolescence-Limited and Persistent Antisocial Behavior," *Development and Psychopathology* 25, no. 4, pt. 1 (2013), 1093–1105.

associated with the failure to develop adequate self-regulation: Michael R. Gottfredson and Travis Hirschi, *A General Theory of Crime* (Stanford, CA: Stanford University Press, 1990).

171   *Parents who use physical force:* Elizabeth T. Gershoff, "Spanking and Child Development: We Know Enough Now to Stop Hitting Our Children," *Child Development Perspectives* 7, no. 3 (2013), 133–37.

172   *parents from lower-class backgrounds:* Erica Hoff-Ginsberg and Twila Tardif, "Socioeconomic Status and Parenting," in *Handbook of Parenting,* edited by Marc H. Bornstein, vol. 2, *Biology and Ecology of Parenting,* 2nd ed. (Mahwah, NJ: Erlbaum, 2002), 231–52.

more controlling and less patient: Vonnie C. McLoyd, "The Impact of Economic Hardship on Black Families and Children: Psychological Distress, Parenting, and Socioemotional Development," *Child Development* 61, no. 2 (1990), 311–46.

"coercive cycle": Gerald R. Patterson, *Coercive Family Process* (Eugene, OR: Castalia, 1982).

worse at providing opportunities to develop self-control: Paul Tough, *How Children Succeed: Grit, Curiosity, and the Hidden Power of Character* (New York: Houghton Mifflin Harcourt, 2012).

174   *obesity is far more prevalent:* Lindsay McLaren, "Socioeconomic Status and Obesity," *Epidemiologic Reviews* 29 (2007), 29–48; Cynthia L. Ogden et al., "Prevalence of Obesity and Trends in Body Mass Index Among US Chil-

dren and Adolescents, 1999–2010," *Journal of the American Medical Association* 307, no. 5 (2012), 483–90.

Premature births: Richard E. Behrman and Adrienne Stith Butler, eds., *Preterm Birth: Causes, Consequences, and Prevention* (Washington, DC: National Academies Press, 2007).

exposure to screen-based entertainment: Ngaire Coombs et al., "Children's and Adolescents' Sedentary Behaviour in Relation to Household Socioeconomic Position," *Journal of Epidemiology and Community Health,* 67, no. 10, (2013), 868–74; Emmanuel Stamatakis et al., "Television Viewing and Other Screen-Based Entertainment in Relation to Multiple Socioeconomic Status Indicators and Area Deprivation: the Scottish Health Survey 2003," *Journal of Epidemiology and Community Health* 63, no. 9 (2009), 734–40; Pooja S. Tandon et al., "Home Environment Relationships with Children's Physical Activity, Sedentary Time, and Screen Time by Socioeconomic Status," *International Journal of Behavioral Nutrition and Physical Activity* 9 (2012), 88.

children from poorer homes have later bedtimes: Brian Crosby, Monique K. LeBourgeois, and John Harsh, "Racial Differences in Reported Napping and Nocturnal Sleep in 2- to 8-Year-Old Children," *Pediatrics* 115, sup. 1 (2005), 225–32; Valerie McLaughlin Crabtree et al., "Cultural Influences on the Bedtime Behaviors of Young Children," *Sleep Medicine* 6, no. 4 (2005), 319–24; M. El-Sheikh et al., "Children's Sleep and Adjustment over Time: The Role of Socioeconomic Context," *Child Development* 81, no. 3 (2010), 870–83; Christine A. Marco et al., "Family Socioeconomic Status and Sleep Patterns of Young Adolescents," *Behavioral Sleep Medicine* 10, no. 1 (2012), 70–80.

Father absence: Mark Mather, *U.S. Children in Single-Mother Families* (Washington, DC: Population Reference Bureau, 2010).

Exposure to bisphenol A: Jessica W. Nelson et al., "Social Disparities in Exposures to Bisphenol A and Polyfluoroalkyl Chemicals: A Cross-Sectional Study Within NHANES 2003–2006," *Environmental Health* 11, no. 10 (2012).

hair-care products: Chandra M. Tiwary, "Premature Sexual Development in Children Following Use of Estrogen- or Placenta-Containing Hair Products," *Clinical Pediatrics* 37, no. 12 (1998), 733–40.

175 *less likely to engage in problem behavior:* Laurence Steinberg, *Adolescence,* 10th ed. (New York: McGraw-Hill, 2014).

Authoritative parenting lessens the risks: Xiaojia Ge et al., "Contextual Amplification of Pubertal Transition Effects on Deviant Peer Affiliation and Externalizing Behavior Among African American Children," *Developmental Psychology* 38, no. 1 (2002), 42–54.

less likely to use successful "management" strategies: Robert E. Larzelere and

Gerald R. Patterson, "Parental Management: Mediator of the Effect of Socioeconomic Status on Early Delinquency," *Criminology* 28, no. 2 (1990), 301–24.

adolescents who aren't supervised after school: Joseph Mahoney et al., "Adolescent Out-of-School Activities," in *Handbook of Adolescent Psychology,* edited by Richard M. Lerner and Laurence Steinberg, vol. 2, 3rd ed. (New York: Wiley, 2009).

176 *antisocial peer groups are more likely to gather:* Robert J. Sampson, "Collective Regulation of Adolescent Misbehavior: Validation Results from Eighty Chicago Neighborhoods," *Journal of Adolescent Research* 12, no. 2 (1997), 227–44.

higher education itself contributes to prefrontal development: Kimberly G. Noble, Bruce D. McCandliss, and Martha J. Farah, "Socioeconomic Gradients Predict Individual Differences in Neurocognitive Abilities," *Developmental Science* 10, no. 4 (2007), 464–80; Kimberly G. Noble and Martha J. Farah, "Neurocognitive Consequences of Socioeconomic Disparities: The Intersection of Cognitive Neuroscience and Public Health," *Developmental Science* 16, no. 5 (2013), 639–40; G. Lawson et al., "Socioeconomic Status and Neurocognitive Development: Executive Function," in *Executive Function in Preschool Age Children: Integrating Measurement, Neurodevelopment, and Translational Research,* edited by J. A. Griffin, L. S. Freund, and P. McCardle (Washington, DC: American Psychological Association Press, forthcoming); Kimberly G. Noble et al., "Higher Education Is an Age-Independent Predictor of White Matter Integrity and Cognitive Control in Late Adolescence," *Developmental Science* 16, no. 5 (2013), 653–64.

177 *In addition to financial capital:* Pierre Bourdieu, "The Forms of Capital," in *Handbook of Theory and Research for the Sociology of Education,* edited by John G. Richardson (New York: Greenwood, 1986).

178 *prefrontal systems become stronger:* Allyson P. Mackey, Kirstie J. Whitaker, and Silvia A. Bunge, "Experience-Dependent Plasticity in White Matter Microstructure: Reasoning Training Alters Structural Connectivity," *Frontiers in Neuroanatomy* 6 (August 22, 2012), doi:10.3389/fnana.2012.00032.

179 *The study that led to this conclusion:* Frederick S. Stinson et al., "Prevalence, Correlates, Disability, and Comorbidity of Personality Disorder Diagnoses in a DSM-IV Narcissistic Personality Disorder: Results from the Wave 2 National Epidemiologic Survey on Alcohol and Related Conditions," *Journal of Clinical Psychiatry* 69, no. 7 (2008), 1033–45.

drawn the same conclusion: Kali H. Trzesniewski and M. Brent Donnellan, "Rethinking 'Generation Me': A Study of Cohort Effects from 1976–2006," *Perspectives in Psychological Science* 5, no. 1 (2010), 58–75; Kali H. Trzesniewski, M. Brent Donnellan, and Richard W. Robins, "Do Today's Young

People Really Think They Are So Extraordinary? An Examination of Secular Trends in Narcissism and Self-Enhancement," *Psychological Science* 19, no. 2 (2008), 181–88.

180   *AmeriCorps:* Information on AmeriCorps can be found at www.nationalservice.gov.

10. BRAINS ON TRIAL

188   *they are* less *guilty:* Elizabeth S. Scott and Laurence Steinberg, *Rethinking Juvenile Justice* (Cambridge, MA: Harvard University Press, 2008).

190   *People are persuaded:* Deena Skolnick Weisberg et al., "The Seductive Allure of Neuroscience Explanations," *Journal of Cognitive Neuroscience* 20, no. 3 (2008), 470–77.
       "formal operational thinking": Deanna Kuhn, "Adolescent Thinking," in *Handbook of Adolescent Psychology,* edited by Richard M. Lerner and Laurence Steinberg, vol. 1, 3rd ed. (New York: Wiley, 2009).

193   *juveniles are more prone to giving false confessions:* Saul M. Kassin et al., "Police-Induced Confessions: Risk Factors and Recommendations," *Law and Human Behavior* 34, no. 1 (2010), 49–52.

195   *the alleged act is played down by the interrogator:* Ibid.

196   *the Miranda warning:* Thomas Grisso, "Juveniles' Capacities to Waive Miranda Rights: An Empirical Analysis," *California Law Review* 68, no. 6 (1980), 1134–66.

197   *black adolescents are judged as more adult-like:* Sandra Graham and Brian S. Lowery, "Priming Unconscious Racial Stereotypes About Adolescent Offenders," *Law and Human Behavior* 28, no. 5 (2004), 483–504.

199   *the minimum drinking age was established at twenty-one:* Jeffery A. Miron and Elena Tetelbaum, "Does the Minimum Legal Drinking Age Save Lives?" *Economic Inquiry* 47, no. 2 (2009), 317–36.
       a point of controversy: Laurence Steinberg et al., "Are Adolescents Less Mature Than Adults? Minors' Access to Abortion, the Juvenile Death Penalty, and the Alleged APA 'Flip-Flop,'" *American Psychologist* 64, no. 7 (2009), 583–94.

200   *whether a minor should be allowed to obtain an abortion:* Hodgson v. Minnesota, 497 U.S. 417 (1990).
       new case about parental involvement in adolescents' abortion decisions: Ayotte v. Planned Parenthood of Northern New England, 546 U.S. 320 (2006).

201   *to help ensure that abortion decisions are not made rashly:* Guttmacher Institute, "Counseling and Waiting Periods for Abortion," *State Policies in Brief,* May 2008, www.guttmacher.org.
       some states have raised the age: Scott and Steinberg, *Rethinking Juvenile Justice.*

202   *the most vehement opponents have been parents:* Martha Irvine, "Teen Driving Age Should Be Raised, Says Auto Safety Group," *Huffington Post,* September 9, 2008.

203   *enlisting older teenagers:* Data on teenagers in the military come from the U.S. Department of Defense, *Population Representation in the Military Services,* 2011.

   the evidence is not as clear-cut: Christopher Carpenter and Carlos Dobkin, "The Minimum Legal Drinking Age and Public Health," *Journal of Economic Perspectives* 25, no. 2 (2011), 133–56.

204   *a decline in auto fatalities was already taking place:* Miron and Tetelbaum, "Does the Minimum Legal Drinking Age Save Lives?"

   significantly lower automobile-fatality rates: International Transport Forum, *Road Safety Annual Report 2013* (Paris: OECD, 2013).

   most countries have far fewer auto fatalities: Ibid.

   the way that drunks use lampposts: Attributed to the Scottish poet Andrew Lang.

CONCLUSION

209   *read up on different stages of development to know what to expect as your child matures:* For a guide to development during adolescence, see my earlier book, *You and Your Adolescent: The Essential Guide to Ages 10–25* (New York: Simon & Schuster, 2011).

213   *Americans' performance was well below the international average:* OECD, *Skilled for Life* (Paris: OECD, 2013).

215   *Transferring adolescents to the adult system:* Scott and Steinberg, *Rethinking Juvenile Justice.*

Index